Addendum

FOR RUSSELL

Acknowledgements

I am indebted to the plethora of people who told me stories and suggested myths and images to pursue, in particular Ursula Masson, Marion Junor, Paul Foley, Val Horsfield, Winifred Kean, Christine Lindley, Susie Mayhew, Nancy Burrows, Bob Jones, Bob Purdie, Nelleke Van Helfteren, Richard Kuper, Rev. Dr Kenneth Greet, Caroline Morrell, Jackie Cameron, Lesley Hall, Felicity Harvest and Teresa Munby. My students at Ruskin College, Oxford, were a mine of characteristically eccentric – and challenging – information. Particular thanks must go to those, such as Rosemary Attack and Peter Thornhill, who forced me to look in different directions, and to Dave Juson, Bill Whitehead, Sean Rothman, Tim Brennan, Sally Morgan and the indefatigable Chris Sladen, who shared ideas and sources.

The pleasures of research owe much to the environment in which documents are read and to the active involvement of librarians, publicity officers and archivists who make rummaging so enjoyable. Apart from the usual thanks due to staff at the British Library and the much-maligned Bodleian (especially in the Upper Reading Room), I am particularly indebted to the following: the staff at the Fawcett Library, especially the inexhaustible David Doughan; the Theosophical Society, which provided electric fans, fascinating ledgers and mint tea in the summer heat; the Wellcome Institute, with its relaxing surroundings and wonderful lunches; the Greater London Record Office (now the London Metropolitan Archives Centre); the newspaper library at Colindale; David Horsfield, Chris Keble and Val Horsfield, undeservedly neglected library staff at Ruskin College; the National Canine Defence League, whose dogs-to-work policy helped provide noisy distractions from work. The national headquarters of the Blue Cross at Burford in Oxfordshire were a researcher's dream: apart from unrestricted and generous access to a splendid archive, a stroll round the rescued dogs, cats and sheep enthused the tired reader. I am also grateful to the many people and organizations who allowed me to use visual images in their possession, especially Nancy Phipps, Clive Howes, Rev. John Newton, Rev. Phillip McFadyen, the RSPCA, NAVS and the Blue Cross.

Many thanks, too, to those with whom I discussed my ideas on animals, even though they may not have shared my point of view: the late Raphael Samuel, Keren Abse, Irene Bruegel, Alison MacNair, Brenda Duddington, Laura Worsley, Kevin Flack, Farhana Sheikh, participants in Women's History Network conferences and especially Russell Burrows. I am particularly indebted to Ken Jones, who once again provided exceedingly helpful comments on earlier drafts. If I have overlooked the input of others, this has not been intentional. Suffice it to say that all errors and interpretations are my responsibility.

ANIMAL RIGHTS

Political and Social Change in Britain since 1800

HILDA KEAN

REAKTION BOOKS

Published by Reaktion Books Ltd
11 Rathbone Place, London W1P 1DE, UK

First published 1998
Copyright © Hilda Kean, 1998

Printed and bound in Great Britain by
Biddles Ltd, Guildford and King's Lynn

British Library Cataloguing in Publication Data:

Kean, Hilda,
    Animal rights: political and social change in Britain since 1800
    1. Animal rights – Great Britain 2. Animal rights – Great Britain – History
    I. Title
    179.3'0941

    ISBN 1 86189 014 1

PHOTOGRAPHIC ACKNOWLEDGEMENTS

The author and publishers wish to express their thanks to the following sources of
illustrative material and/or permission to reproduce it. In a few cases we have been
unable to trace copyright holders; we would be grateful to hear from anyone whom
we have inadvertently failed to credit.

Courtesy of the author pp. 52, 85, 146 (bottom), 167, 189, 196; courtesy of the
Blue Cross pp. 77, 172, 185, 196; Bodleian Library, Oxford pp. 56 (right), 60, 63,
99, 119, 125, 194; British Library, London pp. 28, 49, 74, 78, 83, 104, 151, 152,
155, 193, 198; Brenda Duddington p. 87; Clive Howes p. 209; Rev. Canon Philip
McFadyen p. 178; Mary Evans Picture Library p. 148; courtesy of the National
Anti-Vivisection Society p. 193; National Gallery, London p. 17; courtesy of
Nancy Phipps, p. 214; Plas Newydd/Denbighshire County Council p. 158; Public
Record Office Reference Library p. 146 (top); the RSPCA Photolibrary p. 195;
the Tate Gallery, London pp. 81 (bequeathed by Jacob Bell, 1859), 159 (presented
by Sir Colin and Lady Anderson through Friends of the Tate Gallery); photo
© Rosemary Taylor, 1989, p. 56 (left); and John Wesley's Chapel, Bristol p. 21.

CONTENTS

PREFACE

IN THE LATE twentieth century animals are news. In Parliament discussion of animals proliferates. In private members' bills, parliamentary questions and government legislation animals are accorded attention. The hunting of foxes and deer, the regulations for experimenting on animals, conditions under which puppies are bred, the transportation of animals for export, quarantine rules, and the threat of diseases passed from animals to humans all occupy parliamentary time. The specific debates may not be important; their significance lies in the fact that such issues are accepted as entirely legitimate and proper discussion for those elected to run the country. There may be disagreements on strategies and tactics but no MP would be so rash and dismissive of the views of his or her constituents as to suggest that Parliament was an inappropriate place for the consideration of the treatment of animals. Animals have become an integral part of political, as well as cultural and social life.

Meanwhile on television wildlife programmes vie with the more mundane coverage of animals in the hugely popular series *Animal Hospital*, in which a faded antipodean television star empathizes with people over the fate of their sick and much-loved pets. At the cinema and video shop a re-make of Disney's *101 Dalmatians*, and *Babe*, the tale of a pig with an identity crisis – he thinks he's a dog – do good business. Children are targeted with images of animals in books, like Spot the dog, or Mog the forgetful cat, or Sid, the cat who negotiates himself six dinners and receives his nemesis with six spoonfuls of medicine. And there are images in more concrete form, cuddly toys apart, in 'kitty in my pocket' or 'pony in my pocket'. Here children are introduced gently and persuasively to the possession of animals through toys. Different miniature plastic cats are presented with 'cat specifications' replete with marks for lovability or playfulness. The Conservative MP and diarist Alan Clark, confronted with his wife Jane in tears after returning home from a shopping trip having seen sheep 'stuffed into overcrowded lorries', joined protesters against the live exports of animals: 'It is a distressing sight to see one's wife in tears so I went down to protest.'[1] The comedienne Joanna Lumley supported lobbyists handing in petitions against vivisection and in favour of compassionate farming. Ann Widdicombe, known to many as the former Home Office Minister responsible for the shackling of pregnant prisoners to warders while the women were giving birth, received public support for her impassioned speech suggesting that those who want to hunt should go to Kenya and see what it feels like to be hunted by lions. When Humphrey, the resident cat in Downing Street, was removed to the suburbs 'for his health' the media demanded – and received – images, much like those used in hostage situations, of the cat sitting on newspapers of particular dates to prove that he had not been put down by the Prime Minister's wife.

Can we make any sense of all this? Is there any coherent explanation for such behaviour? In particular can a knowledge of the history of opposition to animal cruelty and of the incorporation of animals into cultural life help us understand the position animals now hold in British life?

In the course of researching and writing this book I spoke to many people, people who told me stories. I heard about the collecting dogs on the London and South-Western railway; the dog which joined the Jarrow March; the statue in Latimer, Hertfordshire, to the Boer War horse; Joe, the fireman's dog at Oxford Fire Station, whose collar still has pride of place in the station; and of films, stories, novels and poems in all of which animals play some part. Animals are a part of public myth and public memory. The stories sprang effortlessly to the tongue, and suggestions for further reading or statues of animals to photograph were plentiful. The stories were invariably public ones, accounts of myths about an animal in a certain time and certain place which 'everyone' knew about. What did Swansea Jack do, I asked one storyteller, since I had never heard of this particular dog before. 'Oh, he rescued people, that sort of thing. Everyone in Swansea knows about him.'[2]

This knowing has a long tradition in Western culture, back to the Greek myths and legends, particularly as later written up by Ovid. The writings of Aesop or Ovid include narratives in which animals and natural objects act in a human way and shapes and identities are transformed with ease. To escape the unwanted attention of Phoebus Apollo, Daphne is changed into a laurel tree. To prevent her rape Arethusa is changed into a stream.[3] It was a part of such story-telling that people recognized that trees, streams or animals might indeed be humans or gods. When his daughter Io is turned into a calf Inachus realizes what has happened, for Io uses her hoof to trace the circumstances of her transformation.[4] Stories of the Minotaur, half-man and half-beast, or of the young Narcissus, so transfixed by his own beauty that he turns into a flower, helped illuminate both the human psyche and the natural phenomenon of change. Import-antly, whatever particular ideas were being explored in this way, animals played a large part in the depiction of human emotions and relationships.

The close relationship between humans and animals in Greek myths was also found in the tales of the Old and New Testament. While the Bible teems with accounts of sacrifice, it also abounds in examples of specific kindnesses to animals, and in the New Testament animals play an important metaphorical role in supporting Christ. Christ is both Lamb of God and Good Shepherd, a protector of his 'flock'. In the Christmas story animals feature prominently. Mary delivers her child among various farm animals that provide warmth and security and the baby is placed in an animal's food trough. Outside the stable, security is further epitomized by the watchfulness of the vigilant shepherds towards their sheep. The relationship between people and animals epitomizing Christ's first days is balanced by that at the end of his life. In the Easter story it is upon a lowly donkey that Jesus makes his fatal entrance into Jerusalem.

Such stories, emphasizing a positive relationship between animals and holy men, were subsequently found in the hagiographical accounts of a plethora of saints. St Jerome, one of the four Latin Fathers of the Church and translator of the Bible into Latin, plucked a thorn from a lion's foot and retained that lion's loyalty for the rest of his life. St Francis of Assisi tamed the terrifying wolf of Gubbio and birds flocked to him, drawn by his humility. An English counterpart is found in Bede's narrative of St Cuthbert, who lived as a hermit on the Island of Farne before being elected Bishop of Lindisfarne in 684. When Cuthbert spent a chilly Northumberland night in the sea prais-ing God, two otters came out of the water, breathed on his feet and

wiped them with their hair.[5] When a generous eagle brought Cuthbert
and his servant a fish, it was Cuthbert who insisted that half of the fish
be given to the eagle in thanks for its kindness.[6] Christian hymns of
later centuries continued to reflect a positive link between animals
and people. 'All things bright and beautiful, All creatures great and
small, All things wise and wonderful, The Lord God made them all'
and 'Once in Royal David's city, Stood a lowly cattle shed' are still
remembered from childhood school assemblies by even the most
atheistic of adults. The existence of animals in the cultural life of
Britain has a long history.

Opposition to cruelty through the use of law, personal testimony
and action has a shorter history, but a history nonetheless. In late
twentieth-century British society there is an assumption that cruelty
to animals, however the individual might choose to define this, is
wrong. But there is little general knowledge that much of this revul-
sion against cruelty has its origins in cultural and social changes of
the last 200 years. Opposition to vivisection did not start with Anita
Roddick and the Body Shop. The concerns of those protesting against
live animal exports are not new but have antecedents over 100 years
ago. The traditions of vegetarianism in Britain owe much less to
Linda McCartney and the advent of soya sausages than to Shelley
and the French Revolution.

Since animals cannot speak they cannot tell us what they feel. The
animal liberationist who rescues animals from a vivisector's laboratory and the 'cat ladies' feeding and neutering stray cats may well
have very different philosophical and political stances. In practice,
however, the cat rescued from a lab or from a difficult life as a stray is
likely to benefit, whatever the intentions of the human agent. A
changing attitude towards animals, whether it derives from a philosophical or humanitarian concern with rights or from a sympathy for
the weak, the vulnerable and exploited, has owed little to animals
themselves. Human concerns, priorities, ideas (and indeed exploitation) have provided the context for the treatment of animals. To
understand why the cause of particular groups of animals has been
promoted at different periods we need to consider the varying uses
and abuses of animals by humans at different times. We also need to
discuss the way in which campaigns about human concerns and
behaviour have incorporated animals for educational, philanthropic

and political purposes. Whether particular aspects of animal cruelty were emphasized or not depended both on current practices towards animals and on wider political campaigns and priorities. When humanitarians rescued stray animals, or deplored the treatment of cattle driven to slaughter, or erected water troughs for thirsty animals, it tells us more about the political and cultural concerns of society at that time than about the plight of animals per se.

In this book I want to start to ask Why? Why was vivisection such a big issue in the 1870s? Why was the National Canine Defence League established in the 1890s? Why was the plight of cats relatively neglected until this century? Why did the welfare of horses and dogs become so important in the 1914–18 war? Why was myxomatosis so reviled in the 1950s? In exploring such questions I want to implicitly reject the debate that has seemed to characterize so much recent academic writing on animals.[7] I am not particularly concerned with the philosophical debate as to whether animals have rights or not, since this does not seem helpful in explaining adequately the nature of the historical practice of people in campaigning to protect animals.[8] My concern is with the sort of treatment meted out to animals and the actions that women and men have taken to change this, often for the most contradictory and inconsistent of motives. How animals have been integrated in different ways into the cultural life of the nation might, I suspect, be a greater source of edification than might a discussion from a late twentieth-century perspective based on the recent preoccupation with rights.

Those who have written about the history of our relationship with animals in the last two centuries have tended to look at specific issues, such as the work of the RSPCA or the growth of vivisection, in a discrete way, rather than setting this against a broader political or cultural background.[9] Moreover, academics have paid scant attention to the role of popular organizations such as the National Canine Defence League, the Blue Cross, the Metropolitan Drinking Fountain and Cattle Trough Association or the Battersea Dogs' Home.[10] Yet, as I shall elaborate, such groups have had a significant cultural and political influence on British society. On the other hand those who have written about the cultural representation of animals have often shown little interest in exploring the cruelty directed towards them.[11] Animals form an integral part of human life and experience.

A study of the stories we weave around them and the way we look at them might tell us about animals; it may also indicate the way in which political, social and cultural changes affecting people's lives have developed in modern Britain.

ONE

Radicals, Methodists and the law for animals in the streets

What returns for their life and faithful service do many of these poor creatures find?[1]

The attitude towards animals did not suddenly change at the start of the nineteenth century. Rather there was a coming together of different ideologies and practices emanating from political activists, philosophers, religious thinkers and artists. During the late eighteenth and early nineteenth centuries animals continued to be a highly visible aspect of British life. Agricultural developments had led to the presence of animals on farms throughout the year: no longer was it necessary to slaughter animals in the winter months, for increased crop production provided fodder all the year round.[2] Wild animals – deer, foxes, badgers, otters – continued to be hunted for sport and some to be routinely slaughtered for food. Animals were seen to be useful. But they were increasingly being depicted as human companions, possessing individual identities and characteristics.

Parrots, fluffy dogs and an exotic cockatoo

In medieval and Renaissance art animals had been routinely painted as symbols of virtues, vices and human characteristics. This practice started to change. Horses were no longer depicted just as symbols of lust, nor dogs merely as embodiments of fidelity;[3] their relationship to humans began to be envisaged in different ways. Thoroughbred horses, particularly in the canvases of Stubbs, or pedigree dogs, as painted by Gainsborough, became representative of the wealth of their owners.[4] The depiction of animals gave a particular status to the people in whose domestic space the animals lived. Animals were increasingly portrayed as loved members of a human family. In the rooms in the National Gallery devoted to British eighteenth-century painting, the walls are covered with images of animals. Alongside the popular Gainsborough painting of Mr and Mrs Andrews with their loyal hunting dog and expanses of agricultural land hang images by Stubbs, Wright, Hogarth and Richard Wilson.[5] In nearly all of these paintings animals are present in different guises: here are hunting dogs, a lady's fluffy terrier, a scavenging mutt, horses pulling a phaeton, and children teasing a cat or chasing a butterfly. Within the separate paintings the animals perform different functions, but they demonstrate collectively that animals were an integral part of the cultural depiction of life in Britain at this time. The wealth of the aristocracy, the respectability of the developing middle class or the immorality of the dissolute subjects of Hogarth's work are all given increased intensity by the inclusion of animals in the image.[6]

Further, the animals depicted in the environs of the wealthy British home are different types of creatures from those seen in some contemporary European images. While rapacious mogs and scavenging mutts eat their way through the kitchens of Dutch paintings of a similar era these are not portrayed as animals with distinct personalities. In contrast, creatures such as the white fluffy-tailed dog accompanying Mr and Mrs Hallett on their morning walk in Gainsborough's eponymous painting is an animal particular to the couple, no doubt bearing its own name, as well as representing canine characteristics of fidelity.[7] Exotic animals, too, start to be portrayed as part of family life. Joshua Reynolds' portrait *Lady Cockburn and her eldest three sons* (1773), for example, contains a splendid image of a huge red and blue parrot on the back of the chair in which Lady Cockburn sits. The parrot is a pet and as much part of the family scene as the little children and the suckling baby. A less benign depiction of household pets is William Hogarth's portrait *The Graham Children* (1742), set within the family's drawing-room. Here is a cat, a family pet, in the room where visitors would be entertained. It is not in the kitchen with the servants, simply performing the role of mouse-catcher. Instead it is in the family space designated for leisure – and about to pounce on the caged bird. The children are alone in the room with no adult to protect them – or their bird – while a statue of Father Time looks knowingly upon the scene. These are children, little adults, who look beyond the years of innocence. Yet the animals used to convey this threat to innocence are not allegories but pets which thrived within the home, a safe domestic terrain, making the scene even more ominous. As Keith Thomas has suggested, by 1700 the keeping of pets was widespread;[8] what has changed is the way in which such practices are acknowledged and validated within art and literature.

Attitudes towards animals, however – including family pets – were complex, as indicated most strikingly in *An Experiment on a Bird in the Air Pump* (1768), by Joseph Wright of Derby. Today it hangs in the National Gallery in London, drawing a great deal of attention from visitors. A regular subject of gallery talks, and pastiches by students and other artists, it is a disturbing image for the late twentieth-century spectator, as it may also have been for an eighteenth-century counterpart.[9] It appears to be a conventional contemporary domestic portrait of a family sufficiently wealthy to employ a servant and to be entertained by a travelling scientist. But at the heart of the painting is a disturbing image of a bird, a rare white cockatoo, struggling for breath within an air pump. The travelling lecturer – an outsider and a scientist – is seeking to demonstrate that animals need air to survive and are unable to do so in a vacuum.[10] The practice of using animals in an air pump had already drawn criticism, and frequently a lung glass with a bladder, demonstrating how the lungs of an animal contracted, was employed instead, because according to a contemporary scientist, 'this experiment is too shocking to every spectator who has the least degree of humanity'.[11]

Here Wright develops the domestic domain to produce a contradictory image. We have the depiction of a family pet, a beautiful cockatoo, which would be kept in the cage next to the window. But we are also watching a scientific experiment performed upon that pet, albeit before respectable men thought to be members of the Lunar Society, a prestigious group of Enlightenment thinkers led by Erasmus Darwin, grandfather of the better known Charles. The site of their scientific enquiry is not a laboratory or lecture hall but a domestic parlour.[12] Simultaneously we are presented with different readings of the cockatoo: exotic object of spectacle, valued pet, subject of scientific research. The bird has been interpreted as an allegory for the phoenix stage of alchemical transmutation, with the lecturer acting as a utopian philosopher enacting Enlightenment rituals for a select audience.[13] It is also a domestic pet, precisely the sort of animal in fact to be protected from danger and experimentation.

This contradiction, coupled with the disturbing object in the chemical jar reminiscent of a memento mori (causing the onlooker on the right for one to ponder on the proceedings) and the presence of distressed children devoid of a mother's protection, asks the viewer of the painting, like the people within, to consider the events critically.

Wright emphasized the shocking nature of the event we are witnessing. The scene is dominated by men, one of the women present being a young girl more keen on flirting with her beau than on watching the experiment. Here the men are not simply rich individuals displaying their wealth, but present us with a narrative dominated by the sense of sight. Only two of the ten seem to be looking directly at the bird: the little girl anxious about its fate and the servant checking to see whether the bird's cage will be needed or not. Others in the painting choose not to see the struggles of the bird for air; even the moon does not want to see and hides behind the clouds to deprive the room of light. The setting for the experimentation then becomes hidden, covert and redolent of shame prefiguring later critical depictions of animal experimentation.[14] Although this painting is a narrative about experimentation and attitudes towards it, it is also about the role of sight in this process. These are men of the Enlightenment, apparently interested in scientific enquiry, yet their night-time activities are hidden from the light and they turn aside to ponder on the spectacle performed for them rather than choosing to witness the struggling bird. As viewers we look both at the suffocating bird but also at those within the painting who choose not to look and turn away. We adopt different roles in our approach to the painting by the very act of looking and identification with a number of the characters in the painting: we too want to look but not to see the distress of the bird.

Most of the commentators on the Wright painting have viewed it within a context of scientific experimentation.[15] They conclude that the bird will live, that the servant is bringing down the cage in which to replace the soon-to-be revived bird – and that the eighteenth-century observer at least would see the image in this way.[16] Such unproblematic reading is very limited: this one painting includes a number of different cultural contexts, reflecting the range of attitudes towards animals at this time. There is the scientist's quest for knowledge, entailing the experimentation on living creatures. There is the

Life or death for the family cockatoo?
Joseph Wright, *An Experiment on a Bird in the Air Pump*, 1768.

observation of animal behaviour imitating the discourse being developed by naturalists.[17] Also depicted is humanity towards creatures, even if in this image such a sentiment is confined to children. In its explicit reference to the choice of whether to acknowledge cruelty or to turn away the painting epitomizes much of the debates to follow. Critical to campaigns for the amelioration of the plight of animals was an emphasis on seeing and acknowledging cruelty as an precondition for positive change. The painting also reminds us that many of the impulses in the interests of animals in the nineteenth century had their origins in earlier decades.

Changing religious views

The questioning stance that Wright depicted in his painting of 1768 was not unique but a visual depiction of an approach being developed by those concerned with religious, moral, and political interpreta-tions of the relationship between animals and humans. In 1776 Humphry Primatt, an Anglican vicar from Swardeston in Norfolk and a doctor of divinity, first published his tract *The Duty of Mercy and the Sin of Cruelty to Brute Animals*.[18] In language which pre-figures that used by parliamentarians in their debates of the early nineteenth century to argue the case for legislative protection of animals, Primatt drew analogies between the plight of different peoples and those of animals:

> It has pleased God the father of all men, to cover some men with white skins, and others with black skins; but as there is neither merit not demerit in complexion, the white man, notwithstanding the barbarity of custom and prejudice can have no right, by virtue of his colour, to enslave and tyrannise over a black man; nor has any fair man any right to despise, abuse, and insult a brown man.

Accordingly if certain groups of men have no authority to abuse others on account of differences of appearance such practice should also apply to animals since 'an animal [is] no less sensible of pain than a man'.[19] Cruelty was practised by all ranks of society, Primatt indicated, giving a range of examples including negligence towards cattle, fox hunting, bull-baiting and boiling lobsters alive.[20] The solution was situated within a religious discourse, namely to practise mercy towards animals, mirroring God's mercy towards humanity.[21] Although such ideas were not prevalent within the established Church, similar views gained greater currency within the growing Non-conformist sects, particularly Methodism.

John Wesley, the eighteenth-century founder of Methodism, offered a vision of a more equal and free community of souls living together on earth.[22] This ideal was reflected in the preaching practices of the Methodists: lay preachers often from working backgrounds delivered their messages, as did their founder, in the open spaces of villages and towns throughout the country.[23] Market squares, the same places where animals lived, worked and were harassed, became the site of Methodist open-air preaching.[24] Wesley emphasized the creation of distinctive moral and religious characters for his followers, centring on the practice of Methodism as a social religion which demanded positive action. As he famously put it, 'It is nonsense for a woman to consider herself virtuous because she is not a prostitute, or a man honest because he does not steal.'[25] Positive change – not merely an absence of wrongdoing – was required in the lifestyle of his adherents, and such change extended to the treatment of animals. In terms which were anathema to Catholics and many Anglicans, Wesley declared that animals did indeed have an afterlife and wrote extensively on the part animals played in the natural world.[26] For it was, he believed, through natural phenomena that God demonstrated his power. Wesley's three-volume *Survey of the wisdom of God in the creation* combined the naturalist's skills of observation with the demagogy of the preacher. Here was an attempt to describe the appearance and habits of animals, fish, birds and reptiles and to introduce the reader to various scientific discoveries, including the invention of the air pump (as painted by Wright). His intention was both to inspire the reader with awe at God's skills and to encourage a recognition of the close relationship between people and their natural surroundings. 'We cannot know much,' he argued. 'In vain does our shallow reason attempt to fathom the mysteries of Nature, and to pry into the secrets of the Almighty . . . But we may love much.'[27]

In his sermons too Wesley specifically instructed his congregations to show mercy to animals, since animals differed from people simply in their incapacity to know love or obey God. His tirade against cruelty, like that of Primatt before him, covered a range of inhumanity. Wesley emphasized both the deliberate cruelty involved in hunting as well as the quotidian ill-treatment of domestic companions:

[Man] pursues [animals] over the widest plains, and through the thickest forests. He overtakes them in the fields of air, he finds them out in the depths of the sea. Nor are the mild and friendly creatures which still own his sway, and are duteous to his commands, secured thereby from more than brutal violence; from outrage and abuse of various kinds. Is the generous horse, that serves his master's necessity or pleasure with unwearied diligence – is the faithful dog, that waits for the motion of his hand, or his eye, exempt from this? What returns for their life and faithful service do many of these poor creatures find? And what a dreadful difference is there, between what they suffer from their fellow-brutes, and what they suffer from the tyrant man! The lion, the tiger or the shark gives them pain, from mere necessity, in order to prolong their own life;

and puts them out of their pain at once: But the human shark, without any such necessity, torments them of his free choice; and perhaps continues their lingering pain till, after months or years, death signs their release.[28]

In his own actions towards animals he made valiant attempts not to act as such a human shark and expected his followers to do likewise. Although not a total vegetarian, Wesley adopted a meat-free diet and advocated the use of simple food, chiefly vegetables, for children.[29] In different vein, he instituted a rule that itinerant preachers were forbidden to seek food and rest for themselves until their horses had been properly fed, rubbed down and bedded for the night.[30] This reflected his own practice. At the New Room in the Horsefair in Bristol where Wesley built the chapel that would be the location for Methodist conferences, stables were built alongside to shelter the horses on which he relied for transport along the country's terrible roads. [31] He travelled extensively, a lone figure on horseback rather than in a carriage, until prevented by infirmity and old age. His very demeanour embodied his attitude towards animals. While Wesley rode, he read and, so the story went, the horse beneath him never stumbled. Musing on the reasons for this equine stability in his diaries, he speculated:

> 'How is it that no horse ever stumbles while I am reading?' . . . No account can possibly be given but this: because then I throw the reins on his neck. I then set myself to observe; and I aver that in riding above a hundred thousand miles I scarce ever remember any horses (except two that would fall head over heels any way) to fall, or make a considerable stumble, while I rode with a slack rein.[32]

He encouraged other travellers to use a slack rein, which allowed the horse to move its neck and mouth freely, rather than the bearing rein which held the horse's neck up high and restricted movement.[33]

Appropriately, the visual image of Wesley treating horses with respect was subsequently formalized through the erection of a statue of the preacher on his horse, complete with slack reins, outside the Methodist premises in Bristol. Being seen publicly to practise compassion – even towards animals – was a distinctive element of Methodism; a corollary of the phrase 'Thou God seest me', the text on the plates that popularly adorned the mantelpieces of respectable Methodist homes.[34] The importance of sight in the development of

John Wesley riding with a loose rein and an open book.
A. G. Walker, *Bronze Statue of John Wesley on a Horse,* 1933,
outside John Wesley's Chapel in Bristol.

moral and religious practices would be acknowledged in later years, not just by Nonconformists but by many concerned with the welfare of animals.

Changing philosophical and religious views

While ideas emanating from new religious sects were to prove influential in the development of animal welfare, so too were ideas coming from political and philosophical domains. The work of the radical philosopher Jeremy Bentham, who defined his Utilitarianism as a new religion, was published a few years after the work of Humphry Primatt.[35] Bentham is one of the few supporters of animals from this period to be remembered today within the animal rights movement. The T-shirt epithet or campaigning slogan for which he has gained this kudos is 'The question is not, can they reason? Nor, can they talk?

But, can they suffer?'[36] But Bentham's work was not primarily concerned with animals. He spent most of his life writing about the reform of the law and prison regulation.[37] The work from which the epithet above is taken, an introduction to *The principles of morals and legislation*, was principally about the basis of legal punishment; the status of animals was employed to exemplify his belief in the encompassing nature of law. The words preceding the statement about animal suffering were devoted to the human and political context of the possible achievement of rights for animals. Like Primatt before him, Bentham drew parallels with the changing treatment of black people, especially the rights recognized for former French slaves. In the same way that previously maltreated people had a right to an absence of pain and to considerate conduct, so too did animals.[38] He suggested that the time would come when the physical appearance of animals, like those of black slaves before them, would be insufficient for abandoning animals to their fate.[39] Bentham embodied a link between religious Dissenters such as Richard Price and Joseph Priestley, who supported the ideals of the French Revolution, and his radical contemporaries, who advocated change in society through legal reform.[40] According to Bentham, the legislator should forbid 'everything which may serve to lead to cruelty'. This would include fox- and hare-hunting, cock-fighting, bull-baiting and fishing, since such 'amusements' produced 'the most painful and lingering death of which we can form any idea'.[41]

The use of the language of 'rights', leading to a different emphasis on the treatment of animals, was similarly found in the writings of both Joseph Ritson and John Oswald, whose dedication to animals was expressed in their practical advocacy of vegetarianism.[42] Joseph Ritson, an antiquarian, argued that extravagant meat-eating had a direct deleterious effect upon the character. Meat-eating was not merely harmful to the animals concerned but led people to engage in the 'barbarous and unfeeling sports . . . [of] horse-racing, shooting, bull- and bear-baiting, cock-fighting, boxing matches, and the like'.[43] He further rejected the eating of meat on economic grounds since the agricultural process itself caused economic waste. The diet of labourers was changing, he argued, from one based on milk, roots and vegetables to meat, causing inefficient farming, 'Bread-corn, which went directly to the nourishment of human bodies, now only contributes to it, by fatening the flesh of sheep and oxen.'[44] Similar moral arguments were found in John Oswald's *The cry of Nature; or an appeal to mercy and justice, on behalf of the persecuted animals*, published in 1791. Although an atheist, in his analysis of meat-eating Oswald was strongly influenced by Hinduism. He maintained that animal food overpowered the faculties of the stomach and clogged the function of the soul.[45] Like Ritson, he argued that meat-eating was the first step to moral ruin, 'From the practice of slaughtering an innocent animal, to the murder of man himself, the steps are neither many nor remote.'[46] Oswald was an active supporter of the French Revolution. Leaving his native Scotland, he went to France and helped repulse the royalist insurrection at Ponts de Cee, for which cause he died in 1793.

The impact of the French Revolution

In some ways such sympathy might be attributed to the actual as well as metaphorical role animals actually played in the Revolution. Prior to the storming of the Bastille, the Estates General, meeting in May 1789 in Versailles (used by Louis XVI as a base for hunting), had debated the abolition of feudal rights, including the hunting rights exclusive to the nobility. Challenging these rights, the Bretons carried out a symbolic massacre of some four to five thousand hares as a challenge to the status quo.[47] In less bloodthirsty vein the animals kept by the king in his menagerie at Versailles were removed by the revolutionary government in 1792 to the Jardin des Plantes in Paris, so that the people could see the animals in public and free of charge.[48] Animals had played a symbolic part in momentous political change; but even more significantly, as Eric Hobsbawm described, 'France provided the vocabulary and the issues of radical and liberal-democratic politics for most of the world.'[49] In France the Jacobin government had offered universal suffrage, support for people's rights and the abolition of slavery in the French colonies.[50] Such policies were warmly welcomed in Britain by supporters organized in Jacobin clubs or Corresponding Societies, which took off in the 1790s after the publication of Thomas Paine's *Rights of Man*.[51] The British Corresponding Societies established in 1791 and 1792 aimed to reform corrupt government, to introduce parliamentary elections based on manhood suffrage and to defend the French National Convention. Supported by skilled working people in groups through-out the country who, as their name suggests, corresponded with each other, and moreover at a time when Britain had declared war on France, the holders of such ideas became subject to violent oppres-sion. But the ideals of the French Revolution would have long-term influence on the treatment of animals, alongside ideas emanating from those who were horrified by events abroad.

Divergence and convergence

Those supporting humane treatment for animals adhered to no one political or ideological set of beliefs. But increasingly the way in which people treated animals became a distinguishing feature of being humane and of membership of a new middle class and respectable working class. That opponents frequently caricatured those of very different political and religious views as part of the same current of dissent does not mean that this was the case. Wesley had himself put forward the rule of no politics, and was no incipient socialist, but this did not prevent clergymen caricaturing Methodists, Jacobins and Atheists alike as 'fruit of the same tree'.[52] The Methodist opposition to gambling and drinking naturally led to opposition to bull-baiting and cock-fighting, in which such practices were endemic. They shunned frivolous amusements and disapproved of performing animals such as dancing dogs.[53] In attempting to change the behaviour of working men towards animals they met opposition, since 'They took away from the pitman his gun, his dog and his fighting cock.'[54] The elision between Jacobinism and Methodism was reiterated by William Windham, the Minister of War in Pitt's government, in a debate in which he defended bull-baiting. The Methodists wanted, he said, to prohibit 'everything joyous . . . to pre-pare the people for the reception of their fanatical doctrines'. If labourers were barred from pleasures they would Jacobinize the whole country, he declared. Nor was this an idle threat, he went on, since within the London Corresponding Society there existed no bull-baiter, fighter nor any man who delighted in manly exercise.[55] This is clearly an extravagant claim, but indicates the way in which different political and religious views superficially had much in common in so far as their outcome benefited animals. The members of the Corresponding Societies and Methodist congregations alike were from respectable, albeit often impecunious, backgrounds. In seeking to create converts they were differentiating themselves from both the rabble and the indolent pleasure-seeking rich. At this time humane attitudes towards animals became a common – and distinguishing – feature of otherwise divergent groups and this trait continued throughout the coming century.

The changing climate in France, subsequent war, and draconian suppression of political opposition led to rapid political realignments in Britain; early supporters of the Revolution like Bentham became hostile opponents a few years later.[56] Meanwhile political organization within Parliament was fluid, and alignment into Whig or Tory groups was by no means fixed although the late 1790s and 1800s saw the early features of what would later become defined as Tory and Liberal parties. It is against such a fluctuating background that treatment of animals starts to move into political, as well as philosophical and religious, debate. But discussion of improved treatment of animals was not confined to one party or religious current. For example, the first meeting of the Society for the Prevention of Cruelty to Animals would be attended by Dr Stephen Lushington, the lawyer who had pressed the case for Queen Caroline to retain her title of Queen Consort in 1820 in her estrangement from George IV, and acted as the executor of her will.[57] Yet Richard Brinsley Sheridan, the playwright and sometime Whig spokesman who would speak in Parliament against the harassment of dogs and the cruelty to horses that he saw daily on the streets, was a close confidante of George when he was the Prince Regent.[58] Such men could, in their attitude to animals at least, make common cause.

The poet's image

At the turn of the eighteenth and nineteenth centuries the cause of animal welfare became prominent across the cultural spectrum. Poets such as Keats, Shelley and John Clare who wrote in the first decades of the nineteenth century took issue in different ways with the plight of animals. Keats condemned the slaughter of seals as a means to accumulate wealth in his narrative poem 'Isabella'.[59] Clare employed his acute observation of the countryside in his native Northampton-shire to reveal empathy towards ill-treated animals ranging from lashed donkeys, beaten dogs, and animals crying beneath the butcher's knife to badgers hunted and baited by his fellow countrymen, whom he castigated as drunkards and blackguards.[60] As he described it in terms not dissimilar to those of Wesley:

> For dogs as men are equally
> A link in nature's chain
> Form'd by the hand that formed me . . .[61]

Shelley's poetry – and political beliefs – were of a more revolutionary character. An atheist, proselytizing vegetarian and exposer of tyranny, he is perhaps best known today for his 'Mask of Anarchy', a scathing condemnation of state brutality at the Peterloo massacre of 1819, in which government troops murdered and maimed people demonstrat-ing for political reform.[62] However his earlier poem 'Queen Mab', written in 1812, which castigated religion, the state and the exploita-tion of the poor and promoted a future world in which nature, animals and humans lived in harmony, had greater impact at the time. His utopia is one in which people and animals are equal:

> All things are void of terror: man has lost
> His terrible prerogative, and stands
> An equal amidst equals . . .[63]

Birds will no longer flee from people but gather round to 'prune their sunny feathers'; no longer will man slay 'the lamb that looks him in the face,/And horribly devour his mangled flesh'.[64] Banned, like much of his other work, popular editions were nevertheless published from the 1820s. The decade that would first witness legislation against animal cruelty would also experience another discourse, a utopian vision in which animals played a key role. Such parallel developments – pragmatism alongside the creation of newly imagined worlds – would continue to underpin different debates in future decades.[65]

Seeing and acting

I have consciously emphasized the poetic images and painted repre-sentations of animals at this time. The changes that would take place in the treatment of animals relied not merely on philosophical, religious or political stances but the way in which animals were literally and metaphorically seen. The very act of seeing became crucial in the formation of the modern person. Who you were was determined by where you were and what you saw – as well as how you interpreted it.[66] This new practice was not confined to the ways in which animals were seen. Notably, there were contemporary parallels in the movement against slavery: the Wedgwood cameo of a kneeling slave or the mass-produced images of packed slave ships hung on walls all over Britain as visual reminders of what was not visible.[67] In different vein, sight was to play an important role in the regulation of society, according to the writings of Jeremy Bentham. His panopticon, based on the design of the animal menagerie at Versailles, was a prison in which prisoners could be under constant observation without being conscious of it; it was a laboratory for experimentation in power, using not physical oppression but the mechanisms of observation.[68]

For the naturalist Gilbert White, personal observation of the area of Hampshire in which he lived was the defining feature of his *Natural History of Selborne*. Reports, classifications and annotations collected in his diaries over 25 years epitomized this new supremacy of observation.[69] For the discerning dog owner, the visualization of a range of dog breeds was found in the 1800 'coffee table' book on dogs, *Cynographia Britannica*. This contained coloured prints and an accompanying text in which dogs were categorized by breed, history, current use and character. Sydenham Teak Edwards, the author, scorned dingoes, praised bulldogs and dismissed dainty Pomeranians as cowardly, petulant and deceitful. 'Although his attachment is weak', the author adds plaintively, 'yet he is difficult to be stolen.'[70] The book combined a sharp observation of the visual features of dogs with a commentary that projected human characteristics relating to the status of their owners:

> The dog may be considered as not only the intelligent, courageous, and humble companion of man, he is often a true type of his mind and disposition: the hunter's dog rejoices with him in all the pleasures and fatigues of the chase; the ferocious and hardy disposition of the bulldog may commonly be traced as the determined brow of this master; nor does the dog of the blind beggar look up to the passing stranger but with suppliant eyes.[71]

Dainty and deceitful Pomeranians with a more reliable New South Wales companion. A print of 'The Dog of New South Wales and the Pomeranian Dog' by Sydenham Teak Edwards, from *Cynographia Britannica*, 1800–05.

Seeing animals in the towns: everyday cruelty

Clearly what animals you saw depended on where you lived. In the country there were, of course, animals on farms, birds and wild animals in the fields and domestic pets in the home. However by the start of the nineteenth century Britain was already an urban country. The cities would be the places in which animals were increasingly seen and where their treatment was most hotly debated. Touring animal menageries would visit cities and in London there were permanent displays of animals at the Tower of London and the Exeter Change.[72] Bull-baiting continued to take place in public places in the heart of towns, particularly Stamford, Wokingham, and Bury St Edmunds.[73] More mundanely, animals traversed the streets of towns to be sold at markets and slaughtered, or to transport people and goods or to fulfil their role as human companions. And it was London, which by 1801 already had a population of over a million, which would be the focus

for campaigns to improve the position of animals.[74] London started
to come into its own as an economic, political and trade centre and
the experience of seeing and engaging in daily life in the city influenced
what aspects of animal ill-treatment were taken up by campaigners. In
London new areas were being laid out and developed precisely
because of the growth in trade. Massive dock construction began in
1799; the Bank of England was designed and erected by Sir John
Soane over a period of some 40 years; and numerous squares were
developed around Old Montague House, the precursor of the British
Museum, in Bloomsbury.[75] Further west John Nash reflected the style
of the stately mansions adjoining Regent's Park in his new shopping
area of nearby Regent Street.[76]

Although London was developing as a centre of new trade and of
new consumer demands, old traditions remained. The Haymarket,
next to the shops, remained a busy market for hay and straw. Most of
the buildings were inns which served farmers, livery stable grooms
and drovers.[77] In nearby Oxford Street the drapery shop that was to
become Debenham's first opened its doors in 1778. But opposite
the store people could still buy asses' milk, a luxury costing twice
the price of the more mundane cows' milk, from asses kept on the
premises. The less wealthy could purchase cheaper fresh cows' milk
from the cows which grazed in Hyde Park and Green Park close by.[78]

Alongside London's development as a trade centre grew the trade
in live animals for which the city became a geographical focus. The
environs of London were used for fattening cattle. Distillers fattened
up pigs on spent grains used in the making of alcohol before selling
them to a butcher.[79] Huge numbers of sheep grew fat on the lush
Romney Marshes before they were driven into London. To the east of
the city in Essex farmers provided veal for the rich tables of London
by nearly bleeding calves to death – and finishing the slaughter the
following day – to ensure that the flesh was white.[80] Cattle were
imported from Ireland and grew fat on British pastures or very cheap
grains before being driven to London for sale.[81] Prior to the introduction first of railways and then of refrigeration live animals were preferred as a meat source to dead carcasses. It meant that animals were
driven from all over the country to their penultimate destination,
Smithfield live animal market, on the borders of the ancient City of
London.

Keith Thomas has argued that the growth of towns led to a new longing for the countryside, precisely because the towns were separate from their environs. Urban isolation from animal farming had nourished emotional attitudes which were hard to reconcile with the exploitation of animals by which most people lived. Brutal country practices were replaced, he suggests, with 'an increasingly sentimental view of animals as pets and objects of contemplation'. A new-found security from wild animals, he continues, had generated an increasing concern to protect birds and preserve wild creatures in their natural state.[82] Thomas's argument rests upon a sharp counterposition of places, which is then deemed to determine the value of the animals in such locations.[83] The countryside is equated with real animals; the town represents sentiment and 'pets'.[84] This analysis fails to recognize the abundance of animals living in cities in the early nineteenth century and their economic, as well as cultural, importance for the inhabitants. It also fails to acknowledge the importance of the role of sight in developing the relationship between seeing ill-treatment and creating change.

The 'farm animals' that lived and worked in London would also be the first type of animal to benefit from legislation. Thomas argues that change did not come from butchers and farmers, those whose livelihoods depended on animals.[85] This is true but simplistic: neither did radical political change emanate from landowners – nor those on the degraded margins of society inhabited by butchers. Those most vociferous in their opposition to animal protection were also characterized by their hostility to progressive human causes. William Windham, fierce critic of the French Revolution, awesome advocate for legislation to outlaw sedition, and Secretary of State for War (against France), was as hostile to political reform as he was to the cause of ill-treated animals.[86]

James Turner has suggested that the animals first protected by legislation were seen as living, tangible relics of the old agricultural way of life. In nostalgic vein people feared the old way of life would slip away completely if they did not protect them.[87] He does not acknowledge that those same animals lived and worked in the cities, especially London; that they, like humans, had become urban creatures. His view also ignores the forward-looking dynamic behind much of the practice of campaigners for animals, who were keen to view cities as modern structures in a modern world. A new humanity towards the animals who lived, worked and traversed the urban domain becomes a distinctive part of modernity.

First attempts at legislation

Debates on the protection of certain animals which started to take place in Parliament from 1800 were, unsurprisingly, not simply about the development of different attitudes towards animals. Rather, such debates were set against a background of contested and suppressed radical ideas, a mood of religious revival, and the development of parliamentary party politics acting as an arena for a complex overlap of competing views. The rise of organized political discussion and then of societies to protect animals became a distinctive part of the creation of new political and moral sensibilities. Changes in the law were invoked not just to defend property nor to regulate the behaviour of the rabble and seditious agitators; they also had the effect of giving protection to those unable to speak for themselves. The role of advocate and protector was being established to invoke the cause of those literally without human speech, dumb animals.

The first animals to be potentially protected by legislation were bulls. On 2 April 1800 Sir William Pulteney sought leave to bring in the first bill in modern Britain to prevent the barbaric practice of bull-baiting in which a bull was set upon by dogs, usually by bulldogs bred for this purpose. The vote was close, the bill being lost by only 43 votes to 41.[88] At that time Parliament was more concerned with other business of the day than with legislation for bulls: the reading of a plethora of bills to enclose common land, to regulate the price of bread – and to approve the Union with Ireland.

Some historians have interpreted the attempted outlawing of bull-baiting as an attempt to deprive the poor of a popular pastime and to regulate hours of work.[89] Certainly drunkenness was rife at such events and did result in mass absenteeism from work, as William Pulteney elaborated: 500 to 600 people in Shropshire alone were enticed away from their work for a week at a time.[90] The parliamentary debate also centred on whether it was possible to change behaviour; those such as William Smith, a Whig MP and Unitarian, clearly thought this was both possible and desirable. To maintain bull-baiting showed '. . . a contempt for the lower class of people . . . if [Parliament] wished to make them rational beings, let them not educate them with one hand, and with the other turn them loose on sports like these'.[91] While clearly the force of law was being invoked to regulate behaviour, it was also designed to underpin a view that change was indeed necessary. Condemnation of brutality, be this towards certain animals or sailors flogged in the navy, became part of the legitimate content of parliamentary debate.

The poor were not the only group who engaged in brutal 'sports'; such bloodlust ranged across classes. Bull-baiting, cock-fighting and dog-fighting were not attended by those of the lowest social standing in society, but by those with the lowest morals: 'The same disposition which leads a man to the raceground, takes him to the ring, the cockpit, and the gaming table, and thus a character is formed of the most revolting description.'[92] The aristocracy was united with the lowest in society by their behaviour towards animals. Cock-fighting was seen as the sport of kings and princes: the Earl of Derby kept 3,000 cocks specifically for fighting. Aristocrats were accused of keeping fighting dogs at dealers on the outskirts of the metropolis: three pits existed in the Westminster area alone which enjoyed royal patronage and the support of MPs. Sir Francis Dashwood, the rake who led the Hell Fire Club, set up a cockpit, especially constructed with a Tuscan arch, at his home in West Wycombe Park in Buckinghamshire.[93] Unsurprisingly, those who practised barbaric sports were amongst the MPs who refused to ban such 'entertainment'.[94]

Parliamentary debates

So who were the first parliamentarians to create support for the welfare of animals and what can this tell us about the relationship between this and other political and religious views? In 1809 Lord Thomas Erskine, former Lord Chancellor in the Whig-dominated 'Ministry of all the Talents' in 1806–7 and popularly known as ' the British Cicero' for his eloquence in court, argued in Parliament that animals had rights and should not just be treated as property; they deserved protection. Erskine employed arguments about rights he had previously espoused in relation to people.[95] In his career as a barrister Erskine had advanced radical views and achieved popular support. In 1792 he had unsuccessfully defended Tom Paine in Paine's absence during the prosecution of the second part of his *Rights of Man*;[96] to great acclaim some two years later he had ensured that leaders of the Corresponding Societies were acquitted when charged with treason.[97] Erskine had also spoken for the abolition of the slave trade and against the Seditious Meetings Bill designed to squash Jacobin sentiment in Britain.[98] His famed eloquence and sense of commitment to radical causes was reflected in his speech to Parliament in 1809 about the plight of animals.[99] As others had previously argued, more humane treatment of animals would have beneficial consequences for people's behaviour towards each other:

> This extension of benevolence to objects beneath us, become habitual by a sense of duty inculcated by law, will reflect back upon our sympathies to one another; so that I may venture to say firmly that [the bill] will not only be an honour to the country, but an aera[sic] in the history of the world.[100]

In contrast to Pulteney's earlier failed attempt, the emphasis in Erskine's bill was upon 'routine cruelty' seen daily in the streets. One would not need to seek out the disreputable venues of bull-baiters or the hidden dens of cock-fighters to witness the cruelty that Erskine was describing. A walk along the streets of any town would provide examples of cruelty towards cattle beaten on their way to market and horses driven furiously. This was not cruelty enacted in arcane country farms but cruelty clearly visible in the cities.[101] Erskine's criticism extended to those of social extremes, from the 'base and worthless' who attended bear-baiting to the indolent rich 'galloping over our roads for neither good nor evil, but to fill up the dreary blank in unoccupied life', thereby causing horses to be ill-treated.[102] Although Erskine's bill was given a second reading by the Lords it was defeated in the Commons, its main opponent – the same man who had led the opposition to Pulteney's bill some nine years before – being William Windham.[103]

It was not until thirteen years later, in 1822, that legislation was first passed to protect animals from cruelty. Radical views continued to be repressed by legislation which outlawed seditious publications and meetings, trade union organization was still illegal, and despite petitions, consumer boycotts of sugar and parliamentary debates, slavery had yet to be abolished in British territories.[104] Although the rhetoric of opposition to slavery was used to promote the 1822 legislation it would be certain breeds of animals, rather than literally enslaved people, that were the first to benefit. On 7 June 1822 in what became known as Martin's Act, after Richard Martin, MP for Galway who promoted the bill, for the first time in Britain it became an offence punishable by fines and imprisonment to wantonly and cruelly 'beat, abuse, or ill-treat any horse, mare, gelding, mule, ass, ox, cow, heifer, steer, sheep or other cattle'.[105] Significantly, the animals afforded protection are those subject to routine cruelty and creatures usually seen in the public domain.[106] They are also domestic animals, being the property of particular individuals. The state was intervening in 'domestic relationships' decades before it would do so on behalf of children or of adult women. Those who could be found guilty of cruelty would normally be those who owned the animals in question or who were employed by the animals' owners to work with them.

Support for the legislation was not confined to any one group or narrow political current. The legislation had been backed in the House of Lords by Lord Erskine but much support had also been aroused by the Society for the Suppression of Vice, the distinctly anti-Radical group in which William Wilberforce, better known for his parliamentary activities against the slave trade, was prominent. This group sought to suppress radical literature and ideas and encourage adherence to the established religion.[107] The perceived links between the anti-slavery movement and the actions of Richard Martin led to Martin's eulogy by the poet Thomas Hood:

> Thou Wilberforce of hacks!
> Of whites as well as blacks,
> Piebald and dapple grey,
> Chestnut and bay –
> No poet's eulogy thy name adorns!
> But oxen, from the fens,
> Sheep in their pens,
> Praise thee, and red cows with their winding horns![108]

Support had been raised outside Parliament amongst the magistracy and clergy of London and Middlesex. As Richard Martin declared,

'There was not a pulpit in London that had not spoken in a pronounced manner in approbation of it.'[109] Martin himself was no Radical. He had warmly welcomed the Union between England and Ireland in 1800 and was a personal friend of the new king, George IV. Yet he was also sympathetic to the estranged queen, a firm supporter of Catholic emancipation and, like other supporters of the animal cause such as Thomas Fowell Buxton, opposed the death penalty for forgery.[110]

The Society for the Prevention of Cruelty to Animals

Two years after Martin's Act had become law the Society for the Prevention of Cruelty to Animals (it became the RSPCA in 1840) was set up in London. The Society did not come into being to campaign for new legislation as such, but rather to ensure that the law which had been passed would be implemented. Whether the law itself was the main motor of changing behaviour or not would henceforth underpin many of the debates of the new organizations set up to protect animals. By considering who attended the first meeting of the SPCA at the Slaughters'[sic] coffee house in St Martin's Lane in central London, we can perhaps start to unravel the different emphases and approaches of the new campaigners. The meeting was called by Thomas Fowell Buxton, MP for Weymouth in Dorset. Buxton, who married into the Quaker Gurney family, was a philanthropist who combined religious impulses with those of parliamentary reform. He was the first treasurer of the famous London City Mission, the ecumenical body which particularly focused on missionary work with cab drivers.[111] Within Parliament he was prominent in introducing motions in 1822 and 1831 to abolish slavery, which finally achieved success in August 1834. He also supported prison reform, the development of popular education for children,[112] and, like Richard Martin, the abolition of the death penalty for forgery. Also present at this inaugural meeting was James Mackintosh, praised as a lawyer by Lord Erskine, who, having issued a polemic against Burke's attack on the French Revolution, quickly adopted his opponent's position, declaring the Revolution to be 'sanguinary history'.[113] Essentially of liberal sentiments, he had introduced legislation to humanize the criminal law and to abolish the death penalty for sedition.[114] Other prominent men at the meeting included William Wilberforce, Stephen Lushington, Queen Caroline's former lawyer, and Richard Martin. Constituting themselves as the new organization's committee, the group went on to elect the Reverend Arthur Broome, an Anglican clergyman, as its first honorary secretary. This was not in initial membership a group embodying radical sympathies, but it sought to implement change pragmatically in the interests of animals. It set itself modest aims in the context of Christian religion, with its overall object 'the mitigation of animal suffering and the promotion and extension of the practice of humanity towards the inferior classes of animated beings'. [115] This was essentially a London middle-class body defining itself against the lowest classes who tortured animals for sport and who were responsible for the 'unmanly outrages daily perpetrated in our public streets on innocent and defenceless animals', which proved so shocking to 'foreigners coming amongst us for the first time'.[116] What is often ignored, however, is that the Society also defined itself against cruelty practised by those of very different social backgrounds, particularly scientists, in its condemnation of 'the practice of dissecting animals alive, or lacerating, mutilating, and inflicting torture upon them in various modes, to satisfy an unprofitable curiosity'.[117]

The SPCA's founding statement is a manifesto of a new rational age, rejecting bull-baiting – and dissection – as a relic of 'rude and obscure ages' and seeking to improve 'moral temper . . . and consequently, social happiness'.[118] From the very first the SPCA was keen to emphasize that it would be guided by sober, rational and practicable principles. It explicitly rejected 'all visionary and overstrained views'.[119] Ironically its secretary from 1826 to 1832, Lewis Gompertz, was one such philosophical visionary. In his *Moral Inquiries on the Situation of Man and of Brutes*, published in the year the SPCA was established, Gompertz outlined a cruelty-free environment for animals. In the book he advocated a vegan diet, and gave practical suggestions about menus. Wheat and barley and vegetables cooked for only a short time were suggested, together with olive oil used as a substitute for butter. Stews and soups, particularly a tasty barley, endive, turnip, parsley and celery stew, were described with the proviso that 'a proper application of the art of cookery' was needed.[120] Gompertz also expressed sympathy for the work of Robert Owen in his co-operative communities. Most significantly, as Peter Singer has suggested, he may well have been the first modern Western thinker to take so strong a stand in favour of equal consideration for animals, to argue for this position in a logical and philosophical manner, and to act accordingly.[121] These far-reaching ideas did not prevent him working in the SPCA, but such a visionary approach did not find favour in the group. Forced out of office in 1832 for allegedly anti-Christian views, Gompertz maintained his ideals in the founding of the Animal Friends' Society.[122]

In 1829, in his capacity as SPCA secretary, Lewis Gompertz had elaborated a wide range of concerns which were not covered by the current law. Some aspects would probably not have been witnessed by the intended readers, 'an enlightened public', namely bull-baiting which continued for days, underground slaughterhouses, pet dogs dissected by 'philosophical butchers' or cats thrown in the ditches at the Tower of London and imprisoned in the drains until they died by drowning.[123] Other cruelties would have been readily seen: the concerns raised were those of visible ill-treatment in the streets and markets.[124] Presciently, Gompertz cautioned against complacency: 'the idea that [the cattle's] sufferings are soon to terminate in the slaughterhouse may afford imaginary ground for consolation to the humane, but there they are subjected to a system of cruelty of a far more revolting kind, of which those alone who have investigated by eye-witness, can be to its full extent convinced.'[125] Although the SPCA had comprehensive paper policies, its reliance on the law to change behaviour and its rejection of visionary ideas would make it a focus of criticism by other groups campaigning for animals, particularly in London.

London continued to be the focus for reform in the treatment of animals. It was into the garden of his London home that Lord Erskine released seven robins purchased in a cage from a boy who had just caught them – and then wrote a poem in their honour, 'The Liberated Robins'.[126] It was in London, not in his constituency of Galway, that Martin personally brought to court men for beating horses tethered outside Smithfield market.[127] It was in Coventry Street in central London that Lord Erskine took direct action and beat a carter ill-treating a horse.[128] In its early years the SPCA did not press for legislation to cover animals kept within the home as pets, since this would involve 'an inquisition into private life'; instead it focused on public cruelty and legislation to 'prevent our streets from being the scenes of cruelty'.[129] The cruelty perpetrated behind closed doors in homes or laboratories would not be tackled in the courts for many decades. In 1822 the law had been used in the interests of 'old' animals in a 'new' context, the city. Legislation against bull-baiting and cock-fighting would follow in the 1830s; but it was the ordinary cruelty of everyday life in public spaces that was tackled successfully first of all.[130]

TWO

Sight, spectacle and education: from Regent's Park zoo to Smithfield cattle market

The increasing instances of cruelty in our streets have now risen to such a height that it is impossible to go any distance from home without encountering something to wound our feelings.[1]

In the 1820s and 1830s new organizations sprung up to complement the work of the SPCA. Unlike the SPCA which emphasized the law as vehicle for change, groups like the Animal Friends' Society, founded by Lewis Gompertz, and the Rational Humanity Group with its strong Quaker influence looked outside the law for change. Here the emphasis was on the creation of change in people's behaviour through the dissemination of information. To this end, *The Animals' Friend* and *The Voice of Humanity* journals were published, which outlined a plethora of cruelties – and action taken against them. In keeping with social mechanisms for change in other areas of public life, the motor for reform was not legal repression but education. The positive effect of education in the creation of a civilized and well-regulated society was part of a wider context for the establishment of public institutions.

The spectacle of the zoo and museum in 'civilization'

The idea of educative spectacle and display was manifest in a variety of forms: museums, galleries, public gardens – and the zoological gardens. The role of sight in achieving behavioural change received state acknowledgement in the establishment both of the National Gallery in May 1824, moving to its current site in 1832, and the British Museum, which increased its public opening hours considerably throughout the nineteenth century. If the eyes of the poor were opened to treasures of the artistic and natural world this would help

to draw them away from the rabble, by incorporating them within
the state and thus adding to the greater happiness of the nation.
Unsurprisingly radicals, reformers, and supporters of Jeremy Bentham
were prominent in such 'civilizing' moves.[2] Galleries and museums
were opened to the public to communicate particular cultural
meanings and to encourage moral behaviour and good conduct.[3]
Specifically, the sight of morally uplifting artefacts might provide
the poor with an antidote to drunkenness, albeit causing anxious
moments for museum staff. When the British Museum first opened
on a Bank Holiday Monday in 1837 the director was worried about
drunkards drawn away from the ginhouse visiting the museum.[4]
Worries were also expressed about the possible misconduct of sailors
from the dockyards and the girls they might bring with them. Late
twentieth-century curators ponder over how to make their institutions more popular; in sharp contrast, at that time the assumption
was that people from even the lowest ranks of society would want
to come to a museum, and the fear of the authorities was then
whether the visitors' behaviour would be appropriate. However, such
concerns proved unfounded. Of the 23,000 visitors attending the
British Museum on Bank Holiday Monday in 1837 none was reported
drunk: an achievement in itself in the educative cause.[5]

Displays of living natural history were also seen as improving.
Previously George III and Queen Charlotte, both enthusiastic botanists,
had been patrons of the Botanical Gardens at Kew, but now such
treasures were being opened to the public.[6] In 1841 Kew Gardens were
open for part of the week on the grounds that instilling a love of
flowers in working people would provide them with an alternative comfort to drink.[7] This followed on from the experiment in
Birmingham in 1832 when the magnificent gardens at Edgbaston
were opened, first as a private garden for the middle-class shareholders and their friends and later, on Mondays and Tuesdays, to
the working classes. This privileged access cost 1d and rules were
issued about inappropriate behaviour: smoking, picnicking – which
smacked of enjoyment rather than education – and entry into the
hothouses, which were banned to the Monday and Tuesday visitors.
The experiment in civilizing was deemed to work; later the hothouses
were opened and no damage was done.

The zoological gardens in Regent's Park were also established to perform a moral and educative role. Influenced by Linnaeus, the Enlightenment's most famous naturalist scientist, the original Zoological Society of 1823 was founded to promote the study of zoology among the specialist and lay person alike. Within a few years it had admitted women to its membership, and issued a prospectus outlining the objects of introducing and domesticating new breeds or varieties of animals likely to be 'useful in common life, and for forming a general collection in zoology'.[8] The Society established a farm for breeding purposes in Richmond and in 1830 laid out the gardens and enclosures for animals in Regent's Park. This would not be a pleasure garden as such but a site of education.

The Regent's Park within which the zoo was to be built had been originally planned by the architect John Nash for the Prince Regent, who had 'talked enthusiastically about eclipsing Napoleon's Paris'.[9] Although the end result did not possess the dramatic intentions of the original designs, the Regency changes in this part of London enhanced the quality of theatricality and of sheer spectacle. Within the Regent's Park area buildings were planned to house panoramas and dioramas and in 1823, a few years before the zoo itself was opened, the first London diorama was opened in the corner of the park.[10] In similar fashion a panorama was established in the extravagantly named Colosseum next to the grand terraces surrounding Regent's Park. Here visitors could experience a view of London as a constructed spectacle which replicated the actual sight witnessed from the lookout point at the top of the building. This part of London, then, had been established as a deliberate site of spectacle even before the animals were introduced in fixed displays. The animals were incorporated into an existing and geographically constructed framework, as the object of the gaze.

This attention to spectacle was also reflected in the specific places in which the animals were viewed. In the same way that the structure and setting of the National Gallery – as much as its contents – was designed to impress, the structures housing the animals were also significant. Although the early buildings have been described as 'follies set in an elegant garden for entertainment and curiosity', the skills of prestigious architects such as Decimus Burton, who had laid out Hyde Park, were used to the spectators' advantage.[11] The emphasis on gardens as a setting is also important; even today the visitor is likely to reach the zoo by leaving the bustle of the Euston Road and strolling across the lawns, paved parades and gardens of the park before reaching the animal enclosures. The positioning of animals within a garden environment helped foster the idea of creatures in a 'natural setting' which also characterized much of the development of the zoo in later decades. The idea of presenting animals in a natural display – albeit one which now seems contrived and restricted – was nevertheless innovatory and broke with the small and featureless cages of the travelling menageries. As a contemporary paper described it, '[The animals] have the luxury of fresh air, instead of unwholesome respiration in a room or caravan.'[12] Moreover, menageries and circuses were established purely as leisure activities; the zoo encouraged the viewing of animals in more uplifting vein.[13] In previous centuries private museums had exhibited exotic animals such as dead polar bears, but now the same animals could be viewed alive in the zoological gardens.[14]

Creating 'nature'

The animals kept there were also likely to enjoy better care than in privately run displays, since qualified vets were employed, most notably William Youatt, the veterinary scientist and SPCA supporter, who was the medical superintendent from 1833 to 1874. Youatt straddled a number of roles: vet at the Middlesex Hospital, lecturer in veterinary science at University College London and horse expert. He believed that animals were to be protected primarily because of their usefulness to humans.[15] In phrases reminiscent of Bentham he argued :

> Although less intelligent, and not immortal, they [animals] are susceptible of pain: but because they cannot remonstrate, nor associate with their fellows in defence of their rights, our best theologians and philosophers have not condescended to plead their cause, or even to make mention of them; although, as just asserted, they have as much right to protection from ill usage as the best of their masters have. [16]

In his pamphlet outlining the obligations of people towards animals Youatt criticized the way fish were caught – they were not stunned first, and lobsters and whelks were boiled alive – and, perhaps surprisingly for such a high-ranking scientist, attacked most animal vivisection, which he dismissed as unnecessary and overrated.[17]

Although the scientific underpinning of the zoo did not prevent it being viewed as a site of leisure as much as instruction, the early pioneers viewed this as a small price to pay if visitors to the zoo were also being educated: 'a fashion has combined with other and more legitimate stimulants to render the menagerie as popular as it is instructive.'[18] Working people had not previously had the opportunity of seeing works of art or archaeological finds, since these would have been displayed in private collections. However they had had the opportunity to see unusual animals, albeit in a context of a non-educational nature. The dilemma facing the managers of the zoo was thus more complicated than that of the director of the British Museum. How were people to be trained to regard animals previously seen in menageries as objects of fun as creatures worthy of awe and wonder? Initially this problem was avoided. Early visitors were members of the Zoological Society, or their friends, and the 'vulgar' were excluded. Benches were especially erected for servants of the middle-class spectators – well away from the animals.[19] In 1833 the essayist Leigh Hunt expressed surprise that the former meadows of Marylebone had been transformed into a place where 'ladies would be amusing themselves with coquetting with monkeys or giving oranges to a bear in a pit'.[20] Later he criticized the keeping of wild animals at all, since they were doomed to lingering deaths.[21] But the zoo authorities encouraged the benign treatment of animals through the feeding of cake and fruit to the bears. While this approach might not seem dignified by late twentieth-century standards, it was far removed from some contemporary treatment of bears, which continued to be baited with legal impunity until 1835.

By 1840 the general public started to be admitted on weekdays and attendance accelerated from 1850 with the arrival of the first hippopotamus, given the name of 'Obaysch'.[22] Charles Dickens was one such regular visitor who knew 'the zoological address of every animal, bird and fish of distinction' in the gardens. He 'chaffed the monkeys, coaxed the tigers and bamboozled the snakes'.[23] By the 1880s over half a million people came annually to stare at animals from all corners of the Victorian empire and a visit to the zoo would become a regular part of social and educational life.[24] As the *Daily*

Telegraph described it, 'We all go to the British Museum for instruction's sake; but we visit the zoological gardens for amusement as well
as for instruction.'[25]

Placed in a fixed place, a zoo, rather than in the wild or a travelling
display, animals could be observed at leisure. Gazing was the only
human activity required: normally fierce animals created no threat.
Animals routinely hunted for sport or used as food now became unob-
tainable by their very siting, capable of being observed but not attacked
by humans. This emphasis on observation followed on as much from
the pioneering work of Gilbert White of Selborne, whose journals cited
his examination of his immediate environment, as from the Jardin des
Plantes in Paris, on which the zoo was directly modelled.[26]

In his influential article on looking at animals, John Berger has
argued that public zoos came into existence at a period in which
animals started to disappear from daily life.[27] This is not the case,
for animals continued to play significant roles in the domestic life of
city dwellers both as objects of affection and as the mainstay of the
transportation system. What changed was that certain animals *outside*
individual ownership became objects of the gaze. As T. H. Huxley, the
scientist and associate of Darwin described it, a country or seaside
stroll became a 'walk through a gallery filled with fine art works'. The
teaching of natural history was analogous, Huxley continued, to
placing a catalogue in the viewer's hand.[28] Nature becomes accessible
and rather than being an object of fear, is transformed into an object
of pleasurable regard.

The educational role of animals in print

The changing perception of animals as focus of the gaze was further
emphasized in the Zoological Society's gazetteer of the animals caged
in the gardens.[29] The authors praised the gardens for the opportunity
they had given for 'our countrymen in general . . . to make themselves
familiarly acquainted with the appearance and manners of a large
proportion of the animal creation'.[30] The menagerie would help to
'eradicate those vulgar prejudices which have in too many instances
usurped the place of truth and to substitute just ideas, drawn from
actual observation'.[31] By observation of real – or pictorially reproduced
– animals, truth could be achieved.

Accordingly, prints were reproduced together with written descriptions of animals in the zoo. In keeping with the emphasis on enlightenment and improvement, animals were endowed with moral characteristics. The brown bear allegedly possessed a high degree of brute force, intellectual stupidity, and insatiable and gluttonous voracity.[32] The relationship between physical appearance and moral qualities was a particular theme: thus the black ape's expression was 'peculiarly cunning'; the leopard had a moral character of suspicion, presenting an air of 'malignity and wiliness'.[33] What was apparently observed in the physical appearance of an animal was also translated into its relationship with humans. The grace of the lesser American flying squirrel made it appropriate as a lady's pet; the pelican's contentedness and familiarity rendered it suitable as a captive bird.[34] Animals were not described as part of social formations which existed within the animal world but in terms of their use to people. The section devoted to birds outlined their characteristics and suitability both as pets and as entrées for the dinner table. The flesh of the greater sulphur-crested cockatoo was apparently very tasty; wild swan was said to resemble beef and duck, but the reader was cautioned from eating pelicans since their flesh was not palatable.[35]

No doubt the popularity of the zoological gardens helped to provide a growing readership for illustrated books of prints of animals.[36] Even if people could not see an exotic animal in the flesh at the zoo, then a visual representation rather than just the written word was available.[37] Those respectable working people who started to frequent the British Museum, and later the zoo, were the same people at whom the mechanics' institutes were aimed. In December 1823, the year the Zoological Society was founded, the London Mechanics' Institution was formally inaugurated with Dr George Birkbeck, a London physician, as its first president.[38] With libraries, lecture and reading rooms and a museum of 'machines, models, minerals, and natural history',[39] it was intended to neutralize working people as a political force potentially antagonistic to the growing middle class.[40] By 1850 there were over 260 such institutions nationally with an attendance of around 60,000, of whom 10 per cent were women.[41] Classes were held on science, literature and the arts. Appropriate treatment towards animals also formed part of such an education, since such behaviour was increasingly an indicator of social status. As one lecturer to the Chester Mechanics' Institute declaimed, 'The love of pets is one of the flowers of civilization.' Such animals embodied particular positive qualities and were empathetic to people: 'Pets cheer the bed of sickness, solace the hours of solitude, bring to mind absent or deceased friends, and soften and render more endurable the trials of poverty and sorrow.'[42]

Similar 'useful knowledge' covering natural and ancient history, geography, science and architecture, was included in the weekly *Penny Magazine* started in 1832 by the Society for the Diffusion of Useful Knowledge. The Society aimed to bring science to the working population, and its popular format, which avoided controversial politics and religion, had much success, claiming a circulation of up to 200,000 copies.[43] Every issue contained prints of animals and birds with accounts of their habits. These ranged from the polar bear and seal to the camel, opossum, beaver, orang-outang, whale and pelican.[44] Articles frequently referred to the relationship between an individual animal and a traveller or scientist. Thus the behaviour is recounted of a particular orang-outang which was brought from Java to England in 1817. The animal is described as a distinct creature with its own characteristics: 'When he first came among strangers he would sit for hours with his hand upon his head, looking pensively all around him; or when much incommoded at their examination, would hide himself beneath any covering that was at hand.'[45] The *Penny Magazine*'s mixture of popular science and natural history was devised as an appropriate vehicle for moral improvement. As a radical commentator scathingly observed, the magazine was 'that easy issue of Whig benevolence, all that kindly supply of juiceless chaff'.[46]

Animals as objects of awe and moral lessons for children

Working people were not the only new readers targeted by the printed word and images of animals. Increasingly books dealing with the appropriate behaviour towards animals were aimed at children, focusing in particular on domestic animals. Mary Wollstonecraft's *Original Stories*, an advice book on conduct for children and servants, argued that people were superior to animals and should prove this by being tender-hearted: 'Let your superior endowments ward off the evils they cannot foresee.'[47] Books with images by the engraver Thomas Bewick became so popular that by the time *Jane Eyre* was published in the 1840s his work was mentioned in the text as a popular signifier of self-improvement – and wonder. Hiding away from the brutalities of the Reed children behind a thick red curtain, the young Jane scanned Bewick's *History of British Birds*, where every picture told a story. 'With Bewick on my knee, I was then happy,' declared Jane.[48]

From the 1850s the numbers of books published specifically on pets and their care escalated.[49] In one of her first books for children, *Domestic Pets: Their Habits and Management,* the prolific writer and gardener Jane Loudon recommended that young people bestow 'unwearied kindness' on pets. They should never forget that the animals 'which they keep in confinement for *their* pleasure, are deprived by that confinement, of all power of helping themselves, and that they are entirely dependent upon those who keep them, not only for their comfort, but for their very existence'.[50]

Pets were not a new phenomenon. What was new was the opportunity to read about an ordinary animal that lived within one's own home as it if were an exotic creature at the zoo, and to see prints too of the most mundane creatures. Children were not merely instructed in the food their pets liked – squeezed tea leaves for rabbits, for instance – but fed with stories about their qualities and information about their origins. Guinea pigs, so they were told, also liked tea leaves, although carrots were better for them – and they came from Brazil.[51] Such popular publications, like *Beeton's Book of Home Pets* issued in weekly pamphlet form, also helped to define cruelty and warn against it. The keeping of singing birds in cages or goldfish in round bowls – or tortoises at all, since they were kidnapped from their warm native land – were all defined as cruel behaviour and thus unbefitting for the respectable child. Definitions too were being challenged about the concept of a pet, which was re-written to be an object of love. Arguing against those who rejected functional animals such as a hen as a pet, the author drew an apparently helpful analogy with the treatment of servants. Since hens were as functional as Mary Jane the all-work maid and John the gardener, and these lowly humans deserved the love of their employers, so too by extension did animals within the same family.[52]

Working animals become visible

What becomes increasingly important in the defining of appropriate behaviour towards animals is not only the perceived or potential status of the human but the situation in which the animal is seen. In the zoo in Regent's Park, in a fashionable part of London, animals were the object of the gaze; in the home they were recipients of kindness; in prints they were examples of the wonders of natural history.

W. H. Pyne's two-volume *Microcosm or a picturesque delineation of the arts, agriculture, manufactures of Great Britain*, however, which illustrated a range of occupations in all parts of the country, presented a more complicated picture. Here animals were not seen as decorative topics for the engraver's pen. These animal images are unlike those in *The Penny Magazine* or the zoo's gazetteer, for they are working creatures – cattle being beaten on the way to market or horses whipped to work faster. As Pyne comments on the wretched existence of post horses, '[Their use] may be stylish but it is not humane.'[53] This is no animal welfare tract but a presentation of the various aspects of daily life in early nineteenth-century Britain. To avoid the depiction of cruelty to animals, however, seems impossible if Pyne is to give an accurate picture of life at the time. Their inclusion in a book of illustrations epitomizes some of the problems facing campaigners at this time. Increasingly their task was to create an awareness of the status and merits of functional animals, drawing on the mechanisms used to render 'exotic' or 'companion' animals objects of attention in the zoo or home. Leaving the task of regulation against cruelty to the law would not by itself achieve this change in awareness of the position of working animals. Different methods were needed.

Working animals, 'farm' animals, were an integral – and visible – part of city life. In North Kensington – now near Holland Park underground – working people, particularly the immigrant Irish, established themselves in outwork laundering for nearby mansions and kept pigs in their back yards. Until the 1850s much of the pork eaten in London was 'home made'. Pigs were fattened in the yards, guarded by dogs before being slaughtered in the self-same spot. The stench and the filth were made more abhorrent by the stink of boiling pig fat. Unsurprisingly, Shepherd's Bush was called the 'pigsty of the

The use of the whip and the lash was routine at cattle markets
Illustration from W. H. Pyne, *Microcosm or a picturesque delineation of the arts,
agricultures, manufactures of Great Britain*, I, 1808.

metropolis':[54] 'In these hovels discontent, dirt, filth, and misery are unsurpassed by anything known even in Ireland.'[55]

Over to the east of the city, in the hay markets of Whitechapel, teams of worn-out horses led a wretched existence which, declared the ubiquitous William Youatt in his authoritative book on the horse, '[would] disgrace the poorest districts of the poorest country'.[56] The metropolis was surrounded by fields and market gardens in the then suburbs of Battersea and Hackney. On the outskirts of London farmers grew hay for the London coach and saddle horses, and for cow keepers.[57] Cows continued to be kept behind shops and burly milk-women with mahogany faces 'handsomely veneered by wind and weather' trekked the streets selling milk 'of a decidedly metropolitan character'.[58]

London was still small enough a city to be seen as an entity to, through and from which people and animals moved in the course of their daily business.[59] Working-class women and men traversed the city in the course of their work.[60] Indeed, the changes in work itself necessitated particular journeys. The growth of sweated labour in the tailoring and garment trades led to an increase in outwork, which itself was often sub-contracted. Women might work at home but they were obliged to move around the streets collecting and delivering goods in various stages of completion.[61] The middle-class woman also ventured from her home either in the pursuit of pleasure or philanthropic activities. As a visitor in the 1840s noted, the middle classes spent their day moving through London. However trifling one's business, over fifteen miles a day might well be travelled through 'the monster city'.[62] This movement provided an opportunity to use and see working animals – and to witness cruelty against them.

Cruelty to horses – seeing and acting

Although the number of cattle, sheep and pigs in cities would decline during the mid-nineteenth century, the number of urban horses would increase. In the first half of the nineteenth century, in which industry and commerce burgeoned, horses became an integral part of the prosperity of the new nation. The numbers of horses employed outside agriculture actually increased: from 487,000 in 1811 to over 500,000 in 1851.[63] Moreover, the number of horses used for transport continued to grow even after the introduction of the railway system. Far from the new cities signifying a break with the rural past, they brought about an increase in the visibility of horses in the centres of mass population. Unsurprisingly, such horses engaged in work in the cities and main roads of the country, rather than the million and a half still working the land, were the ones that seized the attention of humanitarians. 'Urban' horses were treated differently to their rural peers, precisely because of the new tasks they were required to perform in urbanized society. Speed became essential, with firms vying with each other to complete journeys of many miles in the shortest time; consequently horses were regularly flogged in the interests of increased profits. As the Animal Friends' Society put it, there was 'the unceasing sound of the lash in our streets'.[64]

Although the law had previously been used to try to prevent the fierce driving of horses, different strategies were increasingly used to attempt to change human behaviour.[65] In order to implement a prosecution, the name of the offending driver was needed and, unsurprisingly, drivers were unwilling to divulge their names.[66] It was the dishonesty reflected in the refusal to give their names as well as the beating of horses which led to cab and omnibus drivers being viewed as a particularly vile category of being. As Henry Curling raged in his aptly titled *A Lashing for the Lashers* (1851): 'In the whole circle of the habitable globe there does not, perhaps, exist a more uncivil set of beings than the majority of men at present plying their vocation as the cab and omnibus drivers of London.'[67]

Rushing through the congested streets of the capital caused danger to humans and horses alike. In his first book, *Sketches by Boz*, published in 1836–7 when Dickens was in his twenties, the author depicts the vicissitudes of London life endured by travellers and pedestrians. Horses wait at hackney-coach stands 'with drooping heads, and each of them with a mane and tail as scanty and straggling as those of a worn-out rocking-horse'.[68] Horses pulling cabs were expected to go faster than the hackney hacks and consequently suffered frequent accidents. As Dickens extravagantly claimed, 'We are not aware of any instance on record in which a cab-horse has performed three consecutive miles without going down once.'[69] In Dickens's accounts the accidents he describes become humorous anecdotes of London life, as illustrated in the following encounter:

> 'Any body hurt, do you know?' – 'O'ny the fare, sir. I see him a turnin' the corner, and I ses to another gen'lm'n, "that's a reg'lar little 'oss that, and he's a comin' along rayther sweet, an't he?" – "He just is", ses the other gen'lm'n, ven bump they cums agin the post, and out flies the fare like bricks.' [70]

But the subject of Dickens's wit suffered severe distress and premature death. While the search for profits was the main motive for speeding up horses, fashion and slothfulness was another. So fashionable was it to be driven around town that the practice of using horses for leisure descended down the social order. As a colourful pamphleteer put it: 'People now ride who twenty years ago must have walked; but to walk is reckoned vulgar. The fat butcher's wife, flounced and

A hansom cab on a London street.
Anonymous and undated photograph.

furbelowed as fine as Lady Belgravia's lady's-maid; and ten times as fine as Lady Belgravia herself, cannot walk a yard, even to take tea with the wife of a deputy costermonger round the corner!'[71]

Ill-treatment was also caused by the long hours horses were obliged to work. In addition to transporting people around the cities, horses were also used by the dust- and rubbish-carriers under the cloak of the night to remove stinking detritus. Since such work was carried out at night, carriers felt able to use worn-out horses, who had often worked during the day for other employers, with less fear of rebuke from humanitarians who, it was hoped, would not be concerned about injustices they could not see.[72] These creatures were usually cast-offs from brewers and coal merchants carrying out their last service: many collapsed to their death on the streets.[73]

What happened to horses at the end of their life when they were away from the public gaze was approached in a number of ways. The very act of *not* seeing led to vivid imaginings which became as important in the process of stimulating action as the working of sight itself. If horses were ill-treated in public spaces, what even greater horrors happened to them in the hidden recesses of the knackers' yard? *The Times* had complained of horses in such places being so starved that they ate each others' tails and manes;[74] individuals such as Mrs Livingstone of Pentonville brought to the attention of the Animal Friends' Society the appalling conditions at the erroneously named Belle Isle. Here dead animals had been kept with the living, which were deprived of food and drink. If nothing else, her action, resulting in prosecution of the owners of the yard, Parmenters, brought swift death to the horses.[75]

Where the remains of horses – and other urban animals – ended up after death became another concern. As one writer recognized, horses beaten to death became transformed into pet food on the cats' meat barrow.[76] Semi-putrid carcasses did not only end up as cat or dog food but as sausages for human consumption. The principal sausage manufactory of the metropolis was in Sharp's Alley, Smithfield, suspiciously close to the only licensed horse slaughterer in the city, where horses exhausted from driving ended their days.[77] It was also thought that cats themselves were turned into human food. The stories of Dickens's Sam Weller may be fiction but they also reflected popular urban myths. As a prelude to a picnic lunch of veal pie, Sam recounted a tale of the acts of a pieman using pet cats to make meat pies, who explained:

> '[The pies are] all made o' them noble animals', says he, a pointin' to a wery nice little tabby kitten, 'and I seasons 'em for beefsteak, weal, or kidney, 'cordin to the demand. And more than that,' says he, 'I can make a weal a beef-steak, or a beef-steak a kidney, or any one on 'em a mutton, at a minute's notice, just as the market changes, and appetites wary!'[78]

It is perhaps unsurprising that vegetarianism grew in popularity in the 1830s and 1840s. Some pioneering socialists were vegetarians for political and idealistic reasons. William Thompson, the pioneering Co-Operator, supporter of Robert Owen and author of the feminist *Appeal of one half the human race, women*, was one such individual. For the last seventeen years of his life he was a non-smoker, teetotaller and vegetarian who lunched on potatoes and turnips, and drank tea sweetened with honey from his co-operative farm.[79] But the deplorable condition of current food also led others towards vegetarianism. At the founding conference of the Vegetarian Society in Ramsgate in 1847 the MP Joseph Brotherton addressed the assembled women and men, declaring the reasons for his own vegetarianism. It was unnecessary to kill animals and was injurious to happiness and humanity. It was also dangerous to health, he declared, since 'butchers and others who lead very immoral lives, blow up the veal from their disordered lungs'. Human contamination was as significant as idealistic motifs.[80] As members of the Vegetarian Society were wont to explain, animal food was 'second-hand food'.[81]

Changing men: befriending horses

A different, close relationship between the treatment of animals and human health was found in the work of the Metropolitan Drinking Fountain and Cattle Trough Association (MDFCTA), founded in 1859. Public fountains and troughs, founded by public subscription in London and in other major cities including Liverpool and Edinburgh, provided free water for tired animal and human travellers. The erection of such structures created a visible and permanent reminder in public streets of examples of practical humanity.

As is the case today, water was not in the public domain in the mid-nineteenth century. It was a private commodity owned by water companies which required payment for supply to houses and which did not provide water to the streets. The poor were dependent on an intermittent unhealthy water supply from pumps impregnated with faecal matter.[82] It was such circumstances that led to the outbreaks of cholera in London in 1848–9 and 1853–4. The medical officer of the city, John Simon, drew connections between the circumstances governing the lives of people and animals, noting that, 'Animals will scarcely thrive in an atmosphere of their own decomposing excrement, yet such strictly & literally speaking is the air which a large proportion of the inhabitants of the City are compelled to breathe.'[83]

While others hypothesized on whether improved sanitation or compulsory vaccination should be adopted to improve mass health, the Association took practical steps to eradicate the conditions in which 'the poor were left to choose between the poison of the pumps and the poison of their own foul tanks and cisterns'.[84] The actions of the MDFCTA offered some positive remedies to this condition.

The drinking fountains and troughs erected over a century ago are still preserved as local landmarks and have changed the London landscape. Far from animals being marginalized creatures in the new city, the existence of these permanent examples of 'street furniture' for animals indicates the way in which they were viewed as an integral part of city life. Indeed the troughs were used for their original purpose well into the second half of the twentieth century, before being transformed into listed monuments of an earlier age. The first simple fountain was erected in 1859 on the outskirts of the city, precisely on the route cattle drovers took to West Smithfield. Those working with animals had priority in the schedule of the Association. Today the fountain still exists opposite the Old Bailey in the wall of the church of St Sephulchre, complete with instructions to 'replace the cup'.[85] The fountain in the grander Regent's Park, which could be used by sightseers on the way to the zoo, dates from ten years later. It still stands on the main thoroughfare to the zoo, and was presented, as the inscription states, by Sir Cowasjee Jehangir, a wealthy Parsee from Bombay, and opened by Princess Mary, Duchess of Teck.[86] By the mid-1860s over 100 troughs and fountains had been established in London alone. Significantly, there was a similar facility for people and for animals – fresh water in public places. Within the educative process the provision of a common necessity drew together animals and people in a common action, drinking. This theme of commonality found expression in the contributors to the Association. Angela Burdett-Coutts, considered to be the wealthiest woman in England, gave prolifically to good causes which helped both people – with the provision of a market and good housing where the Columbia Road Sunday flower market now stands – and animals. She was a leading member of the ladies section of the RSPCA, a president of the Bee-Keepers Association, an enthusiastic keeper of goats on her Holly Farm (opposite the road now leading to the Ladies' Pond on Hampstead Heath) – and a generous contributor to the MDFCTA. Inside Victoria Park, the huge park in London's East End built to help eradicate cholera in the slums, Angela Burdett-Coutts financed a massive structure surmounted with clocks and an extravagant cupola which could be seen for hundreds of yards, so grand and huge was it. Outside the park, in Lauriston Road, a more mundane trough was erected for the benefit of cattle and horses – and was still being used in the 1950s.[87]

Fresh water for east Londoners in Victoria Park.
A drinking fountain erected in 1862 by Angela
Burdett-Coutts.

Working for horses, cattle, dogs and humans.
An 1886 leaflet from the Metropolitan Drinking
Fountain and Cattle Trough Association.

As with the earlier SPCA, the founders of the MDFCTA were
motivated by a number of underlying concerns, including the practical promotion of temperance in people. At the inaugural meeting of
April 1859 the Earl of Carlisle, the Lord-Lieutenant of Ireland, gave
a presidential address in which he stressed the need for pure water
for all classes of people. 'Perfect purity and coldness' achieved by
processing water through filters would help eradicate disease and
encourage temperate living. The Association was founded and finan-
cially supported by Quaker families such as the brewers Robert
Hanbury and Charles Buxton, and Thomas Fowell Buxton, who had
played an important part in the SPCA. Samuel Gurney, nephew of the
prison reformer Elizabeth Fry, and the Quaker MP for Penryn and

Falmouth in Cornwall, became the chair of the Association from 1859 to 1882. Such philanthropic work existed alongside his membership of the SPCA and his campaigning against slavery: for eighteen years Gurney had been the president of the Anti-Slavery Society.[88] The Association enjoyed wide patronage, with support from Lord Shaftesbury, the evangelical Tory and staunch supporter of the SPCA, Dr Langley, the Archbishop of Canterbury, and John Stuart Mill, the philosopher and politician.[89] In similar ways to the SPCA, the cause of practical support for animals and humans alike led to the making of common cause amongst individuals who would otherwise have disagreed on many aspects of social and political life. Water became a cause that transcended political differences.

The context for the Association was firmly rooted in the specific geography of London. The distances travelled in the course of work and the nature of work undertaken outdoors created thirsty people and animals:

> [It is for] the wayfaring and working classes, and so long as London remains what it is, with its dry and dusty streets, crowded with multitudes of human beings, many of whom earn their livelihoods out of doors, so long will the beneficent operations of the Society be required.[90]

Where the troughs for sheep, oxen and horses were built is significant: they were constructed on the drovers' routes into London at Highgate Hill and Haverstock Hill in the north, Kilburn and Maida Hill in the west, Battersea Rise in the south and Stratford, Plaistow and the Barking Road in the east.[91] In helping animals, the Association would also be influencing the men who worked with them. Before the initiative of the Metropolitan Association the only places where animals could drink water were outside public houses, which the men were then obliged to frequent. The priority of the Association was the promotion of temperance and a clean water supply through practical means, as much as alleviating the particular distress of animals. However the kind treatment of cattle and horses in public places would also act as an impetus towards general kindness to these animals. Here it is changes in behaviour and practical works which are paramount, rather than the implementation of law as emphasized by the SPCA. The same approach was adopted by the evangelical

Christians who established the London City Mission in 1835 to undertake proselytizing work with cab drivers; change was possible even for such reviled people.[92]

'Wild' domestic animals and the Smithfield market

In the late 1820s and 1830s the animals whose cruel treatment was to be the target of campaigners were mainly those already covered by legislation. While some would castigate the treatment of dancing dogs or creatures held in travelling menageries, it was overwhelmingly animals in the public domain performing functional, rather than entertaining or educative, roles that engaged the attention. Although individual campaigners placed different emphasis on strengthening the use of the law, or on personal intervention to change behaviour outside the scope of the law, all recognized that the practices of those employed around the Smithfield cattle market, then a market for live animals, needed attention.

The animals driven to Smithfield were 'domestic' animals; they provided potential food. The fashionable did not venture into the cattle market to gaze at the cattle and sheep as interesting forms of life, as they did in the fashionable Regent's Park zoological gardens on the other side of the capital; this was not a site intended to provide enjoyment or instruction. Instead, it was to be avoided, for here unrestricted acts of cruelty were inflicted on animals. Ironically, while the zoo offered a sanitized spectacle of 'wild' animals, the practices of the cattle drovers ensured that 'domestic' animals became wild and ferocious, particularly in the crowded streets of London.

Smithfield had been a traditional cattle market on the outskirts of the medieval City of London for hundreds of years. There was a regular market on a Monday and Friday at which cattle driven from all over the country were sold. Brought to the then outskirts of London, cattle gathered at Mile End, Islington, Knightsbridge, Newington, Paddington, Bayswater and Holloway on the day before the last lap of their journey.[93] The animals were then transferred to London-based drovers, working for the market, who deprived them of water, food and rest and beat them mercilessly towards their destination.[94] Since such practices took place within a wide radius, those going about their business or leisure activities would have ample opportunity to witness them.

The ill-treatment of the cattle was not new; the environment in which it occurred was. By the nineteenth century Smithfield was surrounded by buildings. Opposite was St Bartholemew's Hospital. Towards the river was Newgate Prison – and the Newgate Shambles where butchers and slaughterers plied their trade.[95] As far back as the fourteenth century there had been complaints about the butchers in the shambles slaughtering animals in the street, fouling the thorough-fares and polluting the water supply, a feature common to butchers' shambles wherever their location.[96] Now the shambles were a mere five minutes' walk away from Cheapside, once the traditional market area of the City, but now a street stuffed with new shops and trades, linen, lace and other luxury goods for the prosperous woman.[97] Smithfield with its old traditions was located in a transitional envi-ronment on the borders of the traditional square mile of the City, with its new Bank of England, stock exchange and trading houses. It was this new geography, this new space – or, as Chris Philo has discussed, a revived animal geography – in which the old customs were prac-tised, which gave rise to a range of grounds for excluding animals from the city.[98]

The campaign to close down the Smithfield market was essentially conducted on two separate but linked themes: the adverse effect on animals and the adverse effect on people, both those who carried out cruelty and those who lived or worked in the vicinity and who were obliged to see it. The anonymous pamphleteer who wrote against the 'fiend-like depravity' exhibited at Smithfield market suggested that humans were distinguished from animals by reason while the latter were creatures of instinct. But, he went on, since humans were abusing this free agency, how were humans superior except in depravity? The 'higher ranks' in society oppressed and persecuted the poor through vagrancy and game laws which led in turn, he argued, to men in the lowest stations of life becoming the persecutors and tormentors of animals as their own inferiors. Christian philanthropists then had a duty to take a stand against the practices in Smithfield as examples of 'malignant moral distemper'.[99]

Animals at the market were exhausted, thirsty and hungry. When they collapsed with fatigue, cattle and sheep were harried by savage dogs trained to worry them. Every week 35,000 or more sheep and cattle were driven to the pens; every week the tails were cut at the tip to distinguish between those sold and unsold.[100] In winter the sheep were frequently sheared brutally in preparation for the special Christmas market and suffered from cold in addition to the usual iniquities.[101]

Although the specific corralling and contingent brutality took place in the tiny streets of West Smithfield, the harassment by drovers took place all over London as they beat on the animals towards the market. The cruelty emanating from this one place thereby rippled out through London. Frances Maria Thompson, a patron of the Animal Friends' Society, explained it thus: 'The increasing instances of cruelty in our streets have now risen to such a height that it is impossible to go any distance from home without encountering something to wound our feelings.'[102]

Even staying at home did not mean that people were immune from witnessing cruelty to animals. On a later occasion Mrs Thompson wrote to *The Voice of Humanity*, 'A poor donkey in a cart has just passed my window, with a man riding, and beating it with a stick as large as my arm most violently on the sides, til it nearly fell in the

Sheep in a slaughterer's den.
From an issue of *The Animals' Friend*, 1840.

slippery frost and snow.'[103] However it was not just cruelty towards defenceless animals in their own environment which provided an impetus for women like Mrs Thompson. Such acts were part of an old world of barbarity, unfit for the new city with its new middle class. Regularly *The Voice of Humanity* contrasted illustrations of the barbaric knackers' yard, the destination of old and worn out horses, with prints of the new abattoir in Paris and the steam engine that could replace the weary horse.[104] Such pleas against cruelty were constructed as part of a modern, city-based society disengaging itself from a former barbarity. As the MP Richard Martin, who also became involved in campaigns to close down the market, declared disapprovingly: 'On a market day a man might as well walk in a country cattle-fair as from Ludgate Hill to Lombard Street.'[105] Such rural scenes were not appropriate for the new space of the city, nor were they part of an idyllic rural past. The threat to order caused by ferocious 'farm' animals in the new city was another cause for complaint:

> Bullocks driven mad by the treatment they receive are afterwards taken through all parts of London, causing many accidents to the passengers and serious frights to females, particularly those who may be enceinte (sic), some of which are occasionally published in the papers but many are never made known at all, but suppressed.[106]

These scenes had no part in a city defining itself as civilized:

> Screams of terrified women and children present scenes of disorder which one could hardly expect to find even in the worst regulated towns in Europe, but which are highly disgraceful to one of the largest, most populous and richest capitals in the universe.[107]

I am not convinced that in seeking to find solutions to the cruelty inflicted upon sheep and cattle within the city, campaigners were attempting to 'feel a sense of kinship with their rural past', as Turner has suggested.[108] Rather, they were looking to the future. London, protesters lamented, was failing to lead the way as a seat of empire and centre of a new enlightened world. Even in New South Wales, Australia, 'that comparatively infant colony', there were proper regulations for the slaughter of cattle and for the driving of animals through the streets of Sydney.[109] Further, so horrific were seen to be the current methods of killing animals that the Jewish method of slaughter, which would be denounced in the future as barbaric, was advocated as a humane improvement.[110] In the 1820s Paris provided the model for killing animals – as well as for preserving them in its new zoo. Decades before Haussmann would blast a network of boulevards through the heart of the old medieval city, Paris would move into the modern world by erecting a public abattoir in the suburb of Montmartre.[111] But in London, abattoirs, unlike zoos, were not fashionable: public slaughterhouses were not established until pressure succeeded in moving the new local government structures later in the century. Ironically, the future model slaughterhouse would not be in London but in Letchworth, the first garden city, in which an idealized relationship between city and countryside would be moulded.[112]

In 1828, six years after legislation had first been introduced to protect farm animals from wanton cruelty, a petition was presented to Parliament about the conditions at Smithfield market. The petition, signed by city merchants, bankers and local inhabitants, with the support of Richard Martin, the MP behind the 1822 Act, sought to establish an inquiry into the manner in which cattle were driven and the conditions in which they were kept at the market . A later report would also emphasize the disruption and distress the market caused to respectable people who traded nearby, including Mr Bullin, a surgeon in Farringdon Street and Mr Lamplough, a chemist of Snow Hill.[113] Campaigners were concerned both with the horrors they witnessed on the streets and with what they could not see, but only imagine.[114] At night local residents could hear the animals' cries of distress as they were rounded into the pens and they were prevented from sleeping 'as the dreadful blows inflicted on the cattle are distinctly heard in their bedrooms'.[115] That it happened on a Sunday night was a 'shocking conclusion to the Christian sabbath':[116] 'Favoured by the darkness of the night, animals scarcely able to walk (literally on their last legs) and in a dying state, are forced by the merciless goad within the pale of the market, if possible, otherwise they remain in the streets adjacent.'[117]

Further, much killing of animals took place underground in cellars into which animals were precipitated to a depth of several feet and 'often [had] their jaws and legs broken by the fall'.[118] Such practices were unseen but conjured up in the evocative illustrations of the journal *The Animals' Friend*. While campaigners did not necessarily

Fiend-like practices in night-time Smithfield. A 'Night View of Smithfield Market',
London, from an issue of *The Animals' Friend*, 1838.

become vegetarians they were horrified about the effect meat butchered
in such circumstances would have on human health: 'The idea of
eating the flesh of animals that have been killed in a state of disease
is revolting to our nature.'[119] The poor condition of meat, it was
argued, was due to butchers who killed animals in a feverish state and
also stirred animals' brains with sticks, allegedly to make the meat
tender.[120] Since slaughterhouses were private property they were
exempt from regulation or inspection. Where the meat went – and its
condition – was also hidden. In the 1850s and 1860s the Gamgee
brothers, a vet and a physician, established that a fifth of meat eaten in
the UK came from very diseased animals – and that such diseases were
transmittable to people. In response, some cities, such as Leeds, introduced vigilant inspection, so diseased meat was instead transferred to
nearby York; in other towns such as Aberdeen meat was taken into the
city at night to escape inspection.[121] The issue of diseased food, which
would occupy the minds of sanitary reformers, humanitarians and
vegetarians alike in late Victorian society, had its precedents in the
debates about the Smithfield market decades earlier.

In 1868, some 45 years after the first lobbies and tracts, the market
was finally replaced by a dead animal market and the Newgate

Shambles were closed down.[122] However, cattle did not disappear from the London streets. A new cattle market was established in 1855 in Islington, between Copenhagen Fields and Camden Town, where it took advantage of the new railway built at King's Cross. Animals continued to be brought into London, but increasingly by rail and they were sold on the outskirts of the city.[123] (As late as the 1960s, as the photographs of Don McCullin testify, sheep, now competing with heavy traffic, were still being herded down the Caledonian Road.) In 1871, in Deptford in south London, a new cattle market was established by the City Corporation exclusively for the live foreign cattle trade. But barbaric methods of slaughter continued, drawing the attention in due course of the Humanitarian League and other late Victorian reformers.[124]

Who was engaged in animal campaigns and why?

On a simplistic level the closing down of the Smithfield market, the establishment of public abattoirs, drinking troughs and fountains with pure water, and streets free of the lash would ameliorate the condition of animals in the city. And further, such changes would improve daily life for people working and living in the city, who were directly or indirectly affected by the presence of animals in the metropolis. But the campaign for animals took on an importance beyond this, for their treatment became bound up with class formation and differentiation. It was not that middle-class people took up the cause of animals; but that by acting in benevolent and charitable ways towards animals people proved themselves to be different from both the degenerate rabble and the indolent aristocrat.

The first years of the century witnessed radical and religious ideas underpinning the thinking on animals. As the century continued animals become the focus of a growing consciousness of new class awareness and distinctiveness. In 1828 William Mackinnon, a Scottish Conservative MP and barrister, published his book, *On the Rise, Progress, and Present State of Public Opinion*, described as the single book most obsessed with the 'middle class' ever to appear in English.[125] In it he expounded on the crucial role 'civilization' and 'progress' must play in the discussion of human affairs; attributes entwined with the rise of the middle class. In practical terms Mackinnon himself exemplified these attributes through his identification with concerns about the position of animals. He was a committee member of the SPCA and also the chair of the Rational Humanity Group, which emphasized the extension of 'temperate, yet efficient legislation' to benefit animals.[126] Mackinnon had been active in Parliament pressing for increased inspection of animal markets, slaughterhouses and knackers' yards. This interest was no anomaly; for him humanity, philanthropy and religion were inextricably linked and he sought to show this through improvements in animals' lives. To this end, he chaired the parliamentary committee on cruelty of 1832, which heard a series of witnesses from all walks of life recount their experiences of witnessing ill-treatment of animals.[127]

The months leading up to the passing of the Reform Act of 1832, which incorporated the male middle class within the parliamentary franchise while explicitly excluding women and working-class voters, saw a plethora of demonstrations and agitations in which middle- and working-class reformers manoeuvred for control of the move-ment.[128] The social divisions were often greater between the skilled artisans and the unskilled masses than between the working and middle class. Large numbers of lower middle-class and even working-class male householders were enfranchised, at least in London, where rents were high.[129] Establishment concern about the extent of agita-tion had been given voice in a lurid publication, *Householders in Danger from the Populace*, brought out in 1831 by Edward Gibbon Wakefield.[130] He exhorted householders in London to arm themselves against the populace of London bent on producing anarchy, seeing the main threat as arising from common thieves and the rabble. What is striking about those defined as rabble is the number of jobs cited which are related to animals in some form. Many of the same jobs under attack from the SPCA, Animal Friends' Society and Rational Humanity Group are the self-same trades that Wakefield vilifies: drovers, slaughterers of cattle, knackers, dealers in dogs' meat and costermongers. All were defined as 'the enemies of law and order and helots of society'.[131]

The approbation that animal campaigners had been keen to apply to those behaving in a humane and civilized way towards animals is replicated explicitly within the political sphere. The treatment of animals becomes a political issue not because of its discussion in

Parliament but because of the incorporation of such sentiments into definitions of respectable working-class and middle-class behaviour. In being prosecuted for cruelty to animals, Brian Harrison has suggested that 'working men were suffering for the humanitarian notions being pioneered by other social classes'.[132] However, distinctions between classes were still being refined prior to the 1832 Act and an orientation towards animals was to play a significant part in the consolidation of class identities. When the French socialist and feminist Flora Tristan, visiting London in 1840, wrote so scathingly of those who promoted better treatment of animals, this was done in the knowledge that such concerns had been adopted by the middle class. It was not the emphasis on humane treatment as such that she derided, but the fact that it was endorsed by those she believed had scant regard for the living standards of working people. 'Fancy', she ironically exclaimed, 'considering the welfare of horses, donkeys and dogs! Think how generous they must be towards their fellow men! . . . Just another piece of humbug . . . [their] aim is to keep a closer watch on the menials employed to tend their precious animals, for as our French proverb says, "He who would travel far takes good care of his mount!"'[133]

Animals become a woman's concern

The appropriation of animals as a focus for political and philanthropic intervention had a distinct gendered dimension. From the 1820s women were involved with men in the main animal welfare groups. In the SPCA this was as patronesses; in the Rational Humanity Group they worked alongside men as benefactors as well as forming local branches, giving donations, writing to the press and fully involving themselves in the propaganda of the organization.[134] The Group's strategy of 'personal interference . . . [and] the reproof of acts of oppression and cruelty, administered with due mildness' was one in which women could readily participate.[135] In the Animal Friends' Society, a Ladies' Association was formed and many women became members and patronesses, attracted by its practical proselytizing emphasis. The Society stressed the importance of the printed and spoken word in changing the behaviour of *all* classes, declaring that upon receiving printed 'admonitions', many responsible for ill-treatment of horses 'frequently desisted, and even forsook their chaises &c in silent shame'.[136]

The involvement of women within the 'umbrella organizations' of the 1820s and 1830s animals' movement is important. I raise this not as a mere counter to the status given to the founding fathers such as Martin, Wilberforce and Erskine, but to attempt to define the nature of these movements for animal welfare historically. In a period in which there was a struggle for hegemony among conflicting visions of a new society, the appropriate role for women in political and social movements was being established.[137] Concurrently, as Clare Midgley has carefully argued, women's establishment of anti-slavery associations from 1825 was an indicator of their involvement in a key movement for political reform. Anti-slavery activity went beyond philanthropy into the public political sphere.[138] In similar vein the activity of women from the developing middle class in the cause of animals involved the laying of a political veneer across activities deemed the concern of women. The relationship between women and animals was being extended beyond their domestic role of responsibility for pets within the home into a broader concern for animals outside the familial unit.

Against the rabble and the aristocrat

By the 1830s and 1840s concern for the condition of animals was established as a distinctive feature of 'the respectable'. But the positive view of human behaviour prevalent in particular among the supporters of the Animal Friends' Society and the Rational Humanity Group led to an awareness that appropriate behaviour was possible, even in those from very poor backgrounds. Further, those working with animals could be reformed, if their job or the conditions under which they carried it out also changed.[139] This position, which did not lump all working people together as cruel, was well illustrated by the evidence which William MacKinnon, the Rational Humanity Group MP, heard when chairing the parliamentary committee against cruelty in 1832. He listened to accounts from supporters of dog-fighting, including the owner of the West Smithfield pit, who protested that he looked after his fighting dogs with brandy, water and beef tea.[140] Former attenders at dog-fights testified that they had broken with the sport and realized it was cruel, while taking care to mention that those generally attending were 'noblemen and governors' or 'gentlemen'.[141] The same committee heard tales of working people exhibiting great attachment to their pets. Thomas Young, for instance, was a porter on the London Docks, engaged in carrying sailors' hammocks and chests. He had had a series of cats, but unfortunately he had lost several to the cat skinners. Young swore that he recognized the skin of a poor creature he had owned ever since he had raised it from a kitten.[142] A humane man, he also testified against butchers who organized dog-fighting in the Mile End Road and Whitechapel.[143] Such working-class affection for pet cats was exhibited in more extravagant fashion by other Londoners. After the introduction of legislation tightening definitions of animal cruelty in 1835, the SPCA successfully sentenced a man to three months hard labour for skinning his neighbours' cats. So fierce was their outrage that the police had difficulty in preventing the cat-owning neighbours from throwing the brute into the Fleet Canal.[144]

Publicity would be given to acts of individual kindness towards animals, across the social scale. Stories were published praising the benign treatment of the Duke of Wellington towards his horse Copenhagen, which had borne him at the Battle of Waterloo, and even towards a frog.[145] In another narrative, an old soldier was depicted as a modern good Samaritan. He had turned on a pump for parched sheep and then borne the wrath of their drover. Such an act served to distinguish him from the rabble. However, a passing gentleman attempted to tip the soldier for his good deed. Annoyed at such a patronizing attitude, the soldier turned down the money saying, 'Sir, do you think I would accept payment for giving a drop of water to them poor sheep? No, never, sir, I couldn't bemoan myself so much . . . I am an old soldier, and many a weary march have I had thirsty and footsore, and I know what these poor sheep feel.'[146]

In more practical vein suggestions were made to improve the conditions in which the poor kept bees. The Apiarian Society, which had been established in Exeter in the later eighteenth century, took off with the publication of Thomas Nutt's book *Humanity to Honey Bees,* which had run to seven editions by 1827. Specifically, 'artificial hives' were suggested. Here the structures could remain – and also the bees – after the honey was harvested, which meant that bees were not killed through smoking and thus survived until the next season.[147] This innovation was reported approvingly in the journal *The Voice of Humanity* as a practical example of 'rational humanity'.[148]

However, although little attention has been previously paid to this, in the early statements of those campaigning for animals in the 1820s and 1830s criticism was specifically directed to the inhumane practices of the aristocracy and wealthy towards animals. In his hugely popular book, *A Practical View of the Prevailing Religious System of Professed Christians*, William Wilberforce of the SPCA had castigated field sports which were designed to 'fill up the void of a listless and languid age'.[149] One of the first instances of cruelty which *The Voice of Humanity* publicized was the flogging to death of a young foxhound belonging to the East Kent foxhounds.[150] The Rational Humanity Group broadened this attack on hunting; particularly the keeping of 'domestic' stags for the purpose.[151] In phrases reminiscent of modern criticism, the group was particularly scathing when it was realized that both stags *and* foxes were bred specifically to be hunted.[152] For its part *The Animals' Friend* declared, 'No one in his senses can think that to hunt and tear a living being to pieces for sport is not wickedness in the extreme.'[153]

Although a new respectability grew by setting itself against both the lower rabble and the dissolute fox-hunting aristocrat, the defining locus of actual campaigns in the 1830s were the streets in the cities, a site redolent of the cruelty of those working with animals, rather than those hunting them. It was the emphasis on personal engagement and observation of cruelty that distinguished the early campaigns. The future emphasis on different locations – and different types of animals – would owe much to people's social, political and cultural preoccupations.

THREE

Continuity and change: fallen dogs and Victorian tales

I wonder who'll have yer, my beauty, when him as you're all to is dead!
There, stow your perlaver a minit, I know as my end is nigh;
Is a cove to turn round on his dog, like, just 'cos he's goin' to die?[1]

The first decades of the nineteenth century saw the animal welfare movement following the Benthamite nostrum, namely that existence of physical pain – or feelings – rather than speech should determine human attitudes towards animals. The inherent ambiguities in the statement grew more apparent. By implication, the distinction between humans and animals was irrelevant if both were to be defined by their possession of feelings. But kind treatment of animals itself became an act which distinguished between people and animals. The ideas of commonality and differentiation shared many features. Both positions were concerned with applauding life and both had the practical outcome of benign behaviour towards animals.[2] Animal campaigners went beyond the earlier strategy of personal witness of perceived cruelty as an impetus to action, towards concern for animals with which they could feel empathy. By the 1840s and 1850s the attention of the middle class became directed towards the animals found within their own homes. As one philosopher, Stephen Clark, has suggested: 'We mind about those close to us, about those like us, about those who embody qualities our evolutionary and historical past have taught us to admire and love. People who lack such sentiments are not rational sages, but psychopaths.'[3]

Charles Darwin's *Origin of Species* was not published until 1859, but his exploration of the continuum of human and animal existence, which underpinned much of the impetus towards animal protection, was evident from his journeys of exploration in the 1830s. Writing in 1837, he suggested that animals were 'our fellow brethren in pain, disease, death, suffering, and famine – our slaves in the most laborious works, our companions in our amusements – they may partake of our origin in one common ancestor – we may be all melted together'.[4] Darwin's theories, and practical examples applied to domestic situations, helped give a scientific authority to demands for a raised status for animals within human affairs.

Darwin suggested that a greater empathy with animal suffering was not only humane, but rational. Moved by its complexity and beauty, Darwin took a holistic view of nature.[5] While seeking to ascertain the nature of their competition, he was also interested in the interdependence of species and the way in which plants and animals were bound together by a web of complex relations.[6] His strong empathy with animals and ascription to them of emotions was particularly reflected in his fondness for dogs; and he used his relationship with his household companions to inform his scientific writing. The devoted behaviour of a dog who remembered him despite his absence for five years on HMS *Beagle*[7] was used to illuminate his theory that dogs had a conscious life: 'But can we feel sure that an old dog with an excellent memory and some power of imagination, as shewn by his dreams, never reflects on his past pleasures in the chase? and [sic] this would be a form of self-consciousness.'[8]

Darwin's empathy extended into his emotional commitment to the objects of his thesis:

> . . . I would as soon be descended from that heroic little monkey, who braved his dreaded enemy in order to save the life of his keeper, or from that old baboon, who descending from the mountains, carried away in triumph his young comrade from a crowd of astonished dogs – as from a savage who delights to torture his enemies . . .[9]

The animals about which Darwin wrote could be seen in the zoological gardens or in the homes of people of all sections of society; he was challenging perceptions about the encounters people had on a daily basis with the animals in their immediate environment. The work of Darwin and his contemporaries was to have a profound influence on cultural and intellectual life – and on the popular perception of animals. Lavishly illustrated books were published between 1838 and 1843, partly financed with treasury support, illustrating Darwin's voyage on the *Beagle*.[10] The writings of his associate, Thomas Huxley, also became popular. Copies of Huxley's *Man's Place in*

Nature were distributed through Mudie's circulating library and reputedly were 'torn from the hands of Mudie's shopmen as if they were novels'.[11] The subsequent debate between Huxley and Bishop (Soapy Sam) Wilberforce during the meeting of the British Association at Oxford University in 1860 received publicity extending far beyond the scientific or religious communities. Ridiculing 'Darwin badly, and Huxley savagely', the bishop bantered to Huxley '[was] it on his grandfather's or his grandmother's side that the ape ancestry comes in?'[12] In his retort Huxley claimed that he felt it no shame to have risen from a monkey, 'But I should feel it a shame to have sprung from one who prostituted the gifts of culture and of eloquence to the services of prejudice and of falsehood.'[13]

In the work of both Darwin and Huxley there was a willingness to be personally identified with 'lower' animals as part of a continuum of living experience. The identification of people with animals had previously been projected onto the lowest sections of human society, who were seen by their brutish behaviour to resemble what was defined as brute creation. Darwin and Huxley allowed for a possible identification of more 'civilized' sections of society with animals, which in turn suggested the differentiated status of certain animals.

Natural history in the home

The growing interest in science went beyond visits to the zoo, or reading the publications of the Society for the Diffusion of Useful Knowledge, or attending classes. Through the craze for vivaria, Wardian glass cases and microscopes, scientific discovery entered into the very homes of the middle class. For Huxley modern civilization itself rested upon physical science, for it made intelligence and moral energy stronger than brute force.[14] Practically, he suggested that a vivarium of tiny living creatures, which mimicked larger displays in the zoo, should be established for children within their own homes.[15] As the naturalist Philip Gosse, the father of the writer Edmund, recommended, if one could grow plants in a closed Wardian glass case, one could also sustain tiny creatures in this environment.[16] Aquaria were also developed with the dual function of keeping fish as pets and enabling the study of marine life. The microscope, which allowed the operator to gaze on aspects of nature previously hidden from the human eye, became fashionable. Although a scientific instrument, it was accessible to the lay middle classes. In turn the fashion for geological and botanical drawing developed, its advocates including the feminist pioneer Lydia Becker, who won a national prize for collecting and drawing dried plants.[17]

New animals on the street

These new ideas took place within an urban environment in which animals still worked and were visible on streets. However the closure of Smithfield as a live cattle market meant that a change took place in the types of animals seen within the cities. Still the livelihood of thousands of people relied on a relationship with 'their distant cousins'. The accounts by the journalist Henry Mayhew in 1861 of the trades of London present a view of employment in which the relationship between animals and people is very close – and not necessarily cruel.[18] Historians have frequently plundered Mayhew's accounts to illustrate a number of arguments about London life, but the extent and range of his subjects' debt to live or dead animals for their employment has been ignored. On page after page of his writings he tells the reader stories of those who worked in the streets and markets of London, and the part that animals played in this. Rat-catchers, dog-stealers, bird-snarers and costermongers all relied in different ways upon animals for their livelihood. Even the street-sweepers were often accompanied by a dog, cat, rabbit or even guinea pig to gain sympathy and bigger tips from passers-by.[19] Although the specific jobs connected with animals that Wakefield had characterized as disreputable in the 1830s were changing, new types of work, also associated with animals, continued to be viewed with disdain.

Furthermore, the change in work patterns was accompanied by a geographical shift in the areas seen as most notorious. The ignominy attached to the environs of Smithfield transferred to parts of east and south London where new trades were being developed. The fur trade in which women worked with dead animals, preparing skins for furriers to make coats for the wealthy, typified for many the lower depths. In his proselytizing tract *The Bitter Cry of Outcast London*, the Congregational minister Andrew Mearns described the process: '. . . here you are choked as you enter by the air laden with

An idealized image of a coster and his 'moke'. 'A Thriving Coster',
from G. Holden Pike, *Golden Lane*, London, 1876.

particles of the superfluous fur pulled from the skins of rabbits, rats,
dogs and other animals in their preparation for the furrier.'[20]

For Mearns, working with animals implied contact with the most
wretched in society. In similar fashion he described Collier's Rents in
Bermondsey, in which the houses were largely occupied by costermongers, bird-catchers, street-singers, liberated convicts, thieves and
prostitutes.[21] Indeed whole districts of London were dominated by
jobs using animals. In the 1830s Smithfield had been a focus for the
live cattle trade; in the mid- and late-nineteenth century most of
the Bermondsey district just south of the river, for example, was taken
up with industries reliant on dead animals. Tanneries proliferated
throughout the area, next to the Bermondsey workhouse, or to a tin

and zinc works, or to a dairy in Abbey Street. The grandly named Neckinger Mills were, likewise, tanneries and a currier. Glue and size works, a rag and bone store, a wool and hides warehouse, a brush manufactory and the Bermondsey leather market were all features of a community as directly and economically reliant for its existence upon animals as were the rural poor.[22] Dog faeces, or 'pure', also provided a livelihood of sorts for the very poor. 'Pure' was collected for use in the Bermondsey tanneries. 'Pure finders' trudged the streets with a bucket to earn a pittance, with a more fortunate few obtaining their product by cleaning dog kennels. Originally this trade had been pursued exclusively by elderly women, but, as Mayhew's female protagonist complained, much of the work had now gone to men, the market was flooded and wages had fallen in consequence.[23]

With the houses of the poor crowded around the workplaces there was nowhere to escape from the stench of dead animals: 'the air reeks with evil smells . . . it is a sight to see the men pouring out from all the works. Their clothes are marked with many stains; their trousers are discoloured by tan; some have aprons and gaiters of raw hide; and about them all seems to hang a scent of blood.'[24] With Southwark Park, a good walk away, the only space for public recreation, it is understandable that the area was subsequently designated as one of the 'blackest' in London by Charles Booth in his survey of the labouring poor.[25] Even the relatively innocuous bird trade in the nearby New Kent Road came in for criticism from the Reverend Maurice Davies, the colourful wordsmith of London eccentricities, who declared that those who dealt in birds were disreputable. On a Sunday in the New Kent Road bets were laid on linnet-singing competitions. It was, he said, 'generally a "birdy" neighbourhood. Its staple products, to judge by the shops, seemed birds and beer'.[26]

Changing character: helping animals

Bird-dealers, tanners and collectors of dog faeces were not specific targets of philanthropists, religious missions or those campaigning explicitly for better treatment of animals. The behaviour of such people was apparently thought incapable of being changed through persuasion. Redemption was seen as possible, however, for those working directly with horses and donkeys. Costermongers who traversed the London streets with their barrows of goods drawn by donkeys were seen as a distinct class of people cut off from the rest of metropolitan society.[27] Costers were not sufficiently tainted by a brutalization endemic to the work – as were butchers and slaughtermen – that it was thought necessary for them to take on new trades. In fact their attitude towards their animals was seen as an important indicator of their potential moral capacities; and their often kind treatment towards their donkeys suggested that change of disposition was possible. Mayhew attributed to costermongers a positive disposition towards their mokes, which they 'almost universally treat with kindness'.[28] Even the religious magazine *The Leisure Hour,* which catalogued the poor principles of the costermongers, nevertheless praised their kindness and humanity towards their animals.[29] They were also indulgent with their pets, who often ate the same food as their owners.[30] For W. J. Orsman, who founded the Golden Lane Mission and Hoxton Costers' Mission in 1861, the costers' treatment of their animals had almost a redemptive character. The changed character of the coster led in turn to changed circumstances for his donkey. Orsman thought that because of their lowly work costermongers were unfairly 'shut out, as it were, from all intercourse of a civilising and moralising kind . . . they are bold, reckless, and sublimely indifferent to public opinion, which alternately brands them as a nuisance, and welcomes them as an indispensable domestic convenience'.[31]

Like the members of the Metropolitan Drinking Fountain and Cattle Trough Association, Orsman was providing support for men and animals alike in practical ways: instituting a barrow club to lend barrows free to those in hard times and encouraging better treatment of animals. Further, costers were encouraged to consider their humble donkeys as a spectacle, an object worthy of visual attention – and humane care. Donkey shows would be held in the People's Palace in the Mile End Road. Opened in the 1880s, the palace was designed to bring West End culture to the East End, particularly in visual form through exhibitions, flower shows, art displays, debates, dances and choral concerts.[32] Baroness Angela Burdett-Coutts regularly presented prizes at the People's Palace and at the Whit Monday cart-horse parade held annually in Regent's Park.[33] The donkey shows, in which the owners would compete for cash prizes or a meerschaum pipe or a

The Costers' and Street Traders' Donkey Show at the People's Palace, Mile End, east London, May 1909. From the show programme, reprinted in the *Twelfth Annual Report* of the Our Dumb Friends' League, 1909.

cup presented by the queen, would continue well into the twentieth century. Awards were also specifically made to donkeys in the form of sacks of crushed oats or forage for the oldest donkey in the show in best condition, or for the donkey owned the longest by one person. Programmes listed the names of donkeys, and their owners, with details of age, value and the sort of work the donkey undertook, in similar vein to racecourse programmes listing the form of thorough-bred horses. The animals which provided a spectacle were the same animals which trudged the streets for up to six days every week working for street traders, coal dealers, fish hawkers and green-grocers. But once a year they performed the same role as the animals in the zoo, providing a source of public spectacle and pleasure. That donkeys were given affectionate names such as Baby, Patsy, Georgie or Trotting Jimmy perhaps gives credence to the influence Orsman was reputed to have had upon costers:[34] 'Now-a-days a respectable coster must have a sleek-coated, well-fed ass, or he will lose prestige among a large proportion of his fraternity.'[35]

While the transformation of donkeys into a spectacle was a strategy for improving costers' moral standing and the treatment of these animals, a different approach was adopted for cab drivers. A stated

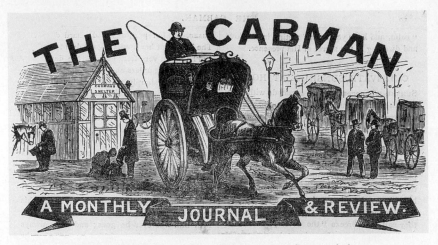

Feeding the horses – and the drivers – at the cabman's shelter.
From the masthead of *The Cabman*, December 1875.

aim of the Cabmen's Mission Hall established at King's Cross in 1871 was the promotion of the spiritual and moral welfare of cabmen; a means of achieving this end was the good treatment of their horses.[36] The journal of the mission thus included articles on both horse management and temperance. Lectures were held in which drivers were told that the difference between men and animals was not of kind, but of degree.[37] A Cab Drivers' Benevolent Association was also established which boasted amongst its patrons Cardinal Manning, known for his support of dockworkers, and the Earl of Shaftesbury, famous for his child protection initiatives and a regular presenter of prizes at the costers' donkey shows.[38] The close relationship between improvement in people's behaviour and a consequent improvement in the treatment of horses was used in different vein by William Booth, the founder of the Salvation Army, in his important book, *In Darkest England and the Way Out*. For Booth, the London cab horse:

> is a very real illustration of poor broken-down humanity; he usually falls down because of overwork and underfeeding. If you put him on his feet without altering his conditions, it would only be to give him another dose of agony; but first of all you'll have to pick him up again.[39]

Analogies worked both ways. The practical solutions which animal campaigners had applied to horses should, he continued, be applied to their human equivalents. While organizations campaigned for the implementation and extension of the law against the ferocious driving of omnibus horses, pamphlets and books were also issued by religious groups against cruel treatment of horses.[40] Organizations such as the Horse Accident Prevention Society also raised awareness about the conditions under which horses worked. The practice of repaving streets with asphalt rather than wood, for example, was dangerous for horses. As the Society declared, the streets of London were never intended for the benefit of shareholders in asphalt companies, a view later shared by the cab drivers' union, which criticized the smooth surfaces of the roads and welcomed the action of those councils that laid down sand to help the horses.[41]

Popular fiction and popular images

Campaigns against fierce driving and the over working of horses were given a massive boost by the publication in 1877 of Anna Sewell's *Black Beauty*. The descriptions of the exploitation of horses, particularly on the London streets, was deemed so realistic that the RSPCA endorsed a number of editions of the book and in the United States George Angell, the founder of the American Humane Society, issued free copies to American cabmen with the subtitle 'The Uncle Tom's Cabin of the Horse'.[42]

Black Beauty, which sold one million copies in the first two years of publication, would also be significant in campaigning against the fashion of bearing reins, which held the horse's head erect and prevented movement, a craze particularly introduced by women, who believed it was stylish.[43] Its use was encouraged by the fad for lavish funerals. In London alone 'Black Masters', those who supplied black horses for funerals, grew in the later nineteenth century to the extent that by the 1890s there were over 700 such horses in London under the control of five firms, one of which, Flemings in East Road, near Old Street, named them after famous people such as Wesley and the locally born atheist MP Charles Bradlaugh.[44] Significantly, the ill-treatment of Black Beauty and his peers cuts across class: the cruel bearing rein is introduced by Lady W–, whereas Jerry, with whom Black Beauty worked as a cab horse in London, is, 'as good a driver as I had ever known'.[45]

While throughout the nineteenth century horses continued to be an object of the animal campaigners' attention, the dog came to the fore in the middle of the century. Dogs became increasingly important in cultural and political life, popularized through fiction and visual images, in particular in the work of one of Queen Victoria's favourite painters, Landseer. His early paintings for the queen included *Queen Victoria's Favourite Pets,* which displayed her King Charles spaniel, Dash, and Albert's greyhound, Eos, as well as a deerhound and parrot.[46] Paintings such as *Dignity and Impudence* remain popular in the 1990s: currently discerning art lovers can purchase fridge magnets of the aforesaid dogs in the Tate Gallery shop.[47] Unlike earlier eighteenth-century paintings where animals were portrayed as part of the family, in Landseer's work they were often depicted as subjects in their own right, and as individual beings with a particular temperament and character. This is particularly evident in the critically acclaimed *Old Shepherd's Chief Mourner,* in which the dog is a substitute for human mourners, and is displaying loyalty even after the death of its owner.[48]

The dog as spectacle

In rather different fashion the focus on dogs was extended to the institution of dog shows. Here was an opportunity for people to display their own domestic animals as objects of the gaze. The relatively mundane animal within the home was elevated to the status of spectacle. As the writer on animals Jane Loudon put it, 'The dog is unquestionably the noblest of all domestic pets.'[49] What was new was the role the dog was playing as visual object as well as family companion or working animal. The functions the dog was required to perform drew both on the paintings of the period and on the growing interest in scientific discoveries. Pure-bred dogs, long established amongst the aristocracy, now became attributes of the middle class. Dogs were judged according to their particular breeds: appearance was all. These were not the mongrels and stray mutts, aligned to the indigent and the rabble, which frequented the streets of the metropolis, but dogs belonging to those who defined themselves as respectable. The first show took place in 1859 in the north of England at Newcastle-upon-Tyne, when 23 pointers and 27 setters were exhibited.[50]

Dogs with individual characters.
Edwin Landseer, *Dignity and Impudence*, 1839.

By 1873 the Kennel Club had been formed to disseminate information and regulate breeds. The human concern with eugenics and the effects of good breeding was clearly reflected in this new form of display. Visual aids were available to help the dog enthusiast. Sydenham Teak Edwards had published his book of dog prints many years before,[51] but the first comprehensive book on the history of the individual breeds of dog was published in 1866 by George R. Jesse, who was to become well known in the animal welfare world because of his vigorous and vociferous opposition to the muzzling of dogs. There were also five editions of John Henry Walsh's *Dogs of the British Isles,* published between 1867 and 1886.[52] Walsh aimed to help the discerning owner define more accurately the different breeds and to be appraised of the rationale for the awarding of marks at dog shows, and the number of editions indicates his success in this venture.[53]

Although the first show was in the north, the fashion for exhibiting took off from the dog show of 1870 at the Crystal Palace. Organizations for specific breeds of dogs flourished: once the breed of dog had been satisfactorily determined by the Kennel Club it could join the ranks of dogs eligible for display. Significantly, two of the first dogs to be exhibited after the Crystal Palace show were those traditionally seen as ladies' dogs, the poodle and the Pomeranian, both of which received Kennel Club status in the 1870s. Teak Edwards had been scathing about the qualities of the Pomeranian, but it became an extremely popular breed, helped by the endorsement of Queen Victoria, who bred them at her kennels in Windsor, for which she won awards.[54] Leading society ladies fussed over Pomeranians too: the feminist anti-vivisectionist Frances Power Cobbe kept one, as would the suffragette Christabel Pankhurst many years later while in exile in Paris, much to the disgust of her socialist sister, Sylvia, who preferred the more lowly Scottish terrier.[55] Queen Victoria also took as pets collie dogs, which had previously been considered shepherd's dogs, quite unpretentious animals.[56] And she gave her name and status to a range of products dealing with dogs. The London Royal Canine Surgery and Hospital in fashionable South Moulton Street enjoyed her patronage, as did Spratt's, the makers of dog biscuits. Spratt's – as the advertisements proudly declared – were used in the royal kennels and the Battersea Dogs' Home alike: the addition of beetroot, appealing to a dog's sweet tooth, encouraged dogs to eat vegetables, which was considered healthy.[57]

Many middle-class and aristocratic women took to dog exhibiting with enthusiasm, and formed the Ladies' Kennel Club, which had the specific remit of preventing cruelty in exhibiting practice and the maiming of particular breeds, which included the cropping of ears and the docking of tails. To this end exhibitions were held specifically for unmutilated toy dogs.[58] Queen Victoria, who had previously given her support to the SPCA, enabling it to adopt the title 'Royal Society', was also influential in changing behaviour towards animals by her refusal to have a mutilated dog in her presence.[59] Visual images of dogs featured prominently, too, in the publications of the Ladies' Kennel Club. *Notable dogs of the year (and their owners)* emphasized the royal connection with pictures of Turi, the queen's prize-winning Pomeranian and of the Irish setter Swell, owned by the Queen of the

Netherlands.[60] However the pictures of terriers, the *Wolverley Duchess* and *Wolverley Dolly*, held on leads by decidedly unenthusiastic domestic staff, indicate that the hard work that went into dog shows was borne in the main by servants and employees.[61]

In the world of dog exhibition and spectacle we have an elision of different cultural interests: a concern with the nature of species and breeding; discussion of the best sorts of breeds and practices for achieving this; combined with a public display of an animal and a keen awareness of the conditions in which animals were kept. The members of the Kennel Club or the Ladies' Kennel Club were neither animal rights activists nor natural historians, but their enthusiasms could not but help them be aware of the conditions in which animals lived.

Dogs were not just objects of the gaze in the spectacle of dog shows. Dogs from various stations in life were a regular sight on the streets of central London. Beggars, especially blind beggars accompanied by dogs, many of whom frequented Lincoln's Inn Fields, were a

Unenthusiastic domestic staff and their canine charges.
Wolverley Duchess and Wolverley Dolly, from 'Notable dogs of the year and their owners', reprinted from *The Ladies' Kennel Journal*, 1896.

constant feature in the middle of the century; as Charles Lamb recalled, 'The mendicants of this great city were so many of her sights, her lions.'[62] Because dogs were popular as pets they also provided a lucrative and often dishonest source of income: those with money would pay much for the return of their stolen dogs. Spaniels in particular could fetch a massive reward of £150.[63] The fashionable shopping area of Regent Street became a favourite haunt of 'dog fanciers', more properly described as dog-thieves, who lurked about the kerbs, 'with the little "dawgs" they have to sell tucked beneath their arms, made doubly attractive by much washing with scented soap, and the further decoration of their necks with pink or blue ribbons'.[64]

Other sights in the streets were dogs working as draught dogs, or carriers of small carts, for example delivering loaves – and warding off bread thieves. The dogs' soft paws were unsuited to the hard roads of the town and their collars and harnesses destroyed the animals' natural posture. Although there had been many attempts to legislate to protect dogs from such ill-treatment it was not until 1854 that dogs were finally protected from such exploitation, under a dog-cart bill which would prevent such working of dogs throughout the country.[65] Furthermore, despite the law against them, illegal dog-fights, frequented by a cross-section of dissolute men, continued, albeit now out of public scrutiny in private houses. Mayhew's interviewees advised him 'it's in private among the nobs';[66] the subjects of prosecutions bore this out. When an illegal international cock-fighting contest between Irish and English cocks was prosecuted in Cheshire, those found guilty included many 'in high social position'.[67]

Gelert and Greyfriars Bobby: two Victorian dogs

The way in which dogs were defined was influenced by scientific ideas, visual images and the growing popularity of dog narratives. In his edifying tome *Duty*, Samuel Smiles, better known for his writing on self-help, opposed cruelty to animals and related a number of stories emphasizing the loyalty of dogs[68] Two particularly popular examples were the tales of Gelert[69] and Greyfriars Bobby, both very much dogs of the nineteenth century in the almost human qualities of loyalty and conviction that they embodied. By the middle of the century there were many versions of Gelert's tale, the essence of which follows.[70]

Gelert was a brave and loyal hunting dog much loved by King Llewelyn. The dog was particularly attached to the baby prince, Morgan. One day the king was out hunting a particularly vicious wolf which had terrorized the neighbourhood, but had left Gelert back at the palace. On his return he saw the baby's cot overturned, the baby gone and Gelert, who welcomed him as usual, covered in gore: 'As Gelert held up his head to lick his hand he stabbed him to the heart. One deep groan the dog uttered – one last dying look he turned upon his master, and fell down dead.'[71] No sooner was the terrible deed done than the child appeared unscathed and the wolf, the real attacker, was found dead thanks to the paws and jaws of the brave Gelert. The king, full of remorse, erected a tomb for the much missed dog and went into perpetual mourning.

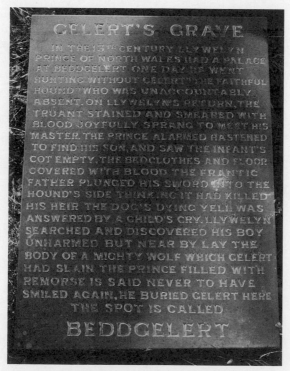

The mythic grave of a mythic dog.
Gelert's gravestone in Beddgelert, North Wales.

As William Robert Spencer described it in his poem on the event:

> There never could the spearman pass,
> Or forester, unmov'd;
> There oft the tear-besprinkled grass
> Llewelyn's sorrow prov'd.[72]

This romantic tale was not part of the *Mabinogion* nor a distant Celtic myth but a specific creation of the early years of the nineteenth century. But it was the right story for the right time – and was hugely popular. By 1860 articles were being written for the Eisteddfod on the true origins of the tale – brought, very mundanely, by the publican of the Royal Goat in Beddgelert in Snowdonia from his home in South Wales.[73] Versions were published for children, a ballad was written, 'as sung by the ancient Britons', and Spencer's poem went into several editions.[74] Prints of the grave proliferated and to this day can be viewed in the National Trust shop and the 'grave' nearby can be visited, complete with its anachronistic bilingual verse in English and Welsh. This modern marketing story follows the earlier tradition, and the fact is that it worked and created tourism in the area and was widely disseminated. It was seen as a story of the grief of a rash man, which came too late to mend matters; the grave became a monument to the 'victims of "well done and ill paid"'.[75]

The story of Greyfriars Bobby has a different content but a similar moral. A Skye terrier, Bobby, owned by a farmer named Grey, visited Traill's dining rooms every Wednesday with his master while they were at the Edinburgh cattle market on business. When Grey died in 1858 the dog continued to visit the dining rooms regularly, taking away the food he was given to eat at his master's grave nearby. Although a new home was found he rejected it and became a vagrant dog. For this Bobby was arrested and the owner of the dining rooms was accused of harbouring him without paying dog tax, a tax which was widely opposed and resented especially by working people.[76] Traill protested that he would have paid the dog tax but Bobby did not acknowledge him as his master because he was still loyal to the dead Grey. This story of loyalty impressed the magistrates, thereby saving Bobby from an untimely end. Bobby continued to live for another fourteen years in the shelter erected for him on his master's grave. On his own death his remains were marked by a rose bush.

His loyalty was also publicly recognized by the Lord Provost of Edinburgh, who presented him with a collar.[77] Tales of his loyalty and steadfastness were published in written form and a statue and drinking fountain were erected in his honour in Edinburgh by Angela Burdett-Coutts, combining practical relief to thirsty dogs with a moral tale for their owners.[78] Even today his grave is visited by adults and children alike who leave the dog messages and flowers.[79]

Here again we have a Victorian dog imbued with a sense of loyalty, but one threatened by forces outside his control, in this instance the state, through the imposition of the dog tax. In addition Bobby was

A Victorian anti-statist dog: Greyfriars Bobby. Statue was erected in Edinburgh by Angela Burdett-Coutts.

loyal even beyond death, as his visits to his master's grave testify. This particular Victorian motif is replicated in a number of contemporary stories such as that of the Newfoundland dog acting as chief mourner for all local funerals, or of the spaniel who visited the grave of his master in St Bride's churchyard, London, where the sexton brought him food and built him a shelter.[80] Greyfriars Bobby appeared both as an embodiment of apparently timeless virtue and as an exemplum of upright standing against unjust laws. In more sentimental vein was the narrative poem 'Told to the Missionary' in which a poor man decided to drown his dog in the canal as he could not afford the dog tax. He subsequently slips and the dog rescues him and, of course, is rewarded with his life. Now on his deathbed, the impoverished man is asking the missionary to look after his dog when he is dead:

> I wonder who'll have yer, my beauty, when him as you 're all to
>   is dead!
> There, stow your perlaver a minit, I know as my end is nigh;
> Is a cove to turn round on his dog, like, just 'cos he's goin' to die?[81]

Fallen dogs and their rescuers

Stories, poems and visual images had the ability to influence the way in which animals were viewed. By the 1860s dogs had been established as both loving members of the family and as animals that could confer a form of respectability on their owners, if they were well looked after. In 1860 the Battersea Dogs' Home was founded. Here was a place to which stray dogs could be taken, looked after well and hopefully be restored to their owners. Significantly, what was established was a 'home', a domestic venue, rather than a place of custody or imprisonment. In its title alone the Battersea Dogs' Home showed the extent to which the status of dogs was inextricably linked with the respectable family. A home was the dogs' proper place. When kindly women saw stray dogs roaming the streets of London they were not simply witnessing fellow creatures in distress, or a putative personal loss from their own family, but they could also witness an animal who had fallen from a position of security into neglect. Mrs Mary Tealby became the first woman to found a British animal welfare organization when she established the Dogs' Home as a response to seeing

dogs dying of 'lingering starvation in the streets'.[82] Mrs Tealby, a
RSPCA supporter,[83] was joined on the first committee of the Dogs'
Home by seven other women, including Emily Tennyson, the sister of
the poet, and four men. All the patrons were titled ladies.[84]

This preponderance of women invites explanation. It reflects both
the domestic nature of the animal at the focus of their attention and
the responsibility which women had for the maintenance and care of
pets within the home. A number of books on the treatment of pets
were written by women and directed towards the female reader as the
person responsible for this aspect of family life.[85] But it suggests more
than this. When the RSPCA, Animal Friends' Society and Rational
Humanity Group had been established in the 1820s they took upon
themselves the promotion of humane treatment towards animals as
an indicator of the new class formations. In the 1860s the work of
the women at Battersea reflects similar ventures undertaken by the
Charity Organization Society (COS) in which women philanthropists
attempted to rescue lost and wretched people.[86] Indeed the Society for
the Relief of Distress, a London group which was a direct antecedent
of the COS, was established in the same year as the Dogs' Home.[87]
The COS saw its charitable works aimed at those on the 'recoverable
verge of pauperism' who could make a quick transition to relative
respectability.[88] A similar ideology was found in the work of the Dogs'
Home, as the story of its founding indicates. One day in the summer
of 1860 Mrs Tealby had been visiting her friend, Mrs Major, who
lived in Canonbury Square, Islington. Ushered into the kitchen rather
than the customary drawing room she was shown a pathetic dog in
the last stages of starvation which Mrs Major had brought home to
nurse, despite its filthy appearance. The dog lived. Inspired by their
successful rescue work, the two women embarked upon their lifelong
venture.[89] Like their human counterparts 'rescued' by the Charity
Organization Society, or religious charities, these animals were the
most wretched of creatures but deserving nevertheless of the attention
of respectable women.

The business of the Home was helped by the publicity given to it
by various writers. Frances Power Cobbe, better known for her anti-
vivisectionist work and activities against wife-battering, penned a
charming piece, *The Confessions of a Lost Dog*, an 'autobiographical'
work by her Pomeranian, Hajjin. He recounted how he got lost and

was persecuted by 'a big hulking bricklayer' who had kicked him, and then defied ruffians trying to steal him. Hajjin escaped from boys throwing stones at him to receive better treatment from women. A poor old woman selling apples gave him a crust of bread and then a lady took him to the Dogs' Home where he was reunited with his mistress.[90] More prosaically, Charles Dickens also endorsed the aims of the Dogs' Home in an article of 1862, contrasting the condition of dogs taken there with those displayed in dog shows:

> For this second dog show [the Dogs' Home] is nothing more nor less than the show of the Lost Dogs of the Metropolis – the poor vagrant homeless curs that one sees looking out for a dinner in the gutter, or curled up in a doorway taking refuge from their troubles in sleep. To rescue these miserable animals from slow starvation, to provide an asylum, where, if it is of the slightest use, they can be restored with food, and kept until a situation can be found for them. . .[91]

Dickens's use of the word lost is telling; for although the dogs there were literally lost, many were also metaphorically lost and wretched, being dogs of humble origin. The links between humane feeling towards dogs and towards the poor is drawn out by Dickens in the same article:

> If people really think it wrong to spend a very, very little money on that poor cur whose face I own haunts my memory . . . if people really do consider it an injustice to the poor, to give to this particular institution let them leave it to its fate; but I think it is somewhat hard that they should turn the whole scheme into ridicule, or assail it with open ferocity as a dangerous competitor, with other enterprises for public favour . . . it is worthy that such a place exists; an extraordinary monument of the remarkable affection with which English people regard the race of dogs; an evidence of that hidden feeling which survives in some hearts even the rough ordeal of London life in the nineteenth century.[92]

Support for the Dogs' Home, as for the RSPCA in earlier decades, was depicted as an indicator of humane feeling.

The politicization of dogs

The Battersea Dogs' Home became more than a philanthropic institution; it was obliged to become involved in political questions when dogs became a focus for national parliamentary debate. When the 1867 Dogs Act was passed to deal summarily with stray dogs the Battersea Dogs Home protested vigorously, ensuring that lost dogs remained under the aegis of the home and not with the police. When ill-founded rumours circulated that the Home sold off dogs to vivisectors, the committee was forceful in its denial. The Home declared its opposition to vivisection, and required all purchasers of dogs to sign a form to the effect that the dog should neither be used for vivisection nor as a performing animal.[93] This forthright stand was strengthened by the subsequent election to the committee of Sidney Trist, the secretary of the London Anti-Vivisection Society.

The committee of the Dogs' Home did not discuss its work in terms of animal rights, nor as a campaign aimed at changing the law, but the Home was, consciously or not, involved in practical politics. This was particularly evident when it intervened against the hysteria surrounding rabies and attempted to educate people that not all stray dogs were rabid.[94] In the 1880s fear was mounting, particularly in London, about the prevalence of rabies. London was regarded as the Mecca of the dissolute, the lazy, the mendicant, the rough and the spendthrift.[95] Stray or rabid dogs, like their human counterparts, epitomized this threatening presence which cried out for regulation – or destruction. Some interpreted rabies scares as symptomatic of the government's need to create a scapegoat for current ills: 'The governing classes find every year that it is more difficult to govern the country, and, therefore, they must have resort to superstition, for rabies in dogs is nothing more than superstition.'[96]

From the 1860s the police had had powers to muzzle dogs in the capital and subsequently nationally as a way of preventing the spread of rabies.[97] Muzzling led, opponents suggested, to difficulty in drinking, and moreover was ineffective. Rabid, often stray dogs could be seen as a threat to the respectable family pet and humans alike. However, in practice all dogs, irrespective of social origin, were potentially affected by the legislation. What today might be a treasured family pet might tomorrow be a lost and neglected stray. As John Walton has persuasively argued, many found the question of state control the most compelling argument for intervention against the legislation. Dogs were part of the family and in intervening here the state was meddling in issues outside its remit.[98] The rabies orders of the 1880s were permissive legislation which could be applied even if rabies had not been identified in the area and were thus a dangerously vague form of control. Millions of dogs, and their owners, were potentially affected by this apparently random measure and there was fear that dogs could be unnecessarily muzzled or killed by the state without any real justification.[99]

Such a fear was not without precedent. In 1860 the Contagious Diseases (Animals) Act had been introduced to stop the import of foreign diseased cattle; animals' movements were restricted to reduce the spread of pleuro-pneumonia and subsequently local authorities were given powers to kill infected animals and to compensate the owners out of local rates.[100] With similar language and emphasis on national strength the Contagious Diseases Acts of 1864 and 1866 had been introduced, ostensibly to contain the spread of venereal disease amongst enlisted men and to act as a form of national defence. Women believed to be prostitutes could be subject to forcible medical examination and incarceration in lock hospitals. These Acts potentially stigmatized and criminalized all women, particularly working-class women, and were fiercely opposed by feminists such as Josephine Butler.[101] Legislation enacted against women on the margins of society in the interests of scientists' notions of cleanliness and good health was now being implemented in similar guise on animals which formed part of the family unit. The family itself was seen to be under threat from a joint attack by science and the law: 'The laboratory, in fact, gives way to Scotland Yard; the "scientist" to the policeman.'[102]

It is important to recognize that scientists did not agree about the origins of rabies nor its possible cure. Although the pioneering work of the French scientist Louis Pasteur in developing the theory that germs caused disease is taken as given today, it was not accepted uncritically in the late nineteenth century. His experiments on animals caused him to be reviled by many animal supporters and his particular work on rabies was seen as highly contentious. Hydrophobia, which was a symptom of rabies, could be controlled in humans through inoculation. In animals, however, it was difficult to ascertain with any precision whether a dog was indeed rabid or merely excitable. Muzzling was introduced to prevent dogs biting each other – and humans – and thereby to contain any spread of the disease. Scientists did not all share this view and many questioned the diagnosis as well as treatment for rabies. Professor Woodroff, a pioneer of distemper research, denounced Pasteur as a quack.[103] The Surgeon-General and honorary physician to Queen Victoria, C. A. Gordon, was also sceptical about Pasteur's methods and believed that many of the so-called symptoms of rabies in dogs were those of other illnesses such as distemper. Victor Horsley, who was to figure so prominently in pro-vivisection debates, became a member of the Society for the Prevention of Hydrophobia and its chief spokesperson on the benefits of muzzling.[104]

Although scientists could not agree, a mood of hysteria overtook otherwise sane people who believed that any excited animal was rabid and thus deserving of summary stoning or execution. The headline-grabbing 'Baker Street Mad Dog Case' even caught the attention of the queen, who intervened to protest against such tyranny and cruelty. In this case a muzzled spaniel owned by a lady in Baker Street was first lassoed and then truncheoned to death in front of a protesting neighbour, Miss Revell.[105] Miss Revell acted like women before her who had remonstrated against the cruel treatment meted out to animals. Only this time the perpetrator was not a cab-driver or cattle drover but an officer in the Metropolitan Police. When her pleas fell on deaf ears Miss Revell took direct action, seized a pitcher full of water and emptied it over the policeman, for which she was summoned and fined. Horrified by the event, the queen asked for a special report. The response of Charles Warren, the Commissioner of Police, highlighted several of the concerns of those who opposed attacks on dogs. First, the law governing rabid dogs meant that the RSPCA was unable to prosecute successfully for cruelty towards a dog where any suspicion of rabies occurred. Second, disputed scientific evidence was employed, in that the police argued that dogs could be healthy at one time of day (as indeed the spaniel was) and rabid at another to justify their interpretation of the law.[106] This incident exemplified the concern that 'science' was being used by the state to interfere in matters outside its proper jurisdiction, particularly as even the scientific community did not agree about the causes of rabies or hydrophobia. Rabies was not a new phenomenon; animal campaigners had written about its existence from at least the 1830s, ascribing its spread to organized dog-fighting.[107] What had changed was the advent of an apparent (and disputed) cure – and the closer integration of dogs within the family. Dogs now, opponents argued, were being sacrificed to the greed and power-mongering of scientists, the police and politicians alike.

Writers such as the novelist Ouida were particularly incensed that muzzling was practised upon dogs, and felt that their qualities of fidelity, courage and submissiveness made it a cowardly and tyrannical policy.[108] The same qualities lauded in the Gelert and Greyfriars Bobby stories were now placed in a context of resistance to state exploitation. The removal of stray dogs from the streets of London was even advanced as a reason for Jack the Ripper being able to commit his crimes without raising suspicion.[109] Moreover organizations like the Kennel Club were forced into taking action on an issue which was essentially outside its remit of defining and regulating breeds of dogs. Such was the concern of its members that it was forced to condemn the arbitrary and inconsistent way in which muzzling orders were applied, especially in London.[110] By 1885 *The Kennel Review* was expressing its opposition to muzzling on the grounds that it caused more cases of hydrophobia than it prevented, since dogs could not drink water properly if muzzled and over-heating could lead to rabies.[111] The National Canine Defence League would also join in opposition to arbitrary muzzling and recognized the strength of opinion held by its supporters: 'the dog lover as a political force is not to be despised'.[112]

From personal witness to taking a stand

The debate around the existence or not of rabies and its effect on animals was a break with earlier approaches to animal cruelty in significant ways. Whether a dog was muzzled or not was clear; what was not evident was whether a dog exhibited particular medical symptoms. More than ever, what was defined as cruel very much depended on who was doing the watching and what they were looking for. Miss Revell, who assaulted the policeman, had witnessed the cruel murder of an excitable dog. The policeman had presumably seen a rabid animal about to attack people, the interests of whom were paramount. How to deal with stray and perhaps rabid dogs became symptomatic of a broader medicalization of social issues and the incorporation of science into state strategies. Science had moved beyond the stage of introducing people to the wonder and beauty of the animal world: it was responsible for creating fear of animals and of advocating action against them, including destruction, in the apparent interests of humans. In this sense the debate around dogs in society was to prefigure the controversy over the value or moral worth of vivisection.

FOUR

Bringing light into dark places: anti-vivisection and the animals of the home

Is it to be seriously maintained that society cannot trust us with dogs and cats? [Are scientists to be treated] as if they were prostitutes under the Contagious Diseases Acts?[1]

Science had developed apace throughout the nineteenth century – but so had the way in which animals were viewed, and cruelty towards them defined.[2] Legislation to regulate vivisection was not introduced until 1876, some 50 years after the practice had first been condemned by the SPCA. In the founding statement of the SPCA in 1824 vivisection was identified as an abuse of animals, alongside cruelty in the streets and torture for sport,[3] but until the 1870s opposition to vivisection had focused primarily on the work of foreign scientists, especially French and Italian vivisectors.

The experiments of the French vivisector Magendie, a compendium of all that is odious,[4] were condemned some 50 years before there was any concerted legislative attempt to restrict or abolish such practices in Britain.[5] Magendie, professor of physiology and medicine in Paris in the 1830s, carried out experiments on animals without anaesthesia and repeated his experiments as demonstrations in lectures. William Youatt, the veterinary scientist, had included vivisection within his own catalogue of cruelty to animals, for many thousands of creatures had died in vain just to illustrate the substance of Magendie's lectures, which made no pretence at revealing new knowledge.[6] Even such a distinguished physiologist as William Sharpey, who became the first full-time professor of physiology in Britain in 1836, and taught at University College London for nearly 40 years, was horrified by some of Magendie's work.[7] The Florence-based physiologist Moritz Schiff, who kept dogs and pigeons in distressing conditions and experimented on them, also incurred the wrath of the sizable local British community.[8]

New animals: new forms of cruelty

Because anaesthetics had been unavailable in the 1830s and 1840s, British scientists had tended to dissect reptiles rather than mammals, although even this invoked ethical discussions within the scientific community. Writing in *The Lancet* in 1847, Marshall Hall, a pioneering physiologist, emphasized the moral problems facing the profession, arguing that experiments should only take place on the least sentient animals and should only involve new work, rather than demonstrations of previously conducted experiments.[9] The experimental physiologist most responsible for the growth of anaesthetics was Sir Benjamin Ward Richardson. He developed carbonic oxide, chloroform and sulphuric ether specifically to prevent pain to animals,[10] established a 'lethal chamber' at Battersea Dogs' Home to ensure animals were put to sleep painlessly, and developed methods of slaughtering animals for food by electrocution.[11] Although his work was designed to alleviate pain, in practice this led to experiments on a wider range of animals. The real growth of vivisection in Britain dated from Darwin's arguing for an understanding of the commonality between species; it also dated from the dissemination of Claude Bernard's pioneering work on physiology within the scientific community. As Coral Lansbury has put it, Darwin changed what people believed; Bernard what they did, through creating a new system by which nature might be examined and controlled.[12]

By the 1870s, those animals that now suffered at the hands of vivisectors were not primarily reptiles but mammals, particularly dogs and cats.[13] Coinciding with the growth in manuals on caring for pets, in 1857 the RSPCA issued its first tract specifically on the treatment of domestic animals, which were depicted as the servants of man and thus entitled to kind treatment.[14] While pride of place in the tract went to the horse, chapters were also devoted to the dog, turkey, lowly hedgehog – which, purchased from Covent Garden market for the purpose, provided a service by eating cockroaches in kitchens – and the cat. As the publication declared, 'almost every household has a cat'.[15] It was estimated that there was one cat to every ten of the London population, as well as thousands of dogs. Unsurprisingly, dogs' and cats' meat dealers did good business, walking up to 40 miles every day selling about a hundredweight of food daily across London.[16] There were also, even then, women who fed stray cats – and annoyed the neighbours.[17] Higher up the scale, Queen Victoria played a significant part in persuading her subjects that cruelty towards cats as well as dogs was reprehensible. In particular she had helped turn the tide of general aversion towards cats by direct-ing the RSPCA to include a picture of a cat in the medal for its supporters.[18] Moreover, when rabies scares flourished and dogs became feared as carriers of disease, the status of cats rose since they were so manifestly clean.[19]

Pets, be they the lowly beneficiaries of Mayhew's cats' and dogs' meat man or partakers of the royally approved Spratt's beetroot-filled biscuits, as fed to Queen Victoria's treasured Pomeranians, were found in the homes of people of all classes. They might destroy rodents and vermin but they were also companions and considered part of the family. Yet it was upon domestic animals, household pets, 'the most loving servants of mankind', that experiments were performed.[20] As pets were stolen for vivisection, it was often the selfsame animals that suffered. While domestic animals were seen as members of the family, meriting affection and good treatment, there was also a growing and changing 'role' for cats and dogs outside the domestic environment, within the vivisector's lab. For although the act of vivisection was hidden, the very animals upon whom such cruelty was perpetrated were the same animals *seen* elsewhere, in the streets and homes of poor and rich alike.[21] Dogs and cats brutalized at St Bartholomew's Hospital were dogs and cats 'straying in the street at night', including pedigree dogs such as spaniels that were scalded and burned in the cause of 'science'.[22]

The mythologizing of family pets in popular narratives played a further part in creating a climate of opinion receptive to anti-vivisectionist ideas. Ouida, the romantic novelist, was a staunch opponent of vivisection. Her 'autobiographical novel' of *Puck*, a tiny Maltese terrier, was a tale of escape from brutality. Puck witnessed cruelty to horses, badgers, dogs and canaries. The use of the autobio-graphical genre helped generate a sense of dogs as creatures with consciousness and almost with a sense of self, a context within which vivisection appeared even more brutal.[23] Gordon Stables's *Sable and White,* another popular dog autobiography, included a diatribe

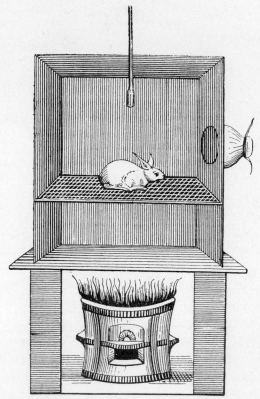

Bernard's *Leçons sur la Chaleur Animale*, p. 347.

*Exposing Claude Bernard's experiments in which rabbits were
roasted alive.* From Frances Power Cobbe, *Light in Dark Places*
(London, 1885).

against vivisection that compared it to the Spanish Inquisition.
Here a mastiff describes the dogs' intended fate: 'We were to
undergo the torture I had often heard poor Professor Huxley speak
about, the torture of vivisection; that, in a word, we would be tied to
a bench or stool and cut to pieces alive, and all for the supposed
benefit of that proud biped, the microbe man.'[24] Within specific anti-
vivisectionist tracts dog stories were also used to win sympathy.
As Frances Power Cobbe wrote, she would not grudge the hard
work of the previous two years against vivisection if 'a certain
hideous series of experiments at Edinburgh have been stopped and a
dozen of Greyfriars Bobby's comrades have been mercifully spared
to die in peace'.[25]

Sight and physiology

In earlier chapters I have stressed the importance of sight in the development of a human awareness of animal suffering. Sight also played a central role in the development of vivisection as an aspect of physiological science.[26] Sight, rather than hearing, became the most important scientific sense in medicine, altering the balance between the ideas and feelings of a patient and the gaze of the medical specialist.[27] No longer did the doctor need to listen to the words of the patient, since the doctor saw, and thus understood, all. As Julia Wedgwood, the writer and niece of Darwin explained, because doctors had not listened to their patients but relied on empirical evidence they had not recognized the validity of certain treatments. For example the open-air cure for consumption would have been effected long before, she argued, if doctors had been willing to respond sympathetically to patients' complaints about the need for air.[28] It was the new science of physiology rather than the growth of science as such that attracted opposition. Louise Lind af Hageby, who would be prominent in later anti-vivisection campaigns, described it thus: 'Physiology is soaring high up in the air like a proud bird of prey. But it carries nothing but the mutilated bodies of weaker and less cruel creatures: the spirit of life which it tried to catch was too subtle for its murderous fangs.'[29]

The new perpetrators of cruelty and their locales

Those who practised vivisection were middle class – and male. Until 1876, the same year that saw the passing of laws to regulate vivisection, women were not allowed to train to be doctors in British universities and medical schools.[30] The middle-class status of the vivisector would normally imply a certain morality and humanity of attitude; so too did the place where such practices frequently took place – in a supposedly safe environment, the middle-class home. The men who perpetrated such acts were the selfsame people with whom the respectable and middle-class family would socialize and invite into their own home as equals. Such behaviour then was more disquieting for the middle class than that of the common cab driver or cattle drover in the streets, outside their own private and social space. Here was an enemy within, threatening assumptions about consensus on humane behaviour. This theme of the enemy within characterizes many anti-vivisection narratives such as Sarah Grand's *Beth Book* and Wilkie Collins's *Heart and Science*. In *The Beth Book*, the heroine finds a little black and tan terrier pinned out in a hidden locked room, on her husband's vivisection table, and puts the poor animal out of his misery.[31] In *Heart and Science* the vivisector Dr Benjulia insinuates himself into the young Carmina's sick-room and uses her, like the dogs in his laboratory, for his experiments.[32]

The microscope had become an essential and innocuous part of any middle-class parlour, but animal experiments heralded scientific enquiry in more melodramatic vein.[33] Traditionally laboratories and experiments had been situated within houses, as Joseph Wright's depiction of the experiment on the cockatoo in the air pump has reminded us.[34] Indeed it was the sight of dogs mutilated by her husband, the physiologist Claude Bernard, wandering in and out of the kitchen of their own home, that led his subsequently estranged wife to establish an asylum for stray cats and dogs in Paris.[35] The home became not just a site for scientific observation of animals but a place for their destruction. George Henry Lewes, more commonly known as the partner of the novelist George Eliot, was an enthusiastic physiologist and conducted experiments at home, enabling George Eliot to exclaim: 'I wish you could have seen today, as I did, the delicate spinal cord of a dragon-fly – like a tiny thread with beads on it – which your father had just dissected! He is so wonderfully clever now at the dissection of these delicate things...'[36]

In some instances the paraphernalia of the dissecting table competed with more jovial pastimes. In the home of Augustus Desire Waller, lecturer in physiology at St Mary's Hospital in fashionable St John's Wood, the table on which apparatus was laid out could be removed by a complicated system of pulleys and ropes to reveal a full-sized billiard table.[37] Even when space for laboratories became more widely available within hospitals and medical schools, physiologists still retained their own private laboratories at home. Sir John Burdon Sanderson, who had witnessed the experiments of Magendie and Bernard, and rose to become, not without controversy and opposition, the first professor of physiology at Oxford University, maintained a laboratory in his own elegant Bloomsbury house off Gordon square.[38] At that time he was in effective control of about three-quarters of physiological laboratory space available in London, but he nevertheless constructed one in his own home.[39]

Ironically, there was a sharp contrast between the 'external' act of seeing, so highly valued in the study of physiology, and the conditions under which such acts of seeing took place. The practice of vivisection was hidden away from sight itself, for animals were experimented upon in private, in 'poor hole-and-corner schools of experimentation for uneducated students'.[40] The campaigners feared that away from any humane gaze, experiments would also take place on vulnerable people: 'If there is any validity in vivisectionist logic, it cannot stay at the lower animals. Why should we not vivisect our idiots, lunatics, babes?'[41] This fear was not groundless. There were close links in Wakefield asylum between experiments on animals and on the brains of deceased 'insane' people. David Ferrier had established a laboratory at West Riding Lunatic Asylum in Wakefield in the 1870s. His experiments there on the cortexes of animals complemented the work of his colleague Sir James Crichton-Browne, the director of the asylum, upon the brains of patients.[42] Within hospitals, observation or the use of post-mortem examinations was being rejected in favour of experimentation on living patients. This was graphically exposed by the humanitarian Edward Maitland, who argued that the ' finest minds' handed over this work to those with the 'hardest hearts and consequently . . . the lowest order of intelligences'.[43] Maitland published lurid accounts of the treatment of the poor in 'public' hospitals: a surgeon delays setting the broken bones of a working man so that the students may manipulate the bones together to hear the sound; a poor woman dying of consumption is subject to violent shaking so that the surgeon might hear the liquid in her chest. If such cruelty could be perpetrated on a vulnerable poor woman in an open (and public) ward of a hospital, how much worse could be the pain inflicted on an even more vulnerable animal, behind the closed doors of a laboratory?[44]

The private nature of hospitals – even those committed to dealing with the 'public' – meant that they were not open to public scrutiny. As anti-vivisectionists realized, hospital porters or other employees would not come forward to testify against cruelty for fear of losing their jobs.[45] Further, the professionalist and secret control of hospitals meant that no one obliged to use them, especially teaching hospitals, was free from potential experimentation.[46] Ouida's fear that vivisection would lead to the 'scientific torture of lunatics' referred at the same time back to the practice of dissecting the brains of hung criminals, and the work of Ferrier in his Wakefield asylum, and forward to the eugenicism of the twentieth century.[47] Of particular concern was the treatment of children by vivisectionists. As one campaigner put it: 'Will the man who has learnt to hear without pity the moan of a tortured dog or the cry of a cat in anguish care very much for the pains of our little ones?'[48]

Making the private public: shedding light on dark practices

What was apparently so new and progressive was conducted in circumstances so disreputable that they could not be seen in respectable society. Experiments instead harked back to the 'worst barbarities of the ruder ages of the past'.[49] Anna Kingsford's dream of a vivisector's laboratory typified these arcane practices. The laboratory was underground in an artificially lighted vault, reminiscent of the places in which sheep had been corralled and deprived of natural light prior to slaughter at Smithfield market.[50] It was the absence of metaphorical light that campaigners focused on, in attempting to bring 'dark practices' into the light. Using the language of the zealous missionary, Frances Power Cobbe issued her powerful pamphlet, *Light in Dark Places,* exposing the tools of the vivisector's trade.[51] His experiments were described in lurid language as 'the deeds of darkness tolerated in Christian countries'.[52] Employing visual images of animals bound, gagged or burned alive from physiologists' own manuals, Cobbe tried to bring about change through shock tactics: '[Vivisection] is the cutting up alive, the flaying, starving, baking, boiling, stewing alive, and creating all manner of gangrenes and other diseases in animals, and notably in the most sensitive animals – dogs, monkeys, cats and horses.'[53] For Cobbe there was little to distinguish such a scientist from a butcher: 'the smooth cool man of science . . . stands by that torture trough'.[54]

The campaigns against vivisection emerge at a time when male explorers were venturing into the unknown reaches of 'darkest

Shedding light on professional cruelty.
'"Publicity." The Light dreaded by all Vivisectors', from
an issue of *The Anti-Vivisection Review*, 1909–10.

Africa', and women in the Charity Organization Society or the
Salvation Army were venturing beyond their own neighbourhoods
into the unknown territories of the slums to conduct their own
philanthropic work. By the 1870s women had 'infiltrated the enemy's
land' of the city slums, mimicking social anthropologists and missionaries alike.[55] In comparable vein others would expose the vivisectors'
work by publicizing their experiments or, later, attending experiments
in the guise of acolytes and calling upon others to do likewise:

The importance of personal experiences of the methods of vivisection for those who throw themselves heart and soul into the battle
against it cannot be exaggerated. We hope that more and more
ardent friends of the cause will enter the laboratories, see the deeds
of darkness tolerated in Christian countries, and tell the world
what they have seen.[56]

Changes in the law

Under pressure of public opinion a royal commission was set up
in 1875 to consider ways of regulating, rather than preventing,
experiments on animals.[57] Its members included two vice-presidents
of the RSPCA and the scientist Thomas Huxley. But the evidence of
witnesses was not clear-cut. While Charles Darwin appeared before
the commission defending vivisection, albeit insisting that anaesthetics should always be used, he also declared that he had personally
never experimented on an animal.[58] Other scientists such as the
Sergeant Surgeon to Queen Victoria gave evidence, backing the anti-
vivisectionists' claim that too many experiments were needlessly
repeated. And the evidence of a lecturer at St Bartholomew's Hospital
supported the campaigners' view that stolen cats ended up in his
labs.[59] In their report the commissioners came out against a complete
ban on experiments. The subsequent 1876 Cruelty to Animals Act
instituted a licensing procedure and general inspection.

One effect of the 1876 Act was to exempt vivisectors from
prosecution for wanton cruelty towards animals under the aegis of
legislation previously established by Richard Martin's Act. Experimentation on animals was not determined by law to be analogous to
deliberate cruelty, a contention campaigners vigorously challenged.
Three times as many vivisectors were licensed in 1878 as were
practising in 1875.[60]

It was not until the 1876 Act became law that specific organizations were established to campaign on vivisection alone, forcing
scientists to account for physiological research both to Parliament
and to the general public.[61] The RSPCA and Battersea Dogs' Home
had little direct involvement in such work; yet their prior activity in
changing the status of particular animals, which were now seen as
creatures in need of protection, was significant.[62] The Victoria Street

Society, the first organization established specifically to oppose vivisection, had much support from women as well as men, thanks in
part to the influence of its founder, Frances Power Cobbe, already an
experienced campaigner in the political field with her work for the
Married Women's Property Committee and the London Women's
Suffrage Society.[63] While Mary Tealby had been the first woman to
found an animal welfare organization, the Battersea Dogs' Home, the
work of Cobbe and her allies was of a different character. These
were feminists who were simultaneously committed to change the
law in the interests of women and animals. Mrs Tealby had been
working within the existing parameters of the woman's sphere, albeit
extending their influence, in her rescue work with animals. Frances
Power Cobbe was operating at the very heart of the political process,
instituting petitions, organizing meetings, lobbying, and writing
pamphlets to change the law.

Many members of the Victoria Street Society had had previous
experience of campaigning on explicitly political questions. Jessie
Boucherett, the brains behind the Society for Promoting the Employment of Women and founder of *The Englishwoman's Review*, was
another anti-vivisectionist.[64] Prior to writing on vivisection Julia
Wedgwood had contributed an article on women's suffrage to the
important early feminist collection edited by Josephine Butler, *Woman's
Work and Woman's Culture*.[65] It is no accident that Georgina Weldon,
a keen anti-vaccinationist, anti-vivisector and dog-lover, should
have been the focus of a *cause célèbre* when her husband attempted
to have her incarcerated in order to acquire her possessions.[66]
Experiences of campaigning against the compulsory vaccination
of children against smallpox and against the Contagious Diseases
Acts, which subjected women to compulsory medical examination,
became linked to the anti-vivisection cause.[67] The links between
these apparently distinct campaigns was recognized in William
Young's *Vaccination Tracts*:

> It is a mark of the hardness of heart and dulness [sic] of mind of the
> scientific nineteenth century; the epoch of the legalized vivisectors,
> legalized vaccinators, and legalized purveyors of clean prostitutes
> for the vaccinated services which defend the United Kingdom from
> domestic disorder and foreign foes.[68]

Campaigners made connections, noting the vulnerability of those subject to state directives: children, working-class women and animals. Opponents also made connections between the campaigns. For John Simon, who as medical officer of the Privy Council had advised against the extension of the Contagious Diseases Acts (though he did not favour their abolition), scientists were being treated with the same disdain and contempt that prostitutes were under the Contagious Diseases Acts: 'Is it to be seriously maintained that society cannot trust us with dogs and cats? [Are scientists to be treated] as if they were prostitutes under the Contagious Diseases Acts?'[69] To this, the anti-vivisectionists answered in the affirmative. For Gladstone, too, the issues were linked, as he recognized while campaigning in Marylebone in 1880, urging voters to put aside 'vaccination, vivisection and the Contagious Diseases Acts' in the impending election.[70]

Feminists, however, were divided on the issue, and certainly those who simply wanted equality with men were less inclined to oppose vivisection. For Barbara Bodichon, editor of *The Englishwoman's Review,* and Emily Davies of Girton College, performing vivisection was the price for women to pay for entry into this male profession.[71] The earliest female doctors, Elizabeth Blackwell, Elizabeth Garrett Anderson and Frances Hoggan, held differing views on vivisection. Elizabeth Garrett Anderson, the pioneer of women's medicine, supported vivisection, vaccination and the Contagious Diseases Acts.[72] Elizabeth Blackwell, who had witnessed Claude Bernard's experiments on dogs in Paris, believed that women were increasingly being used as the subjects for experimentation, and opposed vivisection.[73] Frances Hoggan, who had trained in Zurich and was an enthusiastic vegetarian, was a member of the first executive committee of the Victoria Street Society.[74] If, she argued with some irony, monkeys had been as cheap for experimentation as stray cats and dogs, then 'we should probably have heard much more about the processes of digestion of nuts, grains and fruit'.[75]

Differences and similarities

The twofold claim of animals' similarity to humans was now employed by those opposed to any form of vivisection. Robert Browning's popular poem 'Old Tray' conveys the idea of emotional similarity well. Browning had advised Frances Power Cobbe that so great was his commitment to anti-vivisection that he 'would rather submit to the worst of deaths, so far as pain goes, than have a single dog or cat tortured on the pretence of sparing me a twinge or two'.[76] This strength of feeling is conveyed in the poem. The dog of a 'beggar' rushes to rescue his owner's daughter fallen into a stream, while bystanders 'reason . . . ere they risk their lives'. He subsequently jumps into the stream again to fetch her lost doll. This is cynically seen as irrational behaviour, which a vivisector 'with reason reasoned' needed investigation, so he seeks to buy or steal the dog:

> By vivisection at expense .
> Of half-an-hour and eighteen pence
> How brain secretes dog's soul we'll see.[77]

Here the vivisector's gift of human reason is used for unreasonable ends, and ones which are deemed to be cruel and pointless. Animals, however, were simultaneously seen as very different to people: a mark of man's humanity was his potential for kindness towards animals. To act otherwise was to transgress the very idea of what it was to be human. People had a duty, it was felt, to protect animals as weak and vulnerable.

Class and respectability: new targets

Animal campaigners' previous view that a mark of respectability was the humane treatment of animals was sharply challenged by the class position of the vivisectors. The petition drawn up by the Victoria Street Society and presented to Gladstone in 1879 reflected this view. Signed by a plethora of the (male) great and the good, including the poets Tennyson[78] and Browning, Ruskin, the artist Burne-Jones, a plethora of Radical MPs previously prominent in the anti-vaccination cause, and physicians, religious leaders and headmasters of public schools, the petition drew attention to the ways in which men of comparable social standing to themselves were acting outside the norm:

> Let not the work of Erskine and Martin be undone, and the creatures which they delivered from the lash of the drunken carter be handed over to the scalpel of the physiologist. Let not the name of science be made odious by responsibility for deeds which, if committed openly in our streets, would call forth the execrations even of the roughest of the populace.[79]

The vivisector now took his place alongside the demonized carter and other traditional tormentors of animals, as John Davidson emphasized in his poetic account of the cruelty suffered by a horse at different stages of its life:

> Family physician, coster, cat's-meat-man –
> These, the indifferent fates who ruled his life.[80]

Costermongers, cattle drovers and cab drivers, long the focus of campaigns by the RSPCA, had been seen as separate in sentiment from the respectable. The habits of butchers, donkey keepers, costermongers, goat drivers and poulterers would brand them as 'savages' if they were known to the world, the RSPCA had declared.[81] But vivisectors were more difficult to deal with because of both the secrecy of their acts and their social position. The anti-vivisectionists were conscious of the class aspect and explored the contradictions in their publications:

> We are to go on punishing the poor man who unmercifully beats or over-drives his donkeys, or boys who torment a cat; but the 'learned', the 'open scientific profession', who in cold blood, can cut open (and before those who can bear the sight) the most delicate nerves of a dog or cat, and can let his victim afterwards crawl about the floor for a little rest, until he is fit to be cut open again, such a man is to be a chartered torturer: he is a hero of science.[82]

Indeed similar arguments had been taken up by experimenters themselves in their evidence to the royal commission of 1875. John Simon had stated that the intended regulation conflated professional scientists with a class of unqualified and cruel persons.[83] He declared to the commissioners: 'You are proposing that physiologists shall be treated as a dangerous class, that they shall be regulated like publicans and prostitutes.'[84] It was this very juxtaposition of the civilized lifestyle with barbarous cruelty that was so disturbing and unsettling. No wonder that women were urged to 'ostracise from your society, from your sick room, every man who practices or encourages vivisection'.[85] Moral decline – and social decline – would flow from such practice so that it would no longer be possible to ascertain moral values from social status alone. As the novelist Wilkie Collins outlined in his preface to *Heart and Science*, the practice of habitual cruelty led to the fatal deterioration of man's nature, an argument previously used against the rabble.[86]

The politics of the anti-vivisection movement

While anti-vivisectionists were united in their opposition to the experimentation of the physiologists, there was little else in their views to suggest a political homogeneity. The Victoria Street Society elected Lord Shaftesbury as its first president, and early prominent supporters included Cardinal Manning, the leading Roman Catholic priest and friend of the London dockers in their dispute of 1889, and Frances Power Cobbe, a feminist but also a Conservative and a meat-eater.[87] The movement shortly split into two main umbrella groups, the National Anti-Vivisection Society, led by Stephen Coleridge (great-grandson of the poet), and the British Union for the Abolition of Vivisection, with local branches, in which Cobbe was the leading light, and a number of smaller groups.[88] This plethora of groups give some idea of the problems involved in campaigning against vivisection, for opposition was not united by religious, political or philosophical agreement. Stephen Coleridge, for example, believed science to be vulgar and responsible for a general disintegration and dissolution of society. As late as 1913 he still held Darwin responsible for reducing man, 'once the supreme work of God at the head of His Universe . . . to an accidental development of an arborial ape'.[89] There was also the Church Anti-Vivisection League, whose opposition to vivisection was based on its inherent sinfulness: 'The torture of God's sentient creatures is a sin', stated the first annual report.[90]

The language of anti-vivisectionist campaigners was imbued with religious imagery, although this does not necessarily mean that its supporters were opposed to science in general. When the Bishop of Nottingham ended his speech to an animal rights demonstration with an (apparently) inspirational verse from 'Onward Christian Soldiers', or the wife of a hospital surgeon invoked Christ against the 'powers of darkness', or Charlotte Despard, socialist and feminist, summoned up the words of 'The Master' to reaffirm, 'Life is the product of the Divine and therefore we must have a reverence for life' it did not necessarily signify opposition to science, but support for values others than those held by their opponents.[91] Indeed Wilkie Collins employed such language in his 1883 novel *Heart and Science*, written to spread the word about the horrors of vivisection. As he outlined in his preface, he was 'pleading the cause of the harmless and affectionate beings of God's creation' while reassuring squeamish readers that they would not be subjected to the horrifying scenes within the vivisector's laboratory.[92]

Unsurprisingly, the apparent inconsistencies between those opposed to vivisection – many did eat meat and some prominent supporters like Lord Llangattock, Conservative MP for Monmouth and Master of the Monmouthshire Foxhounds, were keen hunters – were seized upon by scientists.[93] *The Lancet* compared the numbers of cattle despatched daily in slaughterhouses for human consumption, which allegedly raised no protest, with the demise of individual creatures in the name of science: ' . . . but a dog or a guinea-pig must not be submitted to experiment, however tenderly, even if it would advance the art of surgery, both human and veterinary.'[94]

The arguments used by the physiologists, particularly those in the Physiological Society set up in 1876, to castigate anti-vivisectionists as meat-eaters or hunters were acknowledged as valid criticism by new organizations such as the Humanitarian League or the readers of the feminist journal *Shafts*. In his play *A Lover of Animals*, originally published in *The Vegetarian Review* in 1895, Henry Salt, the founder of the Humanitarian League, tackled the contradictions of the anti-vivisectionists head on:

> . . . if we are to fight vivisection, we must rid ourselves of this false 'love of animals', this pampering of pets and lap-dogs by people who care nothing for the real welfare of animals, or even for the welfare of men. Humanitarianism must show that it is not 'bestarian', and must aim at the redress of all needless suffering, human and animal alike – the stupid cruelties of social tyranny, of the criminal code, of fashion, of science, of flesh-eating. . .[95]

Practical politics: anti-vivisection hospitals

In new organizations like the Humanitarian League such ideas were to receive endorsement. In the work of the newly established anti-vivisection hospitals, in which staff were committed to undertaking no vivisection, there was to be practical support for anti-vivisectionist views. The hospitals were specifically located in working-class districts of London – Battersea and the Old Kent Road – where poor patients could attend without fear of personal molestation precisely because they knew that even animals had been treated with kindness by the staff employed there. If educated doctors, normally prepared to dissect animals, had foresworn that cruelty, how much more likely were they in turn to be kind to working people? At the hospital in Battersea there was a management committee which drew together lay anti-vivisectionists and anti-vaccinationists including Joseph Levy, Secretary of the Personal Rights Association, and medical staff who displayed membership of the London Anti-Vivisection Society after their name together with the more conventional medical qualifications.[96] Vivisection and compulsory vaccination were taking place at time when scientific advances were being fiercely debated and contested both in lay circles and among scientists themselves. Ideas about the nature and prevention of rabies, smallpox, cancer and other life-threatening diseases were all being challenged and a range of solutions, including the promotion of a clean environment and healthy food, were put forward. Although vigorous opposition to vivisection continued well into the first decades of the twentieth century, the treatment of vivisection as a single issue was progressively challenged by those opposed to all forms of animal cruelty.

FIVE

Dead animals: spectacle and food

The fashion for birds' wings in ladies dresses has been a woeful
time for birds. They have been shot down in all countries to supply
'gentle woman's' passion for birds' wings.[1]

By the late 1880s and 1890s, although campaigns against the vivisection of domestic animals and the cruel treatment of horses continued,
new issues had emerged. Previous cruelties towards animals had
been perpetrated by men: working men had beaten cattle and whipped
horses; in the cause of science, middle-class men had destroyed
animals in laboratories. Women had not been directly involved in
such acts of cruelty. But by the late nineteenth century many women
became instigators of new forms of cruelty and destruction of animal
life, particularly against birds.

Cruelty towards birds and the first protective legislation

Cruelty towards birds was not new, nor was the outrage of humanitarians who recognized the usefulness to humans and the pleasure
provided by birds. Lord Erskine, the pioneer of legislation against
cruelty to horses, had expressed his appreciation of birds in his poem
'The Liberated Robins': 'Now harmless songsters, ye are free / Yet
stay awhile and sing to me'.[2] The snaring of birds had been such a
commonplace activity that it had been depicted in Pyne's *Microcosm*
of 1808 and criticized in Mayhew's descriptions of London life in the
1850s.[3] In 1869, in one of the first pet manuals devoted to birds,
the author had advised against keeping singing birds, 'the feathered
choristers of our woods and fields', in cages, while refraining from
declaring against all birds as pets.[4] As an alternative she recommended that docile cockatoos and parrots, given restorative chilli
powder in their food in damp weather, could be kept on open perches;
canaries could even be encouraged to fly around the room.[5]

In 1868, fifteen years before any concerted campaign to safeguard birds was established, the first legislation to partially protect wild birds was passed: 'This Act was to wild birds what Martin's Act of 1822 was to animals in general.'[6] The Sea Birds Protection Act, which was amended and extended shortly afterwards, was designed to protect the breeding seasons of birds, including sea birds, because of concern about the decline in the numbers of particular breeds. The habitat of the birds in question, predominantly the countryside and coastal areas rather than the urban environment, was also significant. It represented a shift from the geographical focus of earlier campaigns. Significantly, the legislation protected wildlife, which could not be seen as property. This innovative protection of birds stemmed from an interest in the conservation of wild species rather than from any concern to create order within cities or to ameliorate human behaviour. It corresponded with developments in thinking about the function of zoos. By the 1890s the London zoo saw its prime task as conserving species in danger of extinction, such as the great skua,[7] while at Woburn the Duke of Bedford established a herd of Pere David's deer, in danger of extinction in their native China.[8]

More problematic was the protection of wildlife in Britain since this raised questions about the control and use of land. Laws were introduced to prohibit the deposition of poisonous grains, designed to kill animals defined as vermin, but which in practice destroyed valued domestic and wild creatures.[9] In the 1870s the Land Reform Association, of which the philosopher John Stuart Mill and the Radical anti-vaccinationist MP Peter Taylor were leading members, had campaigned for state control of land with the removal of the vestiges of feudalism through the abolition of hereditary land rights. It had also argued that areas should be left in a state of wild natural beauty in order to allow for the general enjoyment of the community and for encouragement 'in all classes of healthful rural tastes, and of the highest orders of pleasure'.[10] Although not seeking to challenge land rights, the Commons Preservation Society had been established to maintain public land against further enclosure. As Octavia Hill, a leading member of the Society and in 1895 a founder of the National Trust, expressed it, 'Let the grass growing for hay be respected, let the primrose roots be left in their loveliness in the hedges, the birds un-molested and the gates [to paths] shut.'[11] By the 1890s, the interest in the countryside and the creatures therein became a focus of national and parliamentary concern, albeit from different stances.[12] It was against such a background that the organic farmer and writer H. J. Massingham and the naturalist and ornithologist W. H. Hudson would become involved in the protection of birds.[13]

Dead birds and the female body

It was not, however, the treatment of birds in the wild that proved so controversial, but rather the use of their corpses in civilized society. The fashion-conscious female body was becoming a vehicle for the display of dead animal life. The middle-class – and chic – woman was no longer content with gazing at animals at the zoo or within her own home; she now wanted to be seen adorned with the plumage and bodies of small birds. Whole wings of birds, not just feathers, were put on hats; breasts of birds stuck about with beads decorated ever more extravagant outfits.[14] The skins of hummingbirds were used to produce pincushion Valentines and on one ostentatious occasion a dress was displayed sporting the plumage of 800 canaries. This ruthless fashion imperative extended to weddings: eleven bridesmaids at a society wedding wore dresses trimmed with swan's down and the plumage of robins.[15] In a pastiche of 'Who killed cock robin?' a girl 'with her head in a whirl' explained:

> That I went to a ball . . .
> And to make me look colder,
> A bird on each shoulder,
> And all round my skirt
> Robin Redbreasts so pert,
> Shot on purpose for me
> In the midst of their glee,
> With their bright little eyes
> Opened wide with surprise.[16]

Royalty and the aristocracy were specifically criticized for the new craze of wearing toques, 'the advocated headgear for the Jubilee', made of aigrette feathers.[17] The working woman too displayed her finery, often in lurid colours: 'This craze for wearing birds is a universal leveller – mistress and maid must both alike wear them.'[18]

The typical East End factory girl, according to Charles Booth's survey of life among the London poor, wore 'a gorgeous plush hat with as many large ostrich feathers to match as her funds will run to – bright ruby or scarlet preferred'.[19] The cost of such feathers was met by the women, such as match-workers, forming clubs to save up for them.[20] The millinery trade, although supplied by the work of men actually killing birds, was carried out overwhelmingly by women working in the sweatshops of London to provide finery for the brief four months of the 'Season'.[21]

The particular cruelty of women

In the same way that vivisection was seen to be particularly shocking in that it was carried out by respectable middle-class men, so too was the transformation of birds and their feathers into fashion accessories by women. Aigrette feathers (taken from the egret) necessitated killing the mother bird at the very time when she was still caring for young fledglings. The slaughter of the mother meant that there were 'callow fledglings lingering in desolate starvation in the ravished and deserted nest'.[22] The circumstances of the feathers' collection thereby contradicted assumptions about women's role as mothers. As the despairing pamphleteer complained of women, 'If their sense of humanity is too feeble, will not their native sense of maternity arouse them?'[23] Rather than displaying 'motherly' qualities of compassion the 'feathered woman' demonstrated that she was 'a cruel woman'.[24] Scientists might justify killing animals to gain knowledge for humanity. Those sporting birds' bodies or aigrette feathers could make no such lofty claims. Vanity and greed, the detractors argued, were their motivating forces.[25] Such women, another argued, were not 'in earnest except about their own immediate small concerns'. They had a 'selfishly cramped view of life'.[26]

Men such as Henry Massingham or W. H. Hudson, the naturalist, wrote against the use of birds as finery in terms which castigated women exclusively.[27] The former MP Sydney Buxton, of the Buxton family of temperance and animal welfare reformers, also criticized their behaviour in a strongly worded letter to *The Times*. While condemning the wearing of plumes from the white egret and heron by members of the Horse Artillery, King's Royal Rifles and the Hussars, he nevertheless defended the individual soldiers who had no choice in the matter. Women, on the other hand, did. And it was their behaviour, he suggested, that was leading to the extinction of certain breeds of birds.[28] The society painter George Watts[29] did much to oppose in respectable circles the latest fashion whim, dedicating his painting of a kingfisher 'to all who love the beautiful and mourn over the senseless and cruel destruction of bird life and beauty'.[30] Such was his strength of feeling on the matter that he refused to paint women adorned by feathers; his summary removal of a feather from Lillie Langtry, the music hall star, was a well-known example of his anger on this question.[31] The hypocrisy of women was also noted by the humanitarian, Henry Salt, when he complained of women shedding tears for cab horses while wearing skin mantles or condemning the slaughter of songsters while sporting feathered corpses in their hats.[32]

Women organize opposition to 'murderous millinery'

Although women were responsible for the new fashion craze, it was women themselves who established the Plumage League in 1886 and the Society for the Protection of Birds in 1893, in protest against the new fashion. Queen Victoria, as befitted her role as patron of the RSPCA, also condemned the use of birds as trimming on clothing.[33] At the first public meeting of the SPB in March 1893 women again took the lead. The secretary, treasurer and president were all women, and Winifred, Duchess of Portland, was to remain president for the next 63 years. The majority of the officers and committee of the Society were women too, as were the secretaries of the local branches.[34] It was both as perpetrators of cruelty and instigators of political and cultural change that women were to the fore.

The rules of the Society called for the discouraging of the wanton destruction of birds. This covered the shooting of birds for sport and the collection of birds' eggs and nests. In the 1890s county councils received powers to prohibit the destruction of birds' eggs at any time or place within the county area; this was extended in 1896 to prohibit the actual killing of birds.[35] Powers were given to county councils to protect named birds – and their eggs – on the grounds that birds were both useful and gave pleasure.[36] The Society, however, wanted stiffer legal constraints and not just permissive legislation. At the Society's second annual meeting, the MP E. H. Bayley argued that legislation was needed for all birds which were useful, or beautiful or good songsters.[37] His proposal also opposed shooting, which had become fashionable with women as well as men – a fashion that the novelist Ouida deplored: as a young woman she had offered a silver cigar case to be shot for by MPs, but subsequently regretted it: 'It is an act of which I am now poignantly ashamed. When, later on, a wounded bird fluttered down to die beneath a cedar-tree by which I was seated, I realised the full horror of that disgusting sport, and I never again entered the enclosure of the club.'[38] Ouida's sentiments began to be more widely shared and by 1906 the Hurlingham Club, the site of Ouida's conversion, had banned this 'sport'.[39]

Apart from lobbying for changes and extension to the legislation to protect birds, the SPB also put forward practical suggestions to protect the livelihoods of women working in the millinery industry. It attempted to influence the whims of fashion by suggesting that artificial flowers and berries would both save the birds and 'help many poor women hard pressed to find employment'.[40]

Working-class songsters and middle-class birds' nests

Campaigners realized that the wanton destruction of birds was practised across class divides. As W. H. Hudson demonstrated in his *Lost British Birds*, it was difficult to determine which of the following were most responsible for the decline of birds:

> The Cockney sportsman, who kills for killing's sake; the game-keeper who has set down the five-and-twenty most indigenous species as 'vermin' to be extirpated; or third and last, the greedy collector, whose methods are as discreditable as his action is injurious.[41]

Working people were particularly criticized for the conditions in which they kept caged birds. The disreputable area of Seven Dials, near Charing Cross Road, was depicted as a site of animal cruelty: 'Here in this den of smoke and filth/They caged a thrush's broken heart.'[42] In similar vein the Humanitarian League issued a pamphlet against the caging of birds in which images of birds in the open air are

Caged birds in the slums. Alfred Priest, 'The Birds of the back street', from Ernest Bell, *The Other Side of the Bars. The Case against the Caged Bird*, 1911.

juxtaposed with those of birds in cramped cages hanging outside slums with cracked windows and patched washing.[43]

The practice of bird-breeding had a long tradition in city working-class communities. Spitalfields weavers testified to the Royal Commission of Handloom Weavers in 1840 that in addition to establishing botany and entomology classes they had organized a society for breeding fancy pigeons and canaries.[44] Bird shows, which mimicked the more prestigious dog shows, allowed their breeders to display their almond tumblers, pouting horsemen, or nuns – as contemporary breeding guides defined particular pigeons.[45] But even such pastimes could involve ill-treatment. Prize-winning pigeons displayed at the Agricultural Hall in Islington, for example, had their throats stitched at the back to improve their appearance, a practice for which their owner was successfully prosecuted.[46]

The disreputable connotation of working with animals was extended in the 1890s to cover those who caught singing birds. In Oxford, for example, the poor of Headington Quarry village would go bird-catching at night and send down their wares by train to London for sale.[47] At daybreak London street-sellers went to the suburbs of Woolwich, Greenwich and Hounslow and into the green spaces of Hampstead, Epping and Walthamstow to catch their prey. Skylarks were popular but linnets were the cheapest of the birds caught in London, although many died after being caged for just a few days. Nightingales too suffered untimely deaths, and frequently dashed themselves against their cages. Bullfinches and goldfinches, the latter of which were particularly popular with women, were trained to sing, thereby fetching a higher price.[48] Sparrows often had their feathers painted to disguise their commonplace appearance; they died from lead poisoning when grooming themselves.[49] Another new craze was the 'flying' of greenfinches. Caught in the suburbs of Kentish Town, these tiny birds were sold for 1/2d each with strings tied to their legs. They were then flown until they dropped down with exhaustion and died.[50]

The middle classes had moved on from the innocuous spectacle provided by microscopes. No longer were they content to look at live insects or plant life through a lens; they now created their own displays of dead wildlife. Birds' nests and stuffed snakes were kept in glass classes for display.[51] As a bird's-nest catcher described it, 'It's gentlemen I get my order of.'[52] This craze was part of the general enthusiasm for stuffed animals which had been encouraged from the early 1880s by the displays in the Natural History Museum in South Kensington, and in the Bethnal Green Museum in the East End. Even in the ideal farm colony, envisaged by General Booth of the Salvation Army at Whitechapel-by-the-Sea, there was to be a museum complete with a panorama and stuffed whale.[53] So popular was the vogue for stuffed animals that by 1891 the census showed that nearly 1,000 men and women nationally were pursuing the trade of taxidermist.[54]

The consumption of exotic birds

Birds were not simply defined as living or dead fashion statements: certain species also become victims of the discerning palate, eager for new luxury items.[55] Although most middle-class women would not engage personally in the gruesome – and complicated – business of plucking birds, they were nevertheless responsible for the domestic household arrangements, including the planning of meals.[56] While fashionable interiors might display William Morris designs of birds and vines, or the strawberry thief, or birds and anemones upon their dining room walls, the same households would be eating increasingly rare songbirds at their dinner parties.[57] Larks, sold at Leadenhall market in the City of London, became sought after as roast delicacies:

I saw with open eyes
Singing birds sweet
Sold in the shops
For the people to eat.
Sold in the shops of
Stupidity Street.[58]

The selling of larks at Leadenhall had been recorded by Henry Mayhew in the 1850s, but the recent fashion for such delicacies set in train an even greater slaughter of these songbirds.[59] By the 1890s between 20,000 and 40,000 larks were sold in the London markets alone every day. Arriving in sackfuls, these dead birds were sold wholesale to poultry and game dealers by the bushel. Their purchasers were not working people but those with money to spend on fashionable dinners with lark pudding, *mauviettes en suprise aux truffes*.[60] Gourmands, not the hungry poor, were responsible for this slaughter. According to correspondence in *The Times*, while it was wealthy women who wore the feathered hats it was men who were fond of lark puddings, crimped cod and oysters.[61] At this time the only meat the poor in Suffolk could find to eat was sparrow pie. Fuelled by apparent necessity, this not the focus of the SPB's concerns; its contempt was reserved for ostentatious consumption.[62]

You are what you eat

Wesley, Shelley and supporters of the French Revolution had all promoted vegetarianism.[63] Gompertz had published vegan recipes to show that it was possible to implement practically a policy on animal rights, but few had taken this idea up, even though a Vegetarian Society had been established in 1847. It was not until the late nineteenth century that vegetarianism became more popular, and took on new dimensions. The Metropolitan Drinking Fountain and Cattle Trough Association had suggested that the provision of healthy water for cattle, horses and owners alike would help turn men away from an intemperate lifestyle. Those engaged in food reform and the advocacy of vegetarian practices believed that food could also have a beneficial effect on the moral character. Vegetarianism in the late nineteenth century offered many things: a respite from the prevalent contamination of meat and animal produce; a practical alternative to the continuing maltreatment of animals by butchers and slaughterers; and a solution to poverty. Colin Spencer has also suggested that vegetarians started to take up the welfare of animals at this period precisely because of the impact of the vivisection debate, which raised broader questions about the ways in which animals were treated.[64]

Those who suggested that food reform, like temperance, was indeed a solution to the poverty of the working class, couched their message in practical forms. In an interestingly worded article which evoked the religious diatribe against poverty by the Reverend Andrew Mearns in its title – 'The Bitter Cry Answered' – the food reformer F. Pierce described an occasion on which cabmen and their wives partook of a vegetarian dinner at the Alpha Restaurant in Oxford Street. This group was particularly significant, given the notoriety of cabmen in ill-treating their horses and their legendary drunken behaviour. In the same way that the Salvation Army proselytized against drunkenness by entering the very watering holes of the drunkard, here food reformers were working with 'the enemy'. The assembled group feasted on meatless Irish stew, haricot pie, sweet barley stew and tea and coffee before listening to a speech by Symes, an elderly cab driver who extolled the virtues of his own lifestyle. For three years he had abstained from 'beef, beer and baccy' and lived on grapes, potatoes, bread and butter, tea, coffee and eggs; the chairman of the Amalgamated Cabdrivers' Society, Mr Rowlands, endorsed these principles.[65] Changes in diet were also being advanced as ways of creating a more civilized lifestyle. In the same way that kindly treatment to horses indicated a capacity for moral change, so too did a move away from the eating of animals to a temperate vegetarian diet.

Like the work of the SPB, vegetarianism took on a particular female dimension. According to the feminist and socialist Charlotte Despard, giving her presidential address to the Vegetarian Society, 'Vegetarianism is pre-eminently a woman's question because it will do away with the most degrading part of her work.'[66] Anna Kingsford, the anti-vivisectionist and a vegetarian for fifteen years, attributed her vivid dreams to her 'fasting' from meat,[67] and focused her dismay upon those responsible for killing animals for food: 'I think we owe it to civilization to raise the whole class of men now utterly degraded and plunged into barbarism. I mean butchers, slaughtermen, drovers, and all those who have the management and conduct of animals.'[68]

The concern about cruelty perpetrated within the traditional women's domain provided an impetus to women leading the movement for vegetarian food and by the spring of 1895 a Women's Vegetarian Society had been formed.[69] Women who combined philanthropic work with the political membership of school boards or boards of guardians took up the diet of the children in their purview. Florence Nicholson of the London Vegetarian Society established a children's dinner fund for underfed children and distributed cheap meals, comprising one pint of good vegetable soup and thick slices of wholemeal bread and wholemeal currant bread.[70] Anti-vivisectionist Dr Frances Hoggan meanwhile suggested less charitably that the workhouse inmate did not need 'the expensive luxury of animal flesh' in his diet.[71]

Vegetarianism as a personal lifestyle

In adopting vegetarianism not merely as an abstract embodiment of animal rights but as a healthy and humane diet for all, food reformers and vegetarians were changing their own way of life. It was not a case of abstaining from direct cruelty oneself, but of promoting good practice towards animals through positive, and personal, action. Humane behaviour was not something merely urged on others but practised oneself through adopting a vegetarian way of life. Many involved in campaigns to improve the lives of animals were acutely aware that accusations of hypocrisy could be levelled against those who were not themselves vegetarian. 'It seems to me', said a speaker at a Food Reform Society meeting in the Exeter Hall, 'absurd to prosecute a poor uneducated donkey driver for ill treating his beast and complacently to sit down day after day to sirloins of beef and legs of mutton.'[72]

Personal lifestyle became important. When the 'shopping revolution' took off in the 1870s and 1880s this was accompanied by the establishment of tea shops and of vegetarian restaurants.[73] The first vegetarian restaurant had been set up in London on the Farringdon

Road in Clerkenwell in 1876. By 1886 there were twelve others in London: public places where women could – and would – happily go.[74] Such restaurants were also the venue for progressive meetings such as the weekly teas held by the Humanitarian League, where Gandhi first made the acquaintance of Henry Salt.[75] Specialist shops and products flourished. Shearns' Fruit Luncheon Saloon – 'London's Fruit King' – of Tottenham Court Road claimed in its advertisements: 'More fruit and flower shops mean fewer gin and butchers' shops.'[76] Nut-food suppliers, health stores and vegetable oil soaps thrived, and a vegetable face powder entirely free from minerals such as zinc was even produced.[77] Increasingly, vegetarianism was seen as an ethical and moral choice and one which practitioners encouraged others to adopt. A Vegetarian Cycling Club was set up and the improved performance of vegetarian boxers and swimmers was given publicity. The benefits of vegetarianism were deemed to be proved when local vegetarians won a tug of war contest in West Ham against butchers and brewers.[78]

The supporters of food reform

The support for food reform spread across a wide spectrum.[79] The first meeting of the Food Reform Society in 1881 attracted around 700 people. They heard speeches from the anti-vivisectionists Edward Maitland and Anna Kingsford and from Professor Newman, a former professor of Latin at University College London, who endorsed the spread of vegetarian restaurants as a step away from sensuality and towards Christianity.[80] Other prominent food reformers and vegetarians included temperance leaders such as Mrs Florence Bramwell Booth, the Salvation Army leader, who was also against vivisection and a subsequent supporter of the League against Cruel Sports.[81] In the strict temperance homes run by the Salvation Army meat had been phased out of the diet.[82] This was thanks in part to Mrs Bramwell Booth, a vegetarian for twenty years, who explained, 'I have not only emancipated myself but also the seven dear children whom God has given us from the use of animal food.' Looking at the issue from a holistic perspective, she elaborated: 'We cannot divide a human being into watertight compartments, and say the body has nothing to do with the mind, and the mind has nothing to do with the

W. HARWOOD, Weight-Lifter.
Holder of the Heavy Weight-Lifting Championship of the
North of England since 1908.
Third in the British Weight-Lifting Championship at the
German Gymnasium in 1910.
In 1912 at B.W.L.A. Meeting at Camberwell Baths he lifted
301 lbs., being North of England Heavy-Weight Record, and
only equalled by two other men of British birth.
Also won second prize in Open Physical Development
Competition.

The strength of a vegetarian diet. W. Harwood, a vegetarian and a
champion weight-lifter, from Henry Light, *Vegetarian Athletics (What
they Prove and Disprove)*, a Vegetarian Society pamphlet of *c*.1912.

body.' In consequence people drink, eat meat and smoke and 'wonder
they are subject to the temptations of the sins of the flesh.'[83]

For many vegetarians, moral and spiritual dimensions were important, be these taken from the new Theosophy or the Salvation Army.[84]
The emphasis on vegetarianism as abstinence from meat was usually
linked to abstinence from alcohol, and often tobacco. The president
of the Food Reform Society in 1885, for example, was the Reverend
W. J. Monk, a vice-president of the Vegetarian Society and of the

Anti-Narcotic League, secretary of the Canterbury Church of England Temperance Society, and member of the East Kent RSPCA.[85]

At food reform meetings members testified to the personal benefits of vegetarianism. The wholemeal bread advocate, Dr Allinson, reported how his rheumatism had declined with vegetarianism; and he drew upon Darwin's work to highlight the fact that the nearest relative of man, the monkey, was a simple fruit-eating animal.[86] The eccentric Mrs Weldon proclaimed the virtues of bringing her children up without meat and without shoes and stockings. Though dirty 'outside' through playing out of doors, they were 'washed inside'.[87] Lady Paget, the widow of the British Ambassador to Vienna, extravagantly declared that since adopting a vegetarian way of life, 'I have experienced a delightful sense of repose and freedom, a kind of superior elevation above things material.'[88] Obituaries in the vegetarian press lauded the benefits of the diet followed by the deceased. Lady Florence Dixie, a reformed fox-hunter, was remembered by the Vegetarian Society for her diet of only two meals a day: breakfast of watermelon, banana, almonds, raisins and dates accompanied by milk with egg whites; for her other, afternoon, meal she ate pineapple and milk with egg whites.[89]

Such public flaunting of the vegetarian lifestyle led, of course, to satire. In a particularly witty account in his *Heterodox London*, the Reverend Charles Maurice Davies described an interview with a strict vegetarian: '"This," [the vegetarian added] handing me a paper bag containing two or three slices of plum cake, "with a draught of water from yonder decanter will be my dinner" . . .' When Davies questioned whether he might tire of plum cake 'he reminded me that the carte of most men, tied like himself to the city during the day, was almost as monotonously limited to the routine of "chop of steak".' The vegetarian was 'loud in praise of oatmeal and beans'. Davies's irritation is even more explicit in his condemnation: 'These vegetarian people . . . would be uncongenial people to live with, until they shall have levelled the rest of us up to their own lofty ideal.'[90]

Such cynicism was shared, amongst many others, by H. G. Wells who, in his novel *Ann Veronica*, caricatured those engaged with 'the Higher Thought, the Simple Life, Socialism, Humanitarianism.'[91] Miss Miniver, who lives on movements and fourpence a day, and her friends the Goopes are ridiculed for their diet of fruitarian refreshments of chestnut sandwiches buttered with nutter, accompanied by lemonade and unfermented wine.[92] The geographical location of the employment of Mr Goopes, as a manager in a fruit shop in the Tottenham Court Road, suggests comparison with the real Shearns' shop described above. Mrs Goopes's weekly column in *New Ideas* about vegetarian cookery, vivisection, degeneration, lacteal secretion, appendicitis and Higher Thought could also find its real-life counterparts in many vegetarian concerns of the late nineteenth century.[93] Although William Morris often dined with Shaw at the Orange Grove vegetarian restaurant in Rathbone Place,[94] he and Janey nevertheless teased Shaw about his vegetarianism by giving him, unknowingly, suet pudding to eat. When Shaw had eaten a second helping Janey pronounced: 'That will do you good: there is suet in it.'[95]

Shaw was not alone in the literary community in his promotion of the cause of animals. Writers like Thomas Hardy and Ella Wheeler Wilcox, the popular American poet, incorporated their opposition to cruelty to animals in their writing. As Wilcox described it in her poem 'The Voice of the Voiceless':

> I am the voice of the voiceless;
> Through me the dumb shall speak;
> Till the deaf world's ear be made to hear
> The cry of the wordless weak.
> From street, from cage, and from kennel,
> From jungles and stall, the wail
> Of my tortured kin proclaims the sin
> Of the mighty against the frail.[96]

In Hardy's tragic novels and poetry, his empathy with animal life infuses the texts. In *The Mayor of Casterbridge* the death of a caged goldfinch – a wedding present for the estranged daughter of the protagonist – serves to emphasize the tragedy of Henchard's life.[97] It is no accident that contrasting treatments of birds and animals are used by him in his last novel, *Jude the Obscure*, to highlight the emotions of the main protagonists. Jude's antipathy to killing a pig at the behest of his coarse wife, Arabella, and the release of the pet pigeons by Sue to prevent them being sold as food by a poulterer are significant moments in the narrative. Jude's first act of kindness as a child brings him trouble. He is employed to scare away rooks from a farmer's crop but instead encourages 'the poor little dears' to dine on the seeds, saying, 'There is enough for us all'. His harsh treatment at the hands of the farmer evokes a sense of foreboding: such acts of kindness are not to be tolerated in a cruel world.[98]

Contaminated food

Vegetarianism was promoted not just for reasons of health and humanity, but as a practical alternative to the contaminated food which was sold, especially to the poor.[99] Campaigns across political and class divides had long been waged against food contamination. In the 1850s the Chartists reported that bread had been adulterated with rice flour, alum, excessive salt, and potatoes; coffee had been contaminated with chicory and ground horse liver; even mustard had been doctored with flour, turmeric and pepper.[100] In a hard-hitting editorial against unscrupulous traders, the Chartists denounced the 'unprincipled gang of adulterators and dealers in adulterated articles [who] spare no one. From the babe at the breast to the aged being stretched on the bed of death, all are subjected to the destructive power of these heartless impostors'.[101] In different ways, Angela Burdett-Coutts had attempted to tackle the same problem. She had established the Columbia Market – where the Sunday flower market is now based – precisely so that the poor could obtain food direct from producers. When this venture foundered she reopened it as a wholesale fish market, but by 1885 this too had folded, due to the effective opposition of Smithfield and Billingsgate traders alike.[102]

At the end of the nineteenth century widespread food contamination was still rife. Milk was of dubious quality, contaminated and watered down. By 1894 the Local Government Board declared that 'only' 10 per cent of milk nationally was contaminated.[103] However, it was not until the new regulations provided by the Dairies, Cowsheds and Milkshop Order of 1899 that high standards were established and consequently infant welfare improved.[104] Even those who used tinned condensed milk as a safer alternative to cows' milk were not immune from disease: lead used to solder the top of the tin to the sides slipped into the milk.[105]

Meat was often diseased. When the Vegetarian Society declared that 75–80 per cent of meat in London alone was diseased it was building on widespread fears and popular knowledge.[106] As the food reformer Mary Dawtrey explained, decay in meat was more difficult to recognize than contamination in fruit and vegetables.[107] Bad meat was frequently used in sausages, the purchasers of which would be the poor.[108] Ironically, poor immigrants in Italian and Jewish communities enjoyed relatively good health thanks to the lack of meat – of any sort – in their diet.[109]

Bread too was adulterated. Working women's reliance on unhealthy white bread was widespread: they ate bread and tea while their menfolk ate meat or bacon or fish and potatoes.[110] This staple was often polluted by alum.[111] To combat the bad teeth and diseases children developed from eating white bread Miss Yates, president of the Women's Vegetarian Union, established the Bread Reform League to promote wholemeal bread.[112] Physiologist Benjamin Ward Richardson, whose pamphlet on the healthy manufacture of bread endorsed Miss Yates's work, proposed new methods of commercial bread-making and better conditions for the bakers who lived in filthy conditions in the bakehouses.[113] Dr Allinson, the food reformer, developed and marketed wholemeal flour; a branded loaf using such flour still sports his name.[114] Mary Dawtrey advocated that working girls should eat wholemeal bread, fruit, oatmeal, haricots and vegetable soup instead of white bread and tea and the occasional bacon or flesh meat as a 'delicacy'.[115] Vegetarian food was not just healthier than meat, it was cheaper.

Such an interest in the nature of food harked back to the campaigns of the 1830s against the cruelty at Smithfield market: diseased meat came from badly treated and inhumanely slaughtered animals. Improving the conditions under which animals were kept would, in turn, improve human health. The Contagious Diseases (Animals) Act of 1869 had increased inspection of imported cattle but had not resulted in the anticipated improvements in animal or human health.[116] By the 1890s concern about the transmission of TB from cattle to people was widespread.[117] Indeed, the Humanitarian League vigorously opposed the conditions of the transport of cattle from Ireland (and America) in tones reminiscent both of earlier pamphleteers against the iniquities of Smithfield and of the rhetoric of the Kent and Essex campaigners of the 1990s.[118]

New forms of death for the new century

The actual method of killing animals for food had changed little from an earlier, more barbaric age. As the century drew to a close certain animals were still being felled with a pole-axe, penetrating the skull with a crunch,[119] and their brains were then stirred up by a cane inserted through a hole punched in the dying animal's skull, in order to improve the taste of the meat.[120] Although animals were not supposed to see their peers dying in front of them, in practice partition doors between their lairs and the slaughter bays were not closed, so that oxen, for example, 'were evidently on the rack of agonized anticipation'.[121] Animals were rarely stunned before death, pigs being the exception – as a slaughterman reported to the Admiralty Committee on Humane Slaughtering in 1904, 'in crowded cities we could not do with the noise they would create'.[122] This was evidently something not merely to be hidden from sight but from the hearing of the compassionate.

One direction favoured by humanitarians and sanitary reformers alike was to establish municipally run slaughterhouses or abattoirs.[123] In 1883 a London Abattoir Society had been founded to suppress private slaughterhouses, and to centralize the slaughter of animals in humane conditions.[124] The concept of such a society contained its own contradictions, as the founder of the Humanitarian League, Henry Salt, argued. While he recognized that the proposed abattoirs would lead to improvements in the way animals were treated, nevertheless they would, by definition, be killed.[125] Unsurprisingly, Josiah Oldfield, the editor of The Vegetarian, shared his reservations. To show his readers the enormity of his disgust with the notorious Deptford slaughterhouse, a 23-acre complex in south London dedicated to the slaughter of foreign cattle, Oldfield compared it to the hated physiology laboratory.[126]

Writers such as John Galsworthy and Thomas Hardy also campaigned against the horrors of the slaughterhouse:

> Cries still are heard in secret nooks,
> Till hushed with gag or slit or thud;
> And hideous dens whereon none looks
> Are sprayed with needless blood.[127]

Indeed Hardy and other animal campaigners such as Nina, Duchess of Hamilton, George Greenwood and Lady Tenterden became prominent members of the Council of Justice to Animals, an organization formed specifically to lobby for public abattoirs and regulation and inspection of the slaughter process.[128] Recognizing that one of the reasons for the lack of public concern about the slaughter of animals was that 'no one likes seeing it',[129] campaigners entered into one of the 'dark places of the world', as the Deptford slaughterhouse was described, by bribing a slaughterman with cigars to see 'trembling oxen as terrified witnesses of the slaughter of those preceding them'.[130] The tactics used to expose vivisection in the university laboratory were now employed to enter another site of animal death. The human 'witnessing might be of use to aid the cause of slaughterhouse reform'.[131]

The importance of personal experience was stressed. John Galsworthy commented, 'Nearly everyone who witnesses with his own eyes the infliction of unnecessary suffering on an animal, feels revolted, and even hastens to the creature's aid.'[132] One role of the campaigner was to re-create such sights through the use of words and visual images. Gertrude Colmore devoted an entire novel, *The Angel and the Outcast,* to the Deptford slaughterhouse and its environs, casting a slaughterman in the morally ambiguous role of the murderer of a fellow butcher – but one who was cleared since the murder was carried out on the grounds that the dead man was being cruel to the ox he was killing.[133]

Contaminated people

There continued to be concern about the moral character of those associated with the slaughtering of animals. In language reminiscent of observers some 70 years before, the social scientist Charles Booth observed: 'That the men carry on their ghastly trade in a perfectly callous spirit is certain; but sickening as are the sights and sound of the slaughter house to one who enters it for the first time, the most tender-hearted of men would no doubt rapidly become indifferent to them if he could once overcome his initial aversion to such a trade.'[134] Boys entered into the slaughter trade through a debasing route. Bereft of any training in the humane killing of animals, they learnt the craft by collecting the blood of the dying animals.[135] However, in the Deptford market women worked alongside men. 'Gut girls' worked in the offal sheds cleaning out the innards of dead animals.[136]

This 'feminizing' of butchery work was criticized by, amongst others, the *Daily Telegraph*: 'In an ideal world men would not permit women to do work from which instinct of refinement and even decency shrinks . . .' it opined.[137] Deptford had become demonized as a site of animal cruelty and those working in its yards were contaminated by their very jobs.[138] It was precisely because of the morally pernicious influence of the men – and women – who worked in the slaughter trade that Rachel McMillan decided to establish a nursery school for poor children in Deptford at a time when the cattle trade was at its height. Her creation of gardens filled with flowers for the local children was in direct opposition to the 'foul work of the offal trade' which would leave 'its mark on a generation'.[139]

Radicals, Socialists and controversy

By the 1890s socialism as a political ideology had started to challenge any hegemony that radicalism might have earlier had within progressive opinion. But the new socialist movement did not agree about the importance of animal issues, including vegetarianism. William Morris remained critical of vegetarianism, believing that even if the whole dietary system were changed, the poor would still live on 'vegetable cag-mag' and the 'rich on vegetable dainties'.[140] Other socialists, however, saw vegetarianism as a class issue, because of the land (mis)use that the breeding and feeding of animals entailed. The socialist Jim Joynes, the brother-in-law of Henry Salt and translator into English of Karl Marx's *Das Kapital,* linked the vegetarian cause to land control.[141] Referring to the Highland Clearances, which removed sheep to make room for deer-hunting, he claimed: 'slaughter seldom fails to please the high born soul.'[142] Vegetarianism per se, though, would not be a panacea, since Joynes believed, like Morris, that there was a class dimension to the question: landowners should not be allowed to monopolize even the vegetables.[143] Henry Salt drew on the popular work of Henry George, *Progress and Poverty*, to illustrate that food reform alone would not improve the condition of the poor. Other questions also needed resolving which, for Salt, included vaccination, vivisection, temperance and land reform to deal with the 'tangled web of misery and poverty'.[144]

The treatment of animals had little part in the new framework of political debate. Neither the Social Democratic Federation (SDF) nor the Independent Labour Party (ILP), the two main socialist organizations whose members would be influential in future trade union and Labour movement activities, devoted time to considering the position of animals in society. Neither group opposed *individual* members taking up these questions, but they formed no part of conference discussions nor party platforms. The ILP might call for land reform and the SDF for nationalization of land, but this was not linked to party opposition to hunting or shooting.[145] The concentration within socialist groups on particular political issues was no accident but reflected both the priorities of the respective organizations and the way in which they defined politics itself. Scientific socialism, as envisaged by Henry Hyndman, the leader of the SDF, was designed to exclude many causes – and personalities – of the late nineteenth century. He set himself against the radical and humanitarian current in progressive life in Britain. As he (in)famously stated: 'I do not want the movement to be a depository of odd cranks: humanitarians, vegetarians, anti-vivisectionists and anti-vaccinationists, arty-crafties and all the rest of them.'[146] In practice, however, his view was opposed by many of his own supporters – and others in the ILP.

Men and women, especially women, published and campaigned for animals outside their political groups. Isabella Ford, the Yorkshire socialist feminist, for example, was a member of the ILP. She conducted her work for animals through her support of the anti-vivisectionist cause and as chair of the Leeds RSPCA.[147] While she did not introduce her beliefs explicitly into her work for the ILP, nevertheless her understanding of parallels to be drawn between the plights of women and animals appeared in her writing. Her pamphlet *Women and Socialism* is usually analysed in relation to the links she made between class and sex oppression, yet the connections she made between the experience of women and domestic animals are also perceptive: 'In order to obtain a race of docile, brainless creatures, whose flesh and skins we can use with impunity, we have for ages past exterminated all those who showed signs of too much insubordination and independence of mind.'[148]

Peter Taylor, the Radical Liberal MP for Leicester, had been recognized by Marx as the most extreme republican in the House of Commons throughout his parliamentary career until his retirement in 1886, but the concerns that he and his radical friends supported were not embraced by the new socialists.[149] Radicals like the anti-vaccinationist and anti-vivisectionist Elizabeth Wolstenholme Elmy would join the ILP – and new suffrage feminist groups – but their concerns did not fit neatly into the new socialist frameworks. According to Hyndman, such people were to be dismissed as sentimentalists who had no part in his new world of scientific socialism.

Accusations of sentimentality were answered by Henry Salt in 1893. The Humanitarian League spanned concerns for animals and for people within a broad organization committed to 'prevent the perpetration of cruelty and wrong – to redress the suffering, as far as is possible, of all sentient life'.[150] Salt described his approach to humanitarianism:

> By humanitarianism I mean nothing more and nothing less than the study and practice of humane principles – of compassion, love, and gentleness, and universal benevolence. If the word, in the sense in which I use it, is associated in the minds of any of my readers with 'sickly sentimentality' I ask them to divest themselves of all such prejudices.[151]

Far from seeing the work of the Humanitarian League, vegetarianism, anti-vivisection and the SDF as counterposed to each other, Edward Carpenter, the homosexual socialist and friend of Salt, saw all these currents and Theosophy as jointly marking 'the coming of a great reaction from the smug commercialism and materialism of the mid-Victorian epoch, and a preparation for the new universe of the twentieth century'.[152] Carpenter argued that if the Labour movement was to defend itself against the exploitation and tyranny of the propertied classes, it also had to defend animals against the horrible exploitations of so-called science.[153]

In practice this humanitarian view was endorsed by many leading members of the ILP and SDF. In 1896 the Humanitarian League drew up a Labour movement petition against vivisection with the declaration that, 'vivisection is cruel and inhuman, and that all such experimentation on living animals is opposed to the right feelings and true interests of the working classes' and should be entirely prohibited. Those who added their names to this petition were leading members of socialist and feminist groups. They included Social Democratic Federation members, the dockers' hero Tom Mann, Harry Quelch, chair of the London Trades Council, and the gasworkers' leader Will Thorne. They were socialists who had come to the fore in the struggle for new unionism, for organization of unskilled working-class people traditionally outside the remit of respectable unions and political parties.[154] Other signatories included Independent Labour Party members such as Katherine Bruce Glasier, Isabella Ford, the gasworkers' activist Peter Curran, the educationalist Margaret McMillan, and the first Labour MP, Keir Hardie, who also chaired the Humanitarian League conference of 1895.[155]

While the petition did not succeed in its aims it nevertheless repre-sented a high point and a new focus for campaigns against animal cruelty. Despite party political differences, socialists and radicals were still able to join together in common cause for animals, acknowledging that this was an important issue for the new organiza-tions of the growing working class.

SIX

New century: new campaigns

'The old faiths are dying or dead; and we love for some new motive power to take their place in the future.'[1]

The idea of a new age for a new century or, as the writer Edward Carpenter put it, 'a new universe',[2] was variously expressed by a number of organizations, from the Fellowship of the New Life, through Theosophy, the Labour Party, Syndicalism and militant suffrage feminism. An optimistic mood in which change was felt to be imminently achievable had been captured in the first pamphlet of the Humanitarian League in 1893, by Henry Salt, quoted above. A collection of writings on the coming century published by the Labour Press was indicative of the part animals politics would play in this new future.[3] None of the writers mentioned the plight of animals in their particular contributions, yet nearly all were involved in various anti-vivisection, anti-vaccination or Humanitarian League initiatives in the interests of animals: Alfred Russel Wallace, the explorer, scientist and anti-vaccinationist; Tom Mann, the socialist, Syndicalist, vegetarian and anti-vivisectionist; Henry Salt, Fabian and founder of the Humanitarian League; Enid Stacy, member of the executive committee of the ILP and anti-vivisectionist; George Bernard Shaw, Fabian, vegetarian and opponent of both vaccination and vivisection; and Edward Carpenter.[4] Individual support was strong; official endorsement by political organizations was weak.

However, the optimism for the new century, fuelled by new socialist and feminist politics, spilled over into particular concerns about animals. In the early nineteenth century analogies had been made between the plight of animals and slaves; now links of a more complicated kind were being made: 'The same spirit of sympathy and fraternity that broke the black man's manacles and is to-day melting the white woman's chains, will tomorrow emancipate the working man and the ox.'[5]

New age: new optimism

In this new age cruelty towards animals still existed and was still evident on the streets of London. Annie Besant, the Theosophist and former organizer of the female match-workers in their struggle for union recognition, believed that London was so full of cruelty that one would need to wear cotton wool in one's ears and glasses on one's eyes in order to not see or hear it all around.[6] Visible cruelty was still evident in the treatment of horses, which continued to collapse from overwork and harsh beatings.[7] But, in more positive vein, there was growing support for new humanitarian causes. The Our Dumb Friends' League (ODFL) was established in 1897. It particularly aimed to encourage all those who worked with animals to treat them well. Rather than castigate cab drivers as a group, it acknowledged that individuals could – and would – change their behaviour. However, since it was also the case that drivers who behaved benignly were often harassed and sacked by their employers, the League helped to find jobs for those sacked for this reason.[8] It gave financial rewards to those acting with kindness towards animals, such as the cab driver Robert Padwick, who forcibly removed a whip from a costermonger attacking his donkey.[9] Padwick received a small sum and a badge, and the League took possession of the offending whip.[10] The League was endowed by marchionesses, lords and ladies and had local branches in a cross-section of London boroughs including wealthy Chelsea and South Hampstead as well as the less salubrious Bethnal Green and Paddington and Somers Town near King's Cross. There was also a cabmen's branch run by T. Ryan from the cab shelter at Waterloo Station.[11] Within the cab drivers' own union, too, praise was given to members who were kind to horses and who kept them well watered, and castigation piled on those (non-members) who gave horses conditioning powders to overwork them.[12]

Supporters of the ODFL included temperance advocates and those long associated with animal causes such as Lord Llangattock or Mrs Jesse, a founder of the Battersea Dogs' Home. It was also supported by members of new socialist and feminist groups such as Charlotte Despard of the SDF and Gertrude Colmore, the suffrage novelist. The League was primarily philanthropic in its concerns, with its funding

of an animals' ambulance and an animals' hospital for those unable
to pay vet fees, but this did not stop it agitating against the way in
which horses were transported from Ireland or against councils
asphalting streets, thereby causing distress to horses.

In similar vein the National Canine Defence League, set up in
1891, campaigned vigorously and optimistically against vivisection,
declaring that once they knew the situation, 'all the working class, the
masses of voters, will be opposed to vivisection'.[13] Vice-presidents of
the National Canine Defence League included Basil Wilberforce, the
Archdeacon of Westminster, and the vegetarian Lady Paget; Charlotte
Despard and Gertrude Colmore were also members. Individuals
continued to make practical links between campaigns. William Tebb,
the founder of the *Vaccination Inquirer* and chair of Burstow parish
council in Surrey, was a vice-president of the National Canine
Defence League. Sidney Trist, the secretary of the London Anti-
Vivisection Society, was elected to the management committee of the
Battersea Dogs' Home, where he ensured that its policy of never
selling any dog to a vivisector was maintained.[14] John Colam of the
RSPCA had been a member of the Dogs' Home committee and his
son was now its secretary.[15] The Fabian socialist Sidney Webb became
a benefactor of the Battersea Dogs' Home; Beatrice Webb a vice-
president of the newly (re)formed National Food Reform Association,
which also attracted suffrage feminists such as Lady Constance Lytton.[16]
Stephen Coleridge, secretary of the National Anti-Vivisection Society,
was involved in the recently founded National Society for the
Prevention of Cruelty to Children.

The first years of this century saw a mushrooming of activity of
different kinds in support of animals, ably assisted by practical
networks such as these that linked apparently divergent campaigns
through the presence of key individual members. Whether people
ascribed rights to animals or defined them as 'dumb creation' seemed
to matter little to the outcome for animals. The geographical focus for
the work changed in line with the treatment animals themselves
received. In the 1830s and 1840s attention had been focused on the
streets of London and other big cities and the cattle which traversed
them; in the 1860s and 1870s concern shifted to domestic animals
and the way they were dealt with in the laboratories of the middle
class; by the end of the nineteenth century the focus had shifted again

to the iniquity of middle-class women displaying the carcasses of birds on their clothes. By the twentieth century, however, hidden cruelty was still carried out by all classes. The middle-class scientist continued his vivisection away from public view, particularly in the laboratories of the prestigious teaching hospitals in central London. The slaughterman continued to ply his trade in the slaughter yards of Deptford in the south-east of the capital.

New forms of action

Campaigners were faced with the problem of how to maintain interest and support for initiatives started decades before – the same problem as that facing suffrage feminists. The latter realized that new tactics and strategies would be needed if the campaign for the vote, which had commenced a few years before the start of the anti-vivisectionist movement, was to be realized in their lifetimes. Patient lobbying, so reasoned the Pankhurst family, would no longer suffice; rather, disruption of the established order was needed. Women had to enter into the male political arena, to speak out – and be thrown out – at political meetings and to demonstrate in the streets.[17] These were new tactics for new times. They were also used in the cause of animal welfare, particularly since so many of the new feminists and socialists were personally sympathetic to it.

In Manchester, Christabel and Emmeline Pankhurst were discussing a new independent women's movement and organizing headline-grabbing action; in London two young women were initiating similar individual militant action in the cause of animals.[18] In 1903 Louise Lind af Hageby and Liesa Schartau entered one of the most prominent sites of vivisection in Britain, University College London in the heart of central London. In 1836 the college had pioneered the new physiological sciences with the first professorship of its kind in anatomy and physiology, to which it appointed William Sharpey. On his retirement he had advised the government on the workings of the controversial 1876 Cruelty to Animals Act.[19] Sharpey's post had subsequently been filled by Sir John Burdon Sanderson, before his controversial elevation to a professorship at Oxford. When Louise and Liesa enrolled in physiology classes it was to see and record William Bayliss, an acclaimed experimenter, at work.[20]

Louise Lind af Hageby was a young woman in her twenties, the granddaughter of the Chamberlain of Sweden, and a graduate of Cheltenham Ladies' College who, after the traditional humanitarian occupations for women of her class, of philanthropy towards children and the poor and prison reform, had visited Louis Pasteur's institute in Paris and had read Burdon Sanderson's now standard handbook on physiology.[21] In her espousal of humanitarian causes and feminism – she supported the Women's Freedom League, a militant suffrage organization – she epitomized the optimistic spirit of the times. At the annual meeting of the Humanitarian League in 1910 she took the opportunity, amidst discussion of strategy for bringing together a number of humanitarian causes, to emphasize the policy feminists should adopt for their own cause, which was indeed similar to the forceful approach she employed in the cause of animals:

> . . . I feel very strongly – and I am not afraid of saying it – I feel very strongly that it rests with women themselves to make it clear to all humanity that they are worthy of the vote. It rests with women themselves to make themselves intelligent, to make themselves needed, to make themselves humaner beings, so that men would rather die than do without them in the life political.[22]

Although Louise Lind af Hageby prioritized anti-vivisection, she also endorsed vegetarianism, the enfranchisement of women, the abolition of the state regulation of vice and protection for animals.[23] Like Henry Salt of the Humanitarian League she believed that a comprehensive approach to injustice was vital: 'The temptations of the scientific egoist are as real as those of the gourmet, or the dainty lover of soft apparel of fur and feather.'[24] This drawing of connections between different campaigns was increasingly recognized by animal campaigners, who were scathing about those selective in their support of animal rights. Such hypocrisy had been vividly exposed by Shaw in his preface to The Doctor's Dilemma when he recalled speaking at an anti-vivisection meeting in London:

> I found myself on the same platform with fox hunters, tame stag hunters, men and women whose calendar was divided, not by pay days and quarter days, but by seasons for killing animals for sport: the fox, the hare, the otter, the partridge . . . The ladies among us wore hats and cloaks and head dresses obtained by wholesale

massacres, ruthless trappings, callous extermination of our fellow creatures . . . I made a very effective speech not exclusively against vivisection, but against cruelty; and I have never been asked to speak since by that Society. . .[25]

Involvement of animal reformers in a range of progressive campaigns was not new.[26] What was new in the first years of the twentieth century was the political nature of the other causes for which people worked, which reflected the new political situation.

The specific tactics that Louise Lind af Hageby adopted against vivisection were audacious. Recognizing, she said, the need for first-hand knowledge of the process of physiology and vivisection, she ventured into the laboratories of Dr Bayliss to watch him at work and recorded this experience in her book, *The Shambles of Science*. It consists of a lurid narrative of various experiments on cats and dogs which she and Liesa Schartau witnessed during 1903, and was intentionally titled to show this work as 'a sort of butchery'.[27] Frances Power Cobbe, who died in 1904, had exposed the practices of vivisectors by publicizing their experiments through their own words and illustrations; she had not however entered into such places herself. The bringing to light had been achieved through the pamphleteers' pen reprinting for a non-scientific readership extracts from the physiologists' press. The personal witness was not of the act of vivisection itself but of the ordinary domestic animals who might fall prey to such treatment, a witness and knowledge shared by the readership. It was the contrast between the pet seen in the home, or walking in the park with its owner, and the imagined torture which created outrage.

Louise went back to an earlier form of testimony. In the same way that early SPCA or *The Voice of Humanity* supporters had taken up the horrors they had witnessed of cattle tormented in streets or calves in butchers' shops awaiting death,[28] Louise Lind af Hageby used her own words to describe what she herself had seen and to dispel the image of the caring scientist, describing him as a common slaughterman: 'attired in the bloodstained surplice of the priest of vivisection, [the lecturer] has tucked up his sleeves and is now comfortably smoking his pipe, whilst with hands coloured crimson he arranges the electrical circuit for the stimulation that will follow.'[29]

The shocking thing – which led to a successful libel action[30] – was not the depiction of the scientist as a disreputable butcher, but her claim that the vivisector joked throughout his lecture and that this was 'fully appreciated by those around him'. The student onlookers responded in kind: there were 'jokes and laughter everywhere'. To emphasize the point the chapter was headed 'Fun'.[31] The account caused uproar amongst scientists and animal campaigners alike. In an extraordinary counterblast Ernest Starling, professor of physiology at University College, promoted the cause of killing dogs in experiments. Apart from arguing that the dissection of dogs led to knowledge of the human body, he argued that stray dogs were currently put to sleep in their thousands at the Battersea Dogs' Home. To save them from dissection would merely add to this figure. Dogs now merely had an opportunity of 'obtaining euthanasia at the hands of the physiologist'.[32]

Ten years after its first publication *The Shambles of Science* was still referred to with disdain by scientists (in another libel trial), and was used as evidence against vivisection at the hearings of the Royal Commission on Vivisection, which sat between 1906 and 1912.[33] While the book cannot be compared in its influence to *Black Beauty*, which had done so much to create public awareness of cruelty to horses, its publication was nevertheless a key moment in the anti-vivisection campign.[34] Copies of the libellous first edition continued to be sold by the Church Anti-Vivisection League at a stall at the Church Congress, despite its recall by the publishers, and the book was republished on a further four occasions with the offending chapter, 'Fun', excluded. Such was the impact of the rest of text that the Research Defence Society discussed, though to no effect, ways of getting even the revised editions withdrawn from publication.[35] A copy of the book lay on Thomas Hardy's table and, as he informed his friend Florence Henniker, an executive committee member of the NAVS and ODFL, 'everybody who comes into this room . . . dips into it, and, I hope, profits something'.[36] In a sermon given to raise money for the anti-vivisection hospital in Battersea, Archdeacon Basil Wilberforce also recognized the importance of the court case around the book, which had highlighted the 'severe torture of animals'.[37]

The 'moment' of *The Shambles of Science* is significant. The protagonists are young – and female; the perpetrators of cruelty, in this instance, are male and older. In a sense the work and its circumstances epitomize the political mood of the times: new forces of civilization against age-old brutality. There were new methods and a new language reflecting the wider politics of the time. Scientists themselves were not complacent about their opponents. Although the Cruelty to Animals Act of 1876 and subsequent royal commissions upheld the scientists' right to vivisect, the scientists themselves clearly felt that they had not won the moral argument. Ostensibly the Physiological Society had been a dining club, but, tellingly, it had only been established after the passing of the first Act to regulate vivisection in 1876. Early gatherings advised scientists to describe their experiments as generally as possible; subsequent meetings discussed the ways in which the Home Office had 'interfered' with their experiments through inspection.[38] In 1908 the Research Defence Society (RDS) was set up, specifically to counter the impact of the anti-vivisectionists. Holding to the view that the latter could well win in their campaigning, the RDS documented in obsessive detail the meetings, publicity and stance of their detractors.[39]

Political animals

Children became a particular focus of humanitarians in the twentieth century. The Socialist Sunday schools, established to 'unite ethics and religion', also promoted kindly behaviour of children towards animals, and demonstrated against vivisection.[40] Julia Goddard and Edith Carrington both wrote plays and prose for children which depicted animals going on strike to achieve proper recognition of the treatment due to them.[41] In Carrington's tale, the organizing donkey explained to the exploited farm animals that they needed to act like colliers. Accordingly the birds flew away, so insects were not eaten and the crop failed; the horse threw the cruel master, who broke his leg; and the farmer's wife and daughter castigated him, so that the farmer saw the error of his ways and order – and better treatment of animals – was duly restored.[42]

Political initiatives were also taken in public life: demonstrations in the streets, shop displays, international conferences, and the use of the courts to institute libel actions to create a greater public profile. Such moves were contentious and indeed the animal rights and welfare movement in the early years of the twentieth century was strained by similar disputes over strategy as those which beset feminist and socialist groups. There were sharp divisions within the new Labour movement about whether reform of the political system was possible and desirable or whether the status quo should be scrapped in its entirety. Similar arguments were reflected in animal welfare politics.

Sincerely held beliefs – and personal rivalries – about the relative merits of gradualist pragmatism or principled intransigence in the cause of animals had split the Victoria Street Society. The British Union for the Abolition of Vivisection, led by Frances Power Cobbe, intransigently opposed all legal regulation as a sop to brutality. The National Anti-Vivisection Society on the other hand, led by Stephen Coleridge, pursued the regulation of vivisection to ameliorate animals' condition as a step towards abolition.[43] Coleridge himself engaged in a range of tactics including infiltration of the RSPCA to force it to act on vivisection, without much success, and also attempted to join the new Research Defence Society – with no success at all, since the physiologists and vivisectionists who comprised this scientific body rejected his application and duly returned his 5s subscription.[44] Others such as Basil Wilberforce refused to speak on RSPCA platforms because of the organization's pusillanimous attitude to vivisection.[45]

The current which emphasized persuasion of – or action against – individuals guilty of cruelty, and amelioration of the position of animals through the gradual strengthening of the law also continued in the tradition established by Richard Martin. Individual MPs such as George Greenwood, Liberal MP for Peterborough, a believer in evolution and universal kinship, were responsible for leading parliamentary campaigns which resulted in the Protection of Animals Act of 1911,[46] which broadened the remit of cruelty to animals and increased punishments.[47] The National Canine Defence League, which gained much support from the growing Labour ranks in Parliament, also attempted without success to exempt specifically dogs from vivisection, as a first step against all vivisection.[48] The tactic of individuals personally criticizing cruelty and taking a stand was by now well established, if not widespread. Describing the actions of his first wife, Emma, Thomas Hardy stated:

her courage in the cause of animals was truly admirable, surpassing that of any other woman I have known . . . In town or country she would, when quite alone among the roughest characters, beard any man ill-using an animal and amaze him into shamefaced desistence: and she would carry lost or injured cats in London into a house or to some home and insist on their being looked after.[49]

Such behaviour often led to court action. Sentencing a driver who had lashed a fallen horse over its head with a whip to a month in prison, the magistrate thanked a Miss Young who had witnessed and reported the event: 'It was seldom people would take this trouble but it was an act of kindness to the dumb creation.'[50]

The visualization of animals

In the late nineteenth century petitions had been drawn up against vivisection, letters had been written to *The Times* about murderous millinery and MPs had been repeatedly lobbied to change the law. Such acts had been of an individual nature, and, apart from certain meetings, had not broached the realm of public spectacle. This started to change. There was a new focus on the visual to make public what was happening in private spaces. A common device was the use of photographs in animal campaigning publications, echoing the growth of photographic images of animals generally. The image of 'Nipper' the little dog looking quizzically at a gramophone and reproduced on HMV records in Britain, the United States and Russia was increasingly popular.[51] The suffrage movement, keen enthusiasts for the visual and spectacular, issued a Christmas card of the 'catland' genre with a cat displaying a notice 'Votes for women' round its neck, adjacent to Christmas crackers. The verse underneath read:

> I'm a catty Suffragette
> I scratch and fight the P'lice
> So long as they withold the vote
> My warfare will not cease.[52]

The suffrage movement also included animals in its demonstrations, as a form of spectacle. In 1910 the June demonstration was led by Flora Drummond cantering along on a charger, accompanied by women on horseback, the sight of which 'somewhat staggered' the

Advertising new technology.
Francis Barraud, *Nipper and the Phonograph*, c.1899.

I'm a catty Suffragette
I scratch and fight the P'lice,
So long as they withold the vote
My warfare will not cease.

A cat employed for the suffrage cause.
A Christmas card, probably issued by the Womens'
Social and Political Union, c.1908.

onlookers.[53] The image too of a woman posed as Joan of Arc astride a white horse at the head of suffrage demonstrations became ingrained on the memory of those watching and participating in such events.[54] The 'Women's March', which took place some two years later from September to November 1912, in the course of which women travelled from Edinburgh to London, again included a horse, Butterfly.[55] In more sombre vein, in keeping with current funeral customs, black horses were employed by suffragettes for the funeral of Emily Davison in June 1913, a keen horsewoman who had died trying to stop the king's horse at the Derby.[56]

Animal campaigns used the visual devices of the broader political movement in their imagery. The *Animals' Guardian*, 'a humane journal and monthly record of the London Anti-Vivisection Society', sported a serious collie dog and a smart cat with a ribbon around its neck on its masthead. The publication also regularly carried illustrations of animals. Some emphasized good practice: the work of the dog asylum in Saarbrucken, for example.[57] Others were used to illustrate cruelty, such as Gabriel Max's painting of the vivisector at his desk overlooked by Mercy with a puppy and a balance in her other hand.[58] The National Canine Defence League also issued a fund-raising card as part of its anti-vivisection publicity. The image of a real dog sculpturally posed on a stone plinth was accompanied by a verse by Ella Wheeler Wilcox, whose words had also been enthusiastically used by the suffrage movement. The text read:

> The same force formed the sparrow
> That fashioned Man, the King,
> The God of the whole gave a spark of soul
> To furred and to feathered thing.[59]

Anti-vivisectionists hired shops in places frequented by middle-class women – popular shopping areas of London such as Kensington High Street and Piccadilly, and in the provinces, including Plymouth, Newcastle and Leamington. Here they advertised meetings, sold literature and showed grisly replicas of experiments.[60] The emphasis on visual displays in the metropolis had been used a few years before, in 1899, by the National Canine Defence League. Muzzles, which the government intended to be used on all dogs, were nailed up alongside copies of the relevant government bill throughout the capital, and

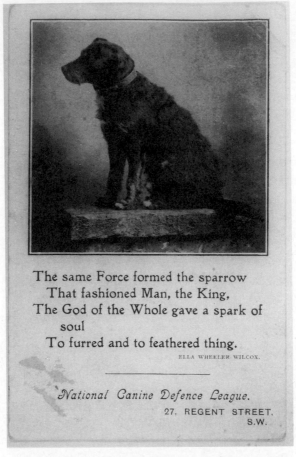

The same Force formed the sparrow
That fashioned Man, the King,
The God of the Whole gave a spark of
soul
To furred and to feathered thing.

ELLA WHEELER WILCOX.

National Canine Defence League.
27, REGENT STREET,
S.W.

Fund-raising for the National Canine Defence League.
Publicity material quoting Ella Wheeler Wilcox, c.1907.

sandwich-board men were employed to parade outside Parliament. That particular spectacle had been undertaken to good effect. A petition of over 100,000 signatures to scrap the bill was presented to the Prime Minister – and the bill was in due course withdrawn.[61]

The spectacle had not lost its impact. In the Piccadilly shop of the Animal Defence and Anti-Vivisection Society there was a stuffed dog stretched out on an operating table to illustrate the circumstances of vivisection. (The dog had been obtained from Battersea Dogs' Home after it had been put to sleep and stuffed by a reputable taxidermist.)[62] Behind it hung a painting depicting a dog begging a vivisector for mercy, apparently based on a story about the French scientist François Magendie.[63] It was a popular image, also used by the National Canine Defence League at its premises in Manchester.[64] Such visual propaganda was apparently effective, causing considerable consternation to the RDS. It in turn employed sandwich-board men to parade outside the offending shops and in Piccadilly hired the adjacent shop and urged the police to take action. Lind af Hageby, who had organized the displays for the Society, was accused 'of having made Piccadilly almost impassable for decent people'.[65] The RDS also issued leaflets specifically against the anti-vivisectionist shop displays protesting that what was seen – dogs tied to boards – was misleading, as the animals would be unconscious: 'they have no pain'. The leaflet went on: 'to die under an anaesthetic is to die in your sleep. It is not possible to die more easily than that.'[66]

Anti-vivisectionists also displayed posters at railway stations, to which the RDS offered different responses, both placing their own posters alongside them and encouraging politicians such as Winston Churchill to use their influence to have the protesters' posters removed by the railway companies. In similar vein the RDS placed pressure on Cruft's dog show to ban the British Union for the Abolition of Vivisection (BUAV) from having a stall at the annual event. So concerned were the scientists by the nature of the public display of vivisection that they even discussed calling on the Home Secretary to ban a demonstration organized by the Animal Defence and Anti-Vivisection Society to coincide with an international congress it had arranged in central London on cruelty to animals.[67] The demonstration, however, duly went ahead along a traditional route, gathering first at Trafalgar Square before proceeding to Hyde Park. Further demonstrations took place; banners covered the plinth of Nelson's Column; some people marched accompanied with their dogs, while others dressed up as the vivisected dog Lind af Hageby had seen at University College, and were transported in a carriage bedecked with flags.[68]

Political and parliamentary support

The intention of all this was, as Louise Lind af Hageby acknowledged, to make 'in a sense, political propaganda'.[69] She was keen to widen this so that anti-vivisection was situated in 'a chain of reforms, prompted by the new spirit of compassion, and fellow feeling towards animals'.[70] To this end she approached the socialist press and the Independent Labour Party for support.[71] The speakers at the International Anti-Vivisection and Animal Protection Congress held in London in July 1909 reflected this coming together of socialist, radical and Liberal campaigners. The brainchild of Lind af Hageby, the congress managed to gain the support in Britain alone of the Humanitarian League, the RSPB, the National Anti-Vivisection Society and the ODFL. Its ambitious programme included a demonstration, mass meeting, church service, theatrical matinée and a garden party at the Battersea Anti-Vivisection Hospital. A number of individuals presented papers and resolutions which were later published. The secretary of the RSPB, Linda Gardiner, RSPCA activist Florence Suckling, the Liberal MP George Kekewich, the Theosophist Annie Besant, president of the Women's Freedom League Charlotte Despard and the journalist W. T. Stead all participated in this venture.[72] Similar support of a more permanent nature was enjoyed by the Humani- tarian League, whose supporters included Keir Hardie, a former chair of the Humanitarian League conference, and Ramsay MacDonald, the future Labour leader who endorsed the work of the organization against the growing 'spirit of gross materialism pushed by an ignorant and pushful [sic] class to justify its own vulgarity and attainments'. Messages of support on the League's twentieth birthday in 1910 were received from a plethora of progressives, including Edward Carpenter, Stephen Coleridge, the illustrator Walter Crane, the philanthropist Passmore Edwards, and Thomas Hardy.[73]

The high-profile action for animals in Parliament and on the streets was entwined with issues of class and gender, which were so important at this period in political life. The eminent surgeon (and vivisector) Sir Victor Horsley had been de-selected as a prospective Liberal parliamentary candidate by the Harborough constituency in Leicestershire precisely because of his support for women's franchise, and subsequently stood for the University of London seat in 1910.[74] He put forward his vivisectional work at the Brown Institute in Battersea as a reason for his candidature. Although militant suffrage feminists would undoubtedly have refrained from support, since the Liberal Prime Minister had called an election precisely to prevent the passing of a suffrage bill, the feminist opposition to his candidature

Campaigning horses in parliamentary action.'Our Anti-Vivisection Van.
Miss Damer Dawson on driver's seat, Miss Evelyn Faulkner, the Hon. Mrs Forbes, and
Miss Warren on their way to the University of London to attend Sir Victor Horsley's
Poll.' From an issue of *The Anti-Vivisection Review*, 1910–11.

focused on the treatment of animals.[75] They held public meetings,
lobbied, and cruised the London streets on a two-horse van driven
by Mary Damer Dawson of the Animal Defence and Anti-Vivisection
Society.[76] Both sides engaged in correspondence in *The Times* debating
the pros and cons of Horsley having vivisected 3,000 animals. Horsley's
subsequent defeat was received by anti-vivisectionists with 'gratifica-
tion and relief'.[77] The next issue of *The Anti-Vivisection Review*
celebrated the victory with a striking cartoon entitled 'Ghosts of
the past: an unforeseen obstacle to parliamentary election', in which
ghosts of animals outside the Houses of Parliament confront a
shocked Horsley emerging from his hidden laboratory in which a dog
is stretched out prone on a table.[78]

Working-class empathy with the plight of vivisected animals grew.
Anti-vivisectionists suggested that although working-class people
desisted from joining societies due to the cost and a general reluctance
to subscribe to societies, they nevertheless supported their cause.[79]
The case of George Radford of Wandsworth illustrates this. George 'a
poor man but a spirited one', was both a dog-lover and opposed to

Victor Horsley: the defeated vivisector.
'Ghosts of the Past: An Unforeseen Obstacle to Parliamentary
Election', a cartoon from an issue of *The Anti-Vivisection
Review*, 1910–11.

vivisection; indeed he refused to pay his dog licence as a protest
against the use of dogs for vivisection. When he was summoned and
fined, the National Canine Defence League paid his costs as part of its
popular campaign against the use of dogs in experiments.[80]

At the instigation of Louisa Woodward and Louise Lind af
Hageby and with the endorsement of Battersea Council and Stephen
Coleridge, a fountain was erected in the Latchmere Recreation
Ground in memory of the brown dog killed at University College
which had found earlier fame in Hageby's *The Shambles of Science*.[81]
This ground was at the centre of a new working-class housing
development built in 1902 off the main Battersea Road in south
London. The surrounding streets had rousing names – Reform Street
and Freedom Street – and were named after George Odger, the first

president (in 1864) of the International Working Men's Association, and John Burns, at that time a socialist on the LCC for the Battersea area and an anti-vivisectionist.[82] The statue represented a coming together of middle-class women and working-class men to commemorate a dog done to death in the cause of science. Erecting images to commemorate animals was not new, but this was the first time in Britain that an animal killed in a scientist's lab had been so recognized. This statue was deliberately provocative, with an inscription which read, complete with capital letters for emphasis:

> In Memory of the Brown Terrier Dog Done to Death in the Laboratories of University College in February, 1903, after having endured Vivisection extending over more than Two Months and having been handed over from one Vivisector to Another Till Death came to his Release. Also in Memory of the 232 dogs Vivisected at the same place during the year 1902. Men and women of England, how long shall these Things be?[83]

On two occasions rampaging students from the offending University College and Middlesex Hospital attacked the statue, lit bonfires in celebration outside their alma mater and attempted to attack the nearby Anti-Vivisection Hospital – and suffrage meetings.[84] When moderates subsequently gained control of the local council they removed the statue, ignoring a petition to the council by over 20,000 local people and acceding, as the former mayor described it, to 'organized violence'. In turn, over 3,000 demonstrated in central London against its removal.[85]

Battersea and the brown dog

In 1871 Sir John Burdon Sanderson, not content with dissecting animals in his private laboratory in Gordon Square, had established the Brown Animal Sanatory Institute, and this practice was continued by Sir Victor Horsley.[86] Less than half a mile away the Battersea Dogs' Home provided shelter of a different kind to lost dogs and cats, while at the junction of Albert Bridge Road and Prince of Wales Drive, five minutes away from the statue, stood the Battersea Anti-Vivisection Hospital.[87] The hospital, housed in a large house opposite Battersea Park,[88] catered for working-class people, 'the suffering poor', although the wealthy were certainly welcomed as benefactors and members of the management committee,[89] which reflected the broad basis of support. They included George Kekewich, former Liberal President of the Board of Education, Louise Lind af Hageby, Joseph Levy of the Personal Rights' Association, the Reverend Campbell of the Nonconformist City Temple, Sidney Trist of the London Anti-Vivisection Society and Battersea Dogs' Home committee, and Mrs Baillie Weaver, otherwise known as Gertrude Colmore, the novelist and suffragette, who depicted the hospital in her novel *Priests of Progress*.[90]

With its outpatient service for the 'suffering poor' and beds for cancer patients and other, non-terminal, cases, it provided a different and more humane treatment than that meted out in more prestigious hospitals north of the river, and attracted hostility from the medical profession for so doing. As a fund-raising leaflet for 1903 put it:

> No vivisection in its schools
> No vivisectors on its staff
> No experiments on patients[91]

The link between vaccination, vivisection and working-class people was made concrete in the establishment of a hospital in this area and by the creation of a management committee reflecting non-professionalist views. Practical opposition to vivisection clouded distinct class-based divisions on the treatment of animals. Coster-mongers, traditionally outside respectable society, were now favourably compared with vivisectors. A medical director of the Runcorn Research Laboratory who had experimented on a donkey he had neglected and maltreated escaped prosecution, arguing in his defence that he was a medical man. The RSPCA had not been allowed into the laboratory since it was a private place and thus not covered by general legislation against animal cruelty, but only the specific regulations of the 1876 Act. Campaigners summarized it thus: 'Legalized cruelty: one law for the vivisector – another for the coster-monger.'[92] As Stephen Coleridge explained, the 1876 legislation 'expressly exempted the vivisector from observing the law of the land, and permitted him to do what cabmen and costermongers remained punishable for doing. It legalized the torture of animals, domestic or wild, if the torture were inflicted by a selected class of persons.'[93]

ABOVE LEFT 'The Brown Dog in the Procession', from an issue of *The Anti-Vivisection Review*, 1909–10. ABOVE RIGHT *Campaigning against vivisection and the removal of the brown dog statue.* 'Major Richardson and his famous Bloodhounds under the Brown Dog Memorial Banner'; 'The Brown Dog's Day in Trafalgar Square.'

'The Demonstration on March 19th [1911].' From an issue of *The Anti-Vivisection Review*, 1909–10.

The first petitions against hunting

Writing in 1903, Lady Augusta Fane imagined that few would would differ from her opinion that 'fox hunting is the finest sport in the world': she was wrong.[94] Primatt, Wesley and Bentham had denounced hunting decades before; *The Animals' Friend* had rejected it in the 1830s: 'No one in his sense can think that to hunt and tear a living being to pieces for sport is not wickedness in the extreme.'[95] But it was not until the twentieth century that hunting started, for the first time, to become a serious campaigning focus for humanitarians. At the Animal Protection Congress in 1909 it was denounced alongside the more usual subjects of vivisection and murderous millinery, even though, as MP George Greenwood suggested, fox hunting was almost part of the British Constitution.[96] It had traditionally been a rural (and upper class) occupation and was considered manly, with grouse shooting and stag hunting being almost exclusively male sports.[97] In 1831 *The New Sporting Magazine* had declared, 'to talk of the decline of the sport is to talk of the decline of the empire'; at that time over 90 different hunts had existed in Britain and Ireland.[98] Fox hunting had reached its peak between 1830 and 1870, made accessible to urban communities through the growth of the railways and, according to some of its supporters, by the final wave of enclosure acts: 'But for enclosure by hedges and the obstacle that these produced, fox hunting might never have been such a challenging and enduring sport.'[99] Then – as now – the argument that fox hunting was needed to keep down foxes was untrue; instead hunting encouraged them. Leadenhall market, the notorious site for the purchase of sackfuls of larks, was also a venue for the purchase of live foxes imported from the Continent and bagged up and thence transported around the country to be chased.[100]

The first national petition against hunting had been organized by the Humanitarian League in 1900. This was directed at Queen Victoria, who owned a pack of buckhounds kept to hunt park deer, that is, deer specifically bred and kept for the purposes of being hunted. The support that the petition received across the political, religious, social and cultural spectrum was impressive and was not confined to any one political party. To the usual animal supporters such as Lord Coleridge and Viscount Harberton were added David Lloyd George, and over 70 other MPs, vicars, headmasters of public schools, Edward Carpenter, Herbert Spencer, and four women: Josephine Butler, the former leader of the campaign against the Contagious Diseases Acts; Mrs Bramwell Booth, the Salvation Army leader; Alice Meynell,the poet and journalist; and Agnes Maitland, the principal of Somerville College, Oxford.[101]

Just as significant was the later petition of 1908, again organized by the Humanitarian League, against the hunting of pregnant hares by the wealthy schoolboys of Eton. The exclusively female document included the signatures of leading suffrage feminists, militant and constitutionalists alike: Christabel Pankhurst, Emmeline Pethick-Lawrence, Millicent Garrett Fawcett, and Charlotte Despard.[102] This suggests both that feminists were opposed to cruelty to animals, and that their position on this subject was seen to be influential. However, little headway on the broader issue of hunting was made with Edward VII, a notorious killer of animals. In a royal visit to India in 1875, when Prince of Wales, he famously killed six tigers in one day. A hagiographic tome dedicated to him as a 'sportsman' explained, without irony, that in the years before his death his shooting was 'really limited' to a few weeks in November, December and January, twelve days at Sandringham, and nine days at Windsor. The last day ever on which he shot, 24 January 1910, the king defined as one of the best days he had known, since 2,400 pheasants had been killed.[103]

The arrival of the cat

The growing influence of women and the working class in political and cultural life was also instrumental in affecting the status of a neglected domestic animal, the cat, which had traditionally suffered much harsher treatment than the domestic dog. The cat was not deemed worthy of displays in shows until 1872, at Crystal Palace, under the aegis of the animal painter and writer Harrison Weir, some thirteen years after the first dog show. Moreover its presence in eighteenth- and early nineteenth-century visual images was less prominent than that of dogs. The art historian Kenneth Clark suggested that this absence was caused by a lack of owner's pride, or perhaps because cats were less part of the family than dogs.[104] It is surely indicative of the status of cats amongst the upper classes painted by Gainsborough and his contemporaries that cats are relatively rare. The notorious Ladies of Llangollen were a well-known example of cat-owners, their tortoiseshell cats being depicted in paint by Maria Taylor; however their lesbian lifestyle was clearly at variance with the norms of eighteenth-century society.[105] With a few exceptions, such as Hogarth's *The Graham Children*, it is only really in the later nineteenth and early twentieth centuries that cats come into their own in art, featuring regularly in French Impressionist works such as those of Pierre Bonnard, Edouard Manet, Berthe Morisot and, later, Henri Matisse: artists concerned more with the everyday than with formal portraits of the wealthy. Moreover, the traditional negative associations of cats – with witches, for example – were transposed into paintings of interior scenes, with cats posing with kept women and prostitutes, most famously in Manet's *Olympia* and, in Britain, in Holman Hunt's *The Awakening Conscience*.[106] In this Pre-Raphaelite painting, which

The cats of Llangollen. Maria Taylor née Spilsbury, *The Ladies of Llangollen's Cats at Plas Newydd*, oil, c.1809.

The predatory cat lurks in the prostitute's domain.
William Holman Hunt, *The Awakening Conscience*, 1853.

depicts a kept woman literally seeing the light and turning towards the viewer away from the constraining arm of her lover, a tortoiseshell cat attacks a bird without pity, apparently echoing the action of the man towards the woman. Moreover, the cat is the woman's own pet: even in her home, presumably paid for by her lover, she is not safe.

In Britain dogs had always had a place in family portraiture but cats, kept to regulate the mice in the kitchen, were less favoured. And while certain breeds of dogs were seen as worthy of human affection, cats tended to be given the role simply of vermin eradicators. Thus the GPO routinely employed cats, for which official payment was allocated for food, although postal workers were advised not to over-feed them: 'They must depend on the mice for the remainder of their emoluments and if the mice be not reduced in number in six months a further portion of the allowance must be stopped.'[107] Cats were often underfed on the assumption that they would catch their own food – or eat boiled and diseased horseflesh.[108]

The idea that cats had simply a use value rather than a place in the family's affections led to their continuing ill-treatment. As Gordon Stables argued, the idea that cats were fonder of places than people originated at the time when cats were kept for their use only, and not as pets.[109] Cats were traditionally compared unfavourably with dogs, since they apparently lacked favoured qualities of faithful-ness, cleverness and docility. To counter such a bad press writers such as Edith Carrington recounted tales of cat loyalty, consciously imitating the Greyfriars Bobby legend. Nevertheless, those who kept cats as companions were seen as unconventional. Cats had tradition-ally faced great cruelty, being stolen and skinned alive like the poor cat belonging to Thomas Young, a porter on the London docks.[110] Recalling life in London in the 1850s and 1860s, Alfred Rosling Bennett claimed:

> Then no boy – of the proletariat – would dream of passing a cat without throwing at it, setting a dog on it, or chevying it in some way. That cats now come on to public pathways and sit and go to sleep on doorsteps and window-sills is eloquent of the softening of manners which has occurred. No mid-Victorian cat would have been such a fool.

He also described the work of merchants in cat-skins allegedly catching cats and skinning them alive to preserve the skins' lustre longer, and thereby command a higher market value.[111] The RSPCA had attempted to prosecute those who skinned cats alive – a particu-larly horrid case involved a young women charged with stealing thirteen cats, the skin of one of which was found to be still warm – very often with vociferous support for their prosecution from neighbours.[112] As one cat-lover noted, those who skinned cats were even lower in the social order than bird-catchers:

> [They] live in the most squalid dens and infamous purlieus of the city, leading an idle, dissipated life; and if not dead of disease before

the age of twenty-five, it is because a grateful country has provided them with board and lodging free, at stony Portland or muddy Chatham.[113]

The popularity of cats with working-class people – according to the RSPCA in 1857, 'almost every household has a cat' – contributed to their lack of status.[114] In Booth's *Survey of London Life* particular reference was made to the condition of cats kept by the very poor as an indicator of their owners' income: 'People are poor indeed whose cats look starved. I have seen the cats' meat man on his round in a very poor street, and no less than a dozen cats were strolling around with raised tails confidently awaiting their turns.'[115]

The 'class nature' of cats had been graphically acknowledged by the London dockers in their great dispute and strike in 1889. These were men deemed to be unrespectable but had been recently organized like their skilled peers into a union. Led by Tom Mann, the socialist and anti-vivisectionist and supported by Cardinal Manning, another opponent of vivisection, they marched through the city of London in what was depicted as a 'carnival of the most downtrodden people of the capital'. Their posters and emblems depicted the contrasting lifestyles of themselves and their employers: for instance, the docker's dinner and the sweater's dinner, the docker's baby and the sweater's baby, and the 'sweater's cats' and docker's cats.[116] This relationship between cats and those connected with sea trades is illustrated in different vein by the work of the missions to Seamen founded in 1856. St Michael, Paternoster Royal, a Wren church in the City of London which is the base of the Mission, recognized the traditional relationship between the seafarer and the cat – which Thomas Young, the porter on the docks, epitomized – in its stained-glass windows. Here Whittington, the future Lord Mayor of London, is depicted with his cat, a lowly animal but one capable of loyalty to Whittington in his rise in the world – and to the seafarers the church embraces.[117] In more popular vein, in Robert Tressell's socialist classic *The Ragged-Trousered Philanthropists*, the socialism and humanity of the hero, Frank Owen, was evident both through his attitude to people – and to a cat. Hurrying home in the rain Frank spots a small black kitten crying piteously, saturated, like him, with rain. He picks up the mewing animal to take home to his son, and as the cat recognizes the safety provided by him, 'the little outcast began to purr'. The elision of circumstances between the working-class hero and the pathetic outcast cat enables Frank to speculate upon the existence of a God that causes so much suffering to all creatures.[118]

Cats still faced cruelty, albeit of a different kind, for they continued to be experimented upon – as Louise Lind af Hageby had testified in her *The Shambles of Science*.[119] Edith Carrington could still declare in 1896, 'The treatment of cats in England is a discredit to a land professedly civilized.'[120] However, action had been taken to establish homes for ill-treated animals. In Hammersmith a society for the protection of cats was established by Mrs Gordon, a committee member of the London Anti-Vivisection Society, and in the Harrow Road the Mayhew Home was established for lost or starving cats and dogs, also supported by Ernest Bell of the Humanitarian League and Vegetarian Society.[121] It received glowing support from the ODFL, which enthused, 'It really is a *home*, and not a cemetery or a mart where they may be bought for the tender mercies of the vivisector.'[122] The League itself instituted a number of shelters for stray cats and established a committee to oversee the work.[123] A home for horses had also been established in Acton where the working animals of the poor could recuperate; elderly horses might also spend their last days in peace rather than suffer an untimely demise as horse meat.[124]

Cats were traditionally identified with women, and their status was subtly affected by the shifting roles of women in society. Bessie Rayner Parkes, the founder of the first British feminist journal, *The Englishwoman's Journal*, was one of the first women to write also about cats. Her short book, *The History of our Cat, Aspasia*, written in 1856, acknowledged the mood of that time: 'I know that people in general like dogs much better.'[125] A similar anonymous autobiographical narrative of a cat was published by Emily Faithfull, the feminist publisher and supporter of the Society for the Promotion of the Employment of Women, in which the cat escaped the vivisector's table, thanks to a carter.[126] When Margaret Thompson, a suffragette and hunger striker, published the diary of her time in Holloway prison she noted with affection the white Persian cat which sat near the chapel entrance, and her concern that on the day she had gone to smash windows her own cat had given birth to two kittens.[127]

A *new age closes*

To understand the optimistic tone of many of the publications issued by animal welfare groups before the First World War we need to look beyond their own writings. The close and growing links between anti-vivisection and animal rights issues generally and the suffrage cause had strong and mutual benefits on the respective campaigns. When Thomas Hardy was asked to write a statement which the suffrage feminists might use, he replied as follows:

> I am in favour of [the vote for women] because I think the tendency of the woman's vote will be to break up the present pernicious conventions in respect of manners, customs, religion, illegitimacy, the stereotyped household (that it must be the unit of society), the father of a woman's child (that it is anybody's business but the woman's own, except in cases of disease or insanity), sport (that so-called educated men should be encouraged to harass and kill for pleasure feeble creatures by mean stratagems), slaughterhouses (that they should be dark dens of cruelty), and other matters which I got into hot water for touching on many years ago.[128]

The corollary of Hardy's linking of the vote to progressive issues in the interest of animals is seen in a letter which Louise Lind af Hageby received after a lengthy libel trial in 1913, which she lost, but for which she gained huge publicity since she insisted on conducting her own case.[129] On this occasion a woman, Maud Hoffman, wrote to her declaring that she knew little of the anti-vivisection question, 'but I feel that you have rendered a great service to the women's movement'.[130] Speaking on the platform of the National Canine Defence League annual meeting of 1910, Charlotte Despard, the president of the Women's Freedom League, declared:

> There is a great change, I believe, coming over us all, and I think this awakening to a sense of true humanity is one of the most hopeful signs of the times . . . this is the desire at the back of our great women's movement [cheers]. Women have always shown sympathy with these causes, and now the best of them are working for them, as are also the best men. The best men and the best women are all the same in one sense. The best men have a great deal of women in them; the best women have a great deal of the man in them [cheers].[131]

In the mid-nineteenth century the crossover in campaigns for the improved position of animals had been with temperance and Radical Liberal involvement. This link had not been broken, but added to it now were the militant campaigns of the new age. Campaigners also had specific grounds for optimism. The long-running campaign against compulsory vaccination had finally achieved its aim, with the report of the royal commission of 1896.[132] This movement against the hegemony of science defied the supremacy of medical practitioners in dealing with disease. Moreover the Liberal government of 1905 had made it relatively easy – and cheap – for people to declare themselves to be conscientious objectors. By 1907 conscientious objectors were no longer obliged to contend with the courts – a simple statement to declare their position to the local vaccination officer would suffice.[133]

This example of a small movement winning against the medical establishment and Parliament was an inspiration to those seeking to challenge the scientists over the use of animals in experiments. It also served to make their opponents conscious of the way in which popular opinion and sustained campaigning could – eventually – win.

SEVEN

Greyfriars Bobby and Black Beauty go to war

Yer loves 'im like yer wife.[1]

The period in the first decade of the twentieth century in which women – and cats – came to the fore in campaigns for animal welfare and rights ended once war was engaged in 1914. Many animals, notably dogs, horses and pigeons, were 'conscripted' into war work. By sharing the deprivations of war with people, they were also integrated in different ways into human life itself at this time. The animals that were directly involved in war work, especially horses and dogs, were those with a cultural history which was being simultaneously disrupted and recalled in images of the war. Black Beauty and Greyfriars Bobby were joining up with their male human companions to defend the nation against the unjust. Former images of loyalty and steadfastness were reflected in the status animals received as participants in the war effort, but also as recipients of compassion, even on the battlefield. In the 1914–18 war soldiers' horses and sentry dogs, as well as strays adopted by the British officers and troops in the trenches, proved to be companions and ciphers of sanity in an insane world.

The South African war and horses

Animals were not new to warfare but now their treatment received greater attention from animal and humanitarian groups and individual soldiers, due in part to the reaction to the appalling treatment horses had suffered in the Boer War.[2] Many had been transported from South America to South Africa to aid in the war effort, but over 16,000 had died on the arduous sea voyage before they even reached a war zone.[3] In the course of military engagement more than 400,000 animals had died, mostly through neglect and lack of food and rest, rather than from injuries in battle.[4] In the two and a half years of the

South African war, so estimated the Army Veterinary Service, only 163 animals died of bullets and a mere three of shellfire.[5] Insufficient vets had been employed to deal with the diseases the horses faced. Brigadier Clabbyd, an army vet and a man well used to the rigours of military life, was nevertheless shocked: 'It has been said that never in the history of any British war has there been such a deliberate sacrifice of animal life and of public money.'[6]

One positive outcome was the creation of veterinary units in the 1914–18 war staffed entirely by veterinary personnel, and the establishment of a number of hospitals for the treatment of military animals.[7] In the same way that the poor physical condition of the men in the Boer War had led to the Royal Commission on Physical Deterioration and in turn to a huge impetus towards medical inspection and school meals for working-class children,[8] so too had the poor treatment of horses led to an awareness of the need for better treatment of animals in warfare, as well as in civilian life, and the establishment of the Army Veterinary Corps. In different ways animal welfare organizations had taken up the poor conditions endured by the horses and donkeys in South Africa. The Humanitarian League had issued campaigning pamphlets; the Metropolitan Drinking Fountain and Cattle Trough Association had erected a magnificent monument in Port Elizabeth in South Africa.[9] In Burstow, Surrey, the anti-vaccinationist William Tebb, who was a member of the parish council, erected a trough to commemorate 'the mute fidelity of the 400,000 horses killed and wounded . . . in a cause of which they knew nothing'.[10] In Latimer in Hertfordshire the grave of the horse ridden by General de Villebois Mareuil at the battle of Boshof was dug alongside the village obelisk to the local war dead. But town or village memorials to local men who had died in war were uncommon: remembrance did not become part of the physical landscape until after the 1914–18 war.[11] The troughs to commemorate the suffering of horses, however, also served to commemorate their human counterparts – and provided much-needed water for thirsty animals.

Domestic animals and the war effort

The First World War introduced a range of animal life – as well as men and women – to new circumstances that were harsh in the extreme.

Commemorating the equine deaths of the South African war. Drinking fountain and cattle trough given by William Tebb, founder of the Anti-Vaccination League and local parish councillor, Burstow, near Horsham, Surrey, 1903.

Far from pushing animal issues to one side, the war heightened them, thanks to conditions both in battle and at home. 'Horses were as indispensable to the war effort as machine guns, dreadnoughts, railways and heavy artillery,' argues John Singleton, 'yet because of our fascination with the history of technology we never give them a second thought.'[12] Such neglect was not shared by contemporary humanitarians, who expressed concern about the fate of the over half a million horses, including those imported from America,[13] the largest group of horses ever assembled together for war purposes, and the 200,000 mules, 47,000 camels and 11,000 oxen that were employed by the British army by the middle of 1917.[14] Horses were used to move heavy equipment: six horses to every field gun; eight to twelve harnessed together to move heavy guns.[15] Horses also carried the wounded on stretchers in mud so deep that human stretcher parties could not get through.[16] Indeed so terrible was the terrain in Flanders that many animals dropped exhausted and died through drowning in the sodden mud.[17] Soldiers directly involved in the fighting were concerned about the animals' condition. As the poet Siegfried Sassoon expressed it, he thought it would be a pity if the cavalry were used on the Western Front – where he too was fighting – 'for I disliked the idea of good horses being killed and wounded, and I had always been soft-hearted about horses'.[18]

While some lessons had been learnt from the Boer War and on-site veterinary hospitals meant that over three-quarters of British horses were returned to duty, yet again the prime cause of loss of life was not enemy attack but debility caused by exposure to the elements.[19]

Attempts to get dogs to engage directly in the fighting by drawing heavy guns in military operations foundered in opposition to protests from the National Canine Defence League.[20] But dogs were trained to act as sentries and to deliver messages and supplies, especially in times of disruption of other means of communication: at Vimy Ridge on the Somme in 1917 they brought news of the state of battle when all the phones were broken and visual signals were impossible.[21] The first cohort of dogs used in the 1914–18 war were Airedales trained by Lt Col Richardson, the commandant of the British War Dog School, as sentry dogs. At his training school at Shoeburyness on the Thames estuary in Essex, dogs from dogs' homes throughout Britain – Battersea, Birmingham, Bristol and Manchester – were sent for training and thus avoided being put down.[22] The incorporation of dogs in the war effort brought home the impact of war into the domestic terrain; it was not just the men who were away fighting, but the whole 'family' was involved in the war enterprise. Lt Col Richardson cited examples of civilian sacrifice in donation of dogs for the cause. One widow apparently wrote to him, 'I have given my husband and my sons, and now that he too is required, I give my dog'; a little girl wrote 'We have let Daddy go to fight the Kaiser, and now we are sending Jack [her dog] to do his bit.'[23] Pet pigeons also joined up. No longer were pigeons viewed by their owners simply as decorative creatures, but as functional birds with a role to play in the war effort. Pigeon fanciers were encouraged by the *News of the World* to donate their birds to the armed services. By the end of the war there were hundreds of stationary and fixed lofts along the English coasts as well as 150 mobile lofts on the Italian and French fronts.[24] In this way civilian pigeon fanciers were directly incorporated into war work. Messages were sent back with pigeons to their owners in lofts near the coast, and then were passed (unopened) from the local post offices to the Admiralty. Information was thus received on shipping losses and other fatalities.[25]

War had a complex effect on animals. In Henry Salt's opinion, more suffering was caused to animals in a day of war than in a year of peace.[26] Yet Salt's encompassing principle that 'all sentient life is akin and that he who injures a fellow being is in fact doing injury to himself'[27] had possibly more complex outcomes than he envisaged.[28] While the war encouraged violence to other humans, ironically it encouraged compassion towards the animals involved. As stated by the Blue Cross, a branch of the Our Dumb Friends' League established in 1912 to help animals in war, 'The Blue Cross does not endow horses with any nationality, and . . . all horses which reach the hospitals, no matter of which of the belligerent powers they belong, are given equal care and attention.'[29] The officers responsible for the veterinary services in the First World War believed that the same criteria should apply to wounded and sick horses as to the men, namely efficiency, economy, and humanity.[30]

War brought brutality – and compassion too– into the centre of social life.[31] This owed much to the physical presence of animals in the same battlefields and trenches as men. Previously the plight of animals hidden in labs or in slaughterhouses had been imagined. Now domestic animals normally seen in the home or street were located in war zones in countries far from home. Just as vivisection of animals was seen by its opponents to lead towards experimentation on humans, similarly the treatment of animals in war was seen to affect directly the treatment of men. When Ernest Bell and Harold Baillie Weaver of the Humanitarian League called for the extension of the Geneva Convention to horses, this implicitly raised questions about the treatment of humans: if horses were accorded respect, this would have a knock-on effect for people.[32]

The president of the Blue Cross carefully justified support for horses as suffering companions in warfare, while acknowledging that the first duty lay in bringing aid to the men at war.[33] The RSPCA and Blue Cross tended wounded and ill animals in battle. The French Minister of War gave the Blue Cross responsibility for the administration of veterinary hospitals for dogs. Bullets were removed, shrapnel wounds dressed and rat bites treated. Operations were performed and convalescence given: by the end of 1917 over 1,604 dogs had been treated.[34] The Blue Cross also brought essential equipment for the equine veterinary corps: syringes, portable forges, withers pads and donations to help the treatment of horses suffering the effects of gas attacks.[35]

Ideas about compassion, humanity, and the nature of the society to strive for after the end of the war permeated all aspects of life. While organizations like the Humanitarian League were rendered less effective, since members had conflicting views on the war, this did not stop them engaging as best they could to improve conditions for the men and animals involved.[36] The Humanitarian League deplored the starvation diet given to horses[37] and to conscientious objectors, who included a number of its own supporters.[38] The Vegetarian Society campaigned for the availability of vegetarian food to both regular soldiers and conscientious objectors; while Fenner Brockway, the pacifist conscientious objector, led a hunger strike in Wormwood Scrubs in support of the right to follow a vegetarian diet.[39] Continuing to publicize the positive effects of the 'food of the orchard, the field and the garden', the Vegetarian Society nevertheless realized that the cheapness of vegetarian food was one of its greatest assets in time of war.[40] The guinea pig, so praised in Victorian times as a clean, harmless creature, the flesh of which was 'by no means a delicacy to the European',[41] was reconstructed as a tasty dish, 'excellent as entrées in various stews with mushrooms cut up and stewed brown'.[42] Rabbits too started to be bred for food, especially in cities.[43] Yet once the effects of gas warfare in the trenches upon men was known, the practice of gassing wild rabbits in their warrens became subject to criticism.[44]

In 1914 Louise Lind af Hageby turned her attention to the human and animal slaughter on the battlefields and attempted to establish a humanitarian service dealing with the suffering of war horses and men at war and the consequent distress and poverty at home.[45] Not content with protesting against the war in London she went to France to 'relieve the hideous mass of human and animal suffering'.[46]

Ironically, the Research Defence Society seemed almost pleased with the war, because it 'had put a stop to the usual anti-vivisection debates, meetings and correspondence'.[47] It declared contemptuously that the public had tired of the anti-vivisectionists 'and is not in the mood to listen to them now . . . We shall have little or no trouble from them, as things are now.'[48] It was clearly proud that the eugenicist Dr Caleb Saleeby was speaking on its behalf to both soldiers and civilians on the benefits of vaccination.[49] A further endorsement of Saleeby's position was offered by Arthur Mee in his publications for children, in which he argued, 'The lives of thousands of little children are more valuable than the lives of dogs. We must save the highest life. Men who study animals are amongst the most humane in the world.'[50]

Images of loyalty: vehicles of emotion

Visual images of horses in war were used to depict the human qualities and emotions of loyalty and resilience thought laudable in war. Thus *The Illustrated London News* published a print entitled 'Fidelity' of a riderless horse, in an exhausted state and entangled in wire, standing over its dead rider.[51] These pictures helped to solicit donations from civilians for horses, initiated by the RSPCA, since 'our dumb allies [are] so faithfully serving us, helping us to win the war'.[52] Compassion towards horses was based in part at least on the horses' inability to resist military involvement. As Ethel Bilbrough wrote in her diary, 'Men fight *voluntarily*, but the horses are dragged into the sickening mêlée to suffer and go through untold agonies all through no fault of their own, it seems so unfair to them.'[53]

Such images printed in papers with a wide circulation also helped create sufficiently sanitized images to evoke empathy, rather than horror, in the reader at home. When Siegfried Sassoon went home on leave, having won the Military Cross in terrifying circumstances, he had intimated (to protect his aunt from the horror of war) that he had merely been working with horses, a 'normal' activity to which she could relate. Death and destruction were outside this framework. On hearing of his decoration, his aunt could only uncomprehendingly exclaim, 'But I thought you were only looking after the horses.'[54]

It was also a feature of the 'genre' of images of animals at war that sketches were deemed to be modelled on true events. Thus Fortunino Matania's *Goodbye Old Man*, a hugely popular image in the postwar period of a soldier tending a dying horse while his battalion moved back behind the safety of its lines, was thought to be based on a number of real events.[55] Reproductions of the watercolour, the original of which is still owned by the animal charity, were sold by the Blue Cross to raise money for its animal hospital in London.[56] A poem based on the same painting, also published by the Blue Cross for fund-raising purposes, again reflected emotional bonds:

The bonds of officer and horse.
Fortunino Matania, *Goodbye Old Man*, 1916.

Goodbye old man; goodbye, my dear old comrade!
At last our true and tender love must cease,
And I, alone and sad, go forth to battle,
While here your war-worn body lies in peace.[57]

The image is literally of man and horse, but metaphorically the division between man and animal counts for little. However this division is important in showing that humanity is displayed, even in war, through caring for an animal. For the officers such compassion was demonstrated towards their horses; for the Tommies in the trenches affection was bestowed on dogs.

The changing terrain for certain animals, from domestic space onto the battlefields of Europe and Africa, demanded new responses. As Jay Winter has persuasively argued in his writing on war and memory, many of the images of war looked back to earlier times; so too did the depiction – and treatment – of animals seen as domestic in a very 'public' world, the battlefields of France. In this most male of terrains, war, animals achieved a new role and new public acknowledgement as worthy recipients of emotion – in men.

Men at the Front, away from their domestic sphere, would still have daily contact with dogs which would remind them of their own pets at home. According to the National Canine Defence League, the love of dogs was not peculiar to any particular class of the community, it pervaded a large proportion of the whole nation – including the nation at war.[58] For the *Times* correspondent on the Western Front in 1917: 'It is the dogs who enlist the men's sympathies more than anything else. Like frightened children they join the ranks, nestling down by the side of the men for warmth and protection.'[59] This reflects a similar image of dogs as children used by Lt Col Richardson, who compared the new canine recruits to his Shoeburyness training centre as new pupils to a large public school, being bewildered and homesick but soon feeling at home due to excellent dinners.[60] Dogs are both substitute pets – and substitute children and wives. In her fascinating writing on the 1914–18 war Joanna Bourke has argued that in the absence of female companionship men bonded together, engaging in intimate and emotional friendships.[61] Animals assisted in providing outlets for a warmth of emotion otherwise frowned upon. The verses collected by the Blue Cross reflect the emotions which the men felt towards the animals. In 'The Silent Volunteers' dogs are portrayed as every bit as heroic as the men who die; in other poems horses take on the role of specific individuals within the family structure.[62] Thus a gunner describes his feelings about his horse affected by gas: 'Yer loves 'im like yer wife';[63] while the emotions of a horse in Egypt towards his former soldier-owner would be expressed in similar language:

> For 'he' loved me like a brother,
> 'He' loved me like a wife.[64]

A relationship with the animals in their immediate environment was a favourable outlet for feelings in a desensitized world, as Geoffrey Dearmer's poem 'The Turkish Trench Dog' epitomizes. Here animals crossed national 'lines', exhibiting an internationalism impossible for their human counterparts in time of war. While the soldier is crawling towards the Turkish lines in the dark he sees a dog following, smelling his trail:

> Nearer and nearer like a wolf he crept –
> That moment had my swift revolver leapt –
> But terror seized me, terror born of shame
> Brought flooding revelation. For he came
> As one who offers comradeship deserved,
> An open ally of the human race,
> And sniffing at my prostrate form unnerved
> He licked my face![65]

Here the 'emotions of war' are replaced with those of normalcy, in an encounter more usually found in a domestic space. The important psychological support given to men at war by animals was acknowledged by a contemporary article in the *Psychoanalytic Review* which explored the role of animals in the unconscious, drawing on the stories of Ovid from centuries before. As the author elaborated, '[Animals] are indispensable today on the battlefields, where their sure instinct brings succor [sic] to the living lying among the dead.'[66]

As C. Rowland Johns, the secretary of the National Canine Defence League during the war, recognized, dogs also had an important emotional role on the home front. They provided protection and consolation to women whose husbands were away fighting.[67]

What was needed was to preserve 'normal' virtues and values in an abnormal time. The NCDL did as much as possible to keep dogs within their domestic setting: discouraging people from putting their dogs down; giving supplies of dog biscuits to needy families; and paying licence fees for the dogs of widowed soldiers.[68]

A memory of experiences with animals at home sustained men at the front. As the refrain of the popular song ended, 'They dream of home'.[69] Further, part of the image of 'Keep the home fires burning' was, surely, the domestic hearth, which included within the family space animals such as dogs and cats. A letter signed by all the staff and patients of a military hospital to the NCDL bore this out: 'Thousands of soldiers at the front look forward greatly to being welcomed home by their pets and companions.'[70] Part of the work of animal welfare organizations during the war was to maintain the status quo in Britain as a place in which the values of companionship, duty and loyalty were safe. The defence of animals at this time was thus an important factor in the maintenance of a 'British way of life'. '. . . for many grieving widows and mothers, the family pet was a vital – sometimes the only – comfort.'[71] One ex-serviceman would describe this sentiment, on being united with the dog he had befriended in the war, as follows, 'After all, this war has been worth winning, knowing that we have people in England who look after our dumb friends whilst we were doing our bit out there.'[72]

Bringing the dogs home

The adoption of dogs, either strays or those trained by the army from dogs' homes, was common in the army and, despite the opposition of the veterinary service, the army council was obliged to allow men to bring back dogs subject to quarantine regulations. This sympathetic response was no doubt due to the recognition that men would smuggle dogs back in any case if it was not regulated, and that in many instances dogs – and cats – had reluctantly been put to sleep when a soldier joined up. Further sacrifices would be damaging to morale.[73] Many soldiers had brought their pets to the London Institute for lost and starving cats and dogs before going to war: 'many a brave soldier lad has broken down at the last parting with his dear four-footed companion of happier days.'[74] Although the charity was able to cater for a lucky few, most animals were put down, due to the cost of keeping them. The adopted war dogs then became a substitute for former pets. As a local paper described it:

> It would be hard to say how many 'regimental pets' have been adopted by British 'Tommies' who have regained territory from the infamous Hun. Still fondly clinging to the ruins of loved homes that they, poor creatures, alone can identify, these faithful four-footed friends of man have brought home to our gallant lads the pathos of war, and the tragedy it also brings into the animal, as well as the human kingdom.[75]

The Battersea Dogs' Home kennels at Hackbridge were prepared in order to take in hundreds of 'adopted' dogs for quarantine purposes. The army established a quota of 'repatriation' (or immigration) with an unstated 'due regard to those having the greatest claims for repatriation', and allocated quotas to the troops in Salonika, Egypt, Italy and France.[76] The army, however, refused to pay the £8 fee for quarantine, which was in turn paid for in needy cases by the Blue Cross, NCDL or RSPCA.[77] While dogs remained in quarantine they were frequently visited by their new owners.[78]

Dog bans at home fail

During the war, panic and food shortages had led to the destruction of dogs, despite the attempt of the Battersea Dogs' Home and NCDL, with its 'Save the dog' campaign, to dissuade people from this course of action.[79] Government attempts to introduce a dog ban in cities, in 1915, was met with more successful resistance. 'Dog haters are not actuated by patriotism,' argued the NCDL, 'nor by the desire to safeguard the food of the people; they are attempting to take advantage of the country's position in order to attain their own selfish and vindictive ends.'[80] The government backed down.[81] Subsequent suggestions voiced in the *Times* letter columns that a fixed percentage of animals should be destroyed to free up food for humans met with no enthusiastic response.[82]

Food specifically for animals was, however, restricted.[83] Manufacturers of dog biscuits were increasingly hard pressed to make palatable food when a regulation of 1917 prevented the use of wheat or rye. Those feeding cereals to dogs would be subjected to large fines or imprisonment. Captain Bathurst, Parliamentary Secretary in the Food Control Department, was unsympathetic: 'People must realise that they keep dogs at their own peril; if they could not keep them without wasting human food the dogs ought to be destroyed.'[84] Writing in her war diary, Ethel Bilbrough deplored the 'great deal of nonsense' about not feeding animals: 'Because we are fighting against brutes must we ourselves become brutes?'[85] To enact legislation against the presence of animals in the domestic spheres of the nation was too difficult to implement. Opposition to the war through the actions of conscientious objectors and revolutionary war resisters was one thing; opposition to the norms of everyday life by dog-lovers would have been much more disruptive, since it would have challenged practices developed over decades.

Honouring the animal war dead

Edith Cavell, the British nurse shot by the Germans in Belgium in October 1915 for smuggling British servicemen and Belgians out of the country, became a national heroine meriting a statue, raised by public subscription, facing Trafalgar Square. She remains the only woman acknowledged in this site of national monuments.[86] It is surely no accident that her dog was awarded a similar honorific posi-tion. His stuffed body still has a privileged place in the galleries of the Imperial War Museum devoted to the First World War – underneath a stuffed flying pigeon.[87] Their inclusion in an exhibition devoted primarily to the human suffering of war adds poignancy to the concept of total war. The role of animals in the First World War was acknowledged in a number of ways within the forms of memorials established to commemorate the war dead. A specific frieze depicting the role of elephants, camels, donkeys and mules, horses, dogs, bullocks and pigeons was cast in 1932 by F. Brook Hitch for the RSPCA dispensary in Kilburn in north-west London.[88] Yet even the honouring of the 'canine soldiers' who had acted as messengers in the war was viewed with alarm by the Research Defence Society, which sought assurances from the RSPCA that such a gesture was not part of anti-vivisection propaganda.[89] The text accompanying the frieze acknowledges the deaths of nearly half a million animals and

*Edith Cavell, some of her nurses and her dog, which is now
stuffed and in the Imperial War Museum.*

the role of the RSPCA hospitals in treating nearly three-quarters of a
million more.[90]

In a more prominent position in Embankment Gardens in central
London an interesting memorial was erected to the Imperial Camel
Corps which depicted camels and men alike from Britain, India, New
Zealand and Australia who had died in Palestine, Sinai and Egypt.[91]
Many animals however, especially horses, had no such public acknow-
ledgement of their role. Horses in Egypt were routinely sold to locals
at the end of the war rather than be repatriated. The 'lucky' few were
shot dead by their officers – a practice later adopted by dog handlers

in Vietnam who chose to do this rather than to abandon their dogs to the victorious Vietnamese people.[92] It was not until Dorothy Brooke, wife of the major-general of the cavalry brigade in Egypt, realized during the 1920s and 1930s that the poor horses overworked by the Egyptians were former British cavalry horses, that action was taken to relieve their suffering. Founding an Old War Horse Memorial Hospital in Cairo, by 1934 she had rescued over 5,000 such animals.[93] In the 1860s the Battersea Dogs' Home had rescued fallen dogs; now some 70 years later thoroughbred horses who faced a similar fall from grace found a similar haven. In the same year and month that Olympia, the huge London arena, witnessed a violent rally by Mosley's fascists, several horses rescued by Mrs Brooke were paraded with due honour at the International Horse Show in a ceremony redolent of the now annual commemoration of the dead soldiers of the First World War.[94]

Although the separate campaigns devoted to the specific welfare of animals emerged intact at the end of the war, the Humanitarian League, which had had more ambitious programmes of action towards humans and animals alike, did not. This organization, like many socialist and feminist groups, had been split asunder by different positions held by its members on the war. It wound up its activities in September 1919.[95] Many of its members would go on to found a new organization against cruel sports and to continue work in the vegetarian and Theosophical movements. But the all-embracing approach to the plight of people and animals would no longer exist. The war had introduced a much more fragmented structure for promoting animals' welfare and rights.

EIGHT

A meeting of the country and the town

We do not hear much to-day of the Non-Conformist conscience
. . . but the things it represented – the awakening, developing,
growing, human corporate soul – is no less, but more alive . . .[1]

In one of their last publications in 1919 the Humanitarian League
had predicted that the 1914–18 war, as an 'orgy of hatred', was likely
to lead to a subsequent revival of animal cruelty.[2] This proved to be
true. The war and the subsequent 1939–45 war would give a massive
impetus to experiments on animals. Although there was evidence
enough of the effects of poison gas from the men disabled by war,
nevertheless animals still had to suffer. Between November 1926 and
July 1929 over 1,300 animals were killed in chemical warfare experiments at the experimental station at Porton Down alone.[3] By 1944
over 1,320,000 experiments would be conducted annually in Britain
on animals.[4] As the Church Anti-Vivisection League described the
new practices: '. . . war atrocities and laboratory atrocities have the
same common denominator.'[5]

Before the war, physiology had been seen as the motor force for
vivisection; now biochemistry took its place.[6] After the 1914–18 war
vivisectors argued that their practices epitomized a new modernity
and a break with the past. Current advances in telegraph communica-
tions, telephones, aniline dyes, dynamos, motors and aeroplanes had
all been achieved, so they argued, by experimentation. Physiology,
pathology and pharmacy – all sciences based on experimentation –
were all part of this new world too.[7] Scientists increasingly criticized
anti-vivisectionists as harking back to the Victorian age, and saw the
post-war period as one in which parliamentarians would have more
important priorities to deal with.[8] When MPs continued to promote
legislation to exempt dogs from vivisection the RDS suggested that
stricter controls should be introduced against private members' bills.[9]

This new world saw the rise of the Labour Party, which included
many individuals committed to the defence and protection of animals.

In the list of honorary vice-presidents of the BUAV, alongside lords, ladies and viscounts, there were now Labour MPs such as Philip Snowden, Chancellor in the 1929 minority Labour government; George Lansbury, the former suffrage supporter and ILP leader; Arthur Henderson, the secretary of the Labour Party; and trade unionist MPs such as J. R Clynes, J. H. Thomas and Will Thorne.[10] The Animal Defence and Anti-Vivisection Society lobbied Labour MPs to prevent the export of worn-out horses and, with little success, the 1924 Labour government to strengthen slaughterhouse reform.[11] Meetings of the Women's Co-Operative Guild or ILP were targeted in turn by the BUAV and by scientists.[12] Such was the sympathy that was felt to exist within the Labour ranks that the RDS made special attempts to influence Labour MPs using the services of Dr Alfred Salter, the Bermondsey MP, calling on him to 'deal with' the MPs who were honorary members of the BUAV.[13]

Women and animals: fanatics and cranks

The suggestion that those who campaigned on behalf of animals were out of tune with the times was increasingly directed towards women. In the same way that the cause of animals had received a boost when linked with suffrage feminism before the war, now in a time of backlash against feminism such women bore the brunt of hostile criticism.[14] Writing in 1911, Judith Lytton had suggested that women who cared for dogs deserved praise; in contrast, 'the man who thoroughly dislikes animals will generally make an indifferent sort of father, and a fondness for animals often goes with understanding and fondness for children'.[15] In the 1920s and 1930s, however, women who undertook animal welfare were seen as part of another time, another earlier era:

> Their fanaticism and crankiness have caused them to take up freak science, freak religions, and freak philanthropy. They are the chief supporters of movements such as anti-vivisection, which does its best to retard the advance of experimental science in this country; of dogs' homes and cats' homes; of missionary societies and 'kill-joy' propaganda.[16]

Scientists now felt confident enough to acknowledge what suffrage feminists had themselves stated before the war: namely, that if women had won the vote at that time, it would have benefited the cause of animals.[17] But times had changed. The Battersea Anti-Vivisection Hospital, which had always faced opposition from the medical profession, now received criticism particularly directed against the women involved in running it. A surgeon called Mr Peart, who had been sacked for wanting to introduce changes against the ethos of the hospital, complained: 'It is the women members of the Board of Management who are mainly responsible.'[18] Even the 'old feminist' novelist Winifred Holtby decried the activities of her sex in supporting the cause of animals, suggesting that the drama which went into animal politics could better be used in the cause of people. In a lovely account of a RSPCA meeting, Mrs Pinto Leite, a leading light in the Our Dumb Friends' League, emerges defiant from her sickbed before the meeting to declare: 'I know that some of you would like to see me dead: but I am going to live – live – live – to fight for suffering animals.' Holtby dryly comments,

> I call that drama ... Whenever two- legged animals meet to discuss the welfare of their four-legged brethren drama descends, like a proprietary goddess, upon the scene. The affection ungrudgingly bestowed on cats, dogs, and horses, by the people of these islands, diverted to human channels, could bring about the reign of brotherly love and goodwill towards men within a fortnight.[19]

Such hostility, however, did not prevent women continuing to campaign for animals. The National Council of Women, to which the ODFL was affiliated, established a committee with the specific remit of humane treatment of animals, pursuing legal changes in their status, opposing zoos for profit, and championing the humane slaughter of animals. The League's representative was the vilified Mrs Pinto Leite.[20] In the same way that women with different views on women's suffrage had joined together some years before to petition against the hunting of pregnant hares by Eton schoolboys, women from all parts of political life united to testify against hunting in a special issue of the journal *Cruel Sports* in July 1927. These included Eleanor Barton, the general secretary of the Women's Co-operative Guild; Mrs Platon Drakoulous, the former treasurer of the Humanitarian League; Louise Lind af Hageby; Ellen Wilkinson; and the novelist and former hunter Radclyffe Hall who explained: 'I could no longer kill for the sake of pleasure . . . I could, in fact, no longer ignore the victim, for imagination had led to understanding, and understanding to compassion.'[21]

New politics: new demons

By the 1920s drunken cattle drovers and cruel hansom cab drivers were becoming part of history. But the vilification of a working-class group of 'outsiders' seen to be cruel to animals continued. In a pamphlet issued even before the unrest in the coalfields, a former inspector of mines for the Midlands area, A. H. Stokes, had declared that the gloomy picture painted by humanitarians of conditions of ponies in pits had been exaggerated.[22] However in the wake of the miners' disputes of 1921 and 1926, the plight of pit ponies, previously of little interest to Parliament, was brought to light by those hostile to the miners' cause. Colonel Lowther suggested in Parliament that while miners had been seduced by 'Bolshevik agitators paid by German gold', ponies were at that very moment drowning bit by bit or gradually starving to death in the pits.[23] Prime Minister Lloyd George, who had previously shown scant interest in the condition and protection of animals, suggested, with press support, that mines would be flooded and ponies' lives thus endangered, to bring miners to discussions in 1922.[24] Yet it was not until 1927 that a Pit Ponies' Protection Society was founded, and pit ponies existed in their thousands in mines until the 1970s.[25]

In the same way as many individual drivers were kind to their horses, challenging the stereotype of the cruel cab driver, so too did the ranks of allegedly hard miners contain those who cared for their pit ponies. Most famously Keir Hardie, the first Labour MP, had worked as a child in the mines and formed a strong bond with his pony, Donald, in whose crib he had sought refuge during a mining accident.[26] A humanitarian miner wrote to Gertrude Colmore, declaring that it was the money-grubbing and commercialism of the times that was the root of the cruelty inflicted on ponies. He, like so many humanitarians before him, remonstrated with cruel pony lads but also recounted a story of boys insisting that their ponies had adequate oats when the owners had tried to reduce them. His response to the ponies with which he worked in the mines is reminiscent of the language used by soldiers in the First World War: 'How [the pony] will nestle its head on one's breast like a child when you pet and pat on it!'[27] The owners' greed was also stressed by B. L. Coombes in his popular autobiographical novel *These Poor Hands*, a story of a miner's hard life in South Wales between the wars. Coombes acknowledged the cruelty suffered by horses underground owing to the nature of the work: ponies were required to work sixteen hours in one shift, often without water.[28]

Kindness to animals by working-class people was not rare, but often went unreported. During a strike by farm workers in Ireland in the 1930s the union organizer was busy dispatching pickets to various farms when a voice from the back boomed out, 'What about the cows?' It was the socialist Jim Larkin. Everyone was nonplussed and more so when Larkin demanded to know who was going to milk the cows. The organizer responded that the cows were the responsibility of the farmers. The angry Larkin retorted, 'If men can't arrange their affairs so that they don't fight each other, that doesn't mean that dumb animals have to suffer.' And he made them arrange squads to go and milk the cows as well as to picket.[29] In their long trek to London in the summer of 1936 from the derelict shipyards of the north-east, the Jarrow marchers were accompanied by a stray but now loyal dog. Men and dog were at one in their arduous journey.[30] More routinely, the National Canine Defence League was keen to publicize the careful attention that the poor who attended their clinics directed towards their dogs. The 1933 *Annual Report* describes a man, 'a typical product of unemployment ... In the surgery [his dog] will be revealed – probably better fed and groomed than his owner, who trembles on the verge of destitution. Yet he cannot part with his dog.'[31]

The People's Dispensary for Sick Animals (PDSA), founded by Maria Dickin in Whitechapel in 1917 to provide free veterinary treatment for the sick and injured animals of the poor, established itself nationwide. Seventeen dispensaries were set up throughout Britain and an animals' sanitorium – the first of its kind in Europe – was opened in Ilford in 1928. Its Busy Bees club for children encouraged humane treatment and fund-raising activities.[32]

Slum clearance between the wars in working-class areas often resulted in pets being abandoned. The RSPCA responded by destroying homeless animals at the rate of 50,000 a year in its Islington premises

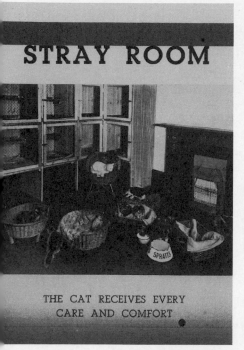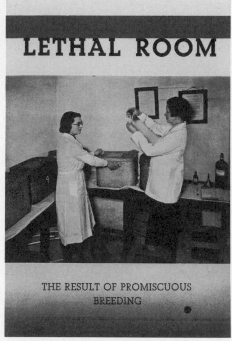

STRAY ROOM

THE CAT RECEIVES EVERY
CARE AND COMFORT

LETHAL ROOM

THE RESULT OF PROMISCUOUS
BREEDING

Home comforts and responsible breeding.
From an Our Dumb Friends' League leaflet of the 1930s.

alone.[33] The ODFL acted less brutally, liaising with local authorities, instituting a slum clearance fund to buy ambulances and animal handlers and bringing strays into its shelters. It provided the comforts of home with comfy armchairs and cosy gas fires alongside a spaying service to reduce the number of neglected animals in the future.[34]

New organizations: old cruelties

Organizations established after the First World War against cruel sports significantly shifted the geographical locus of concern with animal welfare from the cities to the countryside. The League for the Prohibition of Cruel Sports, founded in 1925 by former members of the now defunct Humanitarian League, Ernest Bell and George Greenwood, and by Henry Amos of the Vegetarian Society, implicitly shifted attention away from the cruelties perpetrated by working people to those of the middle and upper classes, who hunted for sport.

The war had seen a decline in fox hunting and the destruction of packs of hounds due to food shortages. Although certain hunts had determined to keep going 'for the sake of the boys at the front', even Eton had suspended its beagle pack 'for the duration'.[35] But popular opposition to hunting had been based, the Humanitarian League had argued, on criticisms of extravagance rather than cruelty. A new campaign was needed.[36] Fox and deer hunting became particular targets on the grounds that 'it is iniquitous to inflict suffering upon sentient animals for the purpose of sport'.[37]

Such was its impact that the British Field Sports Society was founded in 1930 to counter the League's campaigns. The League's immediate aim was to prohibit the hunting of fox, deer, otter and hare, and to oppose rabbit and hare coursing.[38] The League's opposition to fox hunting was shared by, amongst others, the National Anti-Vivisection Society which believed that the sport was itself responsible for the numbers of foxes that might damage farmers' property.[39] In 1937 supporters of the Our Dumb Friends' League campaigned without success for the National Trust to prohibit all hunting and shooting for sport on its lands.[40] As Mrs Pinto Leite argued, it was only a very small minority who indulged in blood sports and it was unreasonable that they should be considered the majority.[41] Even the magazine *John Bull* recognized the hypocrisy of the National Trust, the charter of which expressly forbade blood sports on its land. It had prosecuted a working man for shooting eight wood pigeons on its land but had officially endorsed fox hunting: 'Why should the working man be prosecuted for taking wood pigeons, or a camper for killing a rabbit for his supper, when others can buy shooting rights to bang away over Trust lands as hard as they please?'[42]

Campaigns in the *Daily Herald* and *Daily Express* drew widespread opposition to hunting. In a carefully conducted poll in 1936 the *Daily Express* found that 55.2 per cent of those interviewed were against hunting.[43] Organizations joined forces to lobby MPs to ban carted stag hunting. Although a private member's bill received a second reading in 1938 it failed to become law.[44] The campaign continued through the Second World War. As the president of the League for the Prohibition of Cruel Sports, Hamilton Fyfe, a former editor of the *Daily Herald*, declared: 'I do not see how anyone who considers it justifiable to torment and kill animals for fun can ever really look with horror or shame at the killing and wounding of men in battle, and until those are the feelings aroused by war we shall never be rid of it.'[45] However although the League had obtained nearly a million signatures on its 1948 petition against hunting it was unable to move the new Labour government into action. In the following year when Seymour Cocks presented his second reading of the Protection of Animals (Hunting and Coursing Prohibition) Bill it was rejected by 214 to 101 votes.[46]

From the towns into the countryside

The growth of class-based organizations, in particular the Communist Party and industrial unions, helped raise awareness about the ownership of land and access for recreational purposes. The blurring of the boundaries between countryside and town was emphasized by the formation of the Ramblers Association in 1935. Developed from the many local federations of walkers, mainly from working-class backgrounds, who ventured from industrial towns into the country at weekends, it campaigned for legislation to provide access to moors, mountains and hillsides. The mass trespass of Kinder Scout in Derbyshire in 1932 led by the Communist Benny Rothman, the secretary of the Lancashire British Workers' Sports Federation, drew wide attention to the privatization of land, particularly in view of the prison sentences imposed on the protesters, charged with riotous assembly and assault.[47] Arthur Creech Jones, former secretary of the powerful Transport and General Workers' Union, honorary treasurer of the Pit Ponies' Protection Society and a BUAV supporter, introduced a private member's bill in 1938 to extend access to land which, although containing restrictions for ramblers, nevertheless provided the basis for the post-war legislation to establish national parks.[48]

While certain tracts of land were being opened up to naturalists and walkers, other land was being set aside by the RSPB to provide a sanctuary for birds. On the isolated promontory of Dungeness in east Kent, the largest shingle formation (with Cape Canaveral) in the world, the RSPB established its first sanctuary in 1931.[49] The more famous sanctuary at Minsmere in Suffolk followed after the Second World War. Potential landing strips had been flooded as a counter-invasion strategy; these provided ideal nesting and safety areas for birds, especially bearded tits.[50] From a tiny membership in the 1950s, the RSPB grew to 200,000 by the 1960s and recruited its millionth member in 1997.[51]

The relationship between people and animals, particularly in the countryside, was developed by Bertram Lloyd, a socialist friend of Henry Salt, and a keen rock climber, vegetarian and Fellow of the Linnean Society who founded the National Council for the Abolition of Cruel Sports.[52] He wrote on birds and vegetarianism, thereby embodying much of the earlier range of issues taken up by the Humanitarian League. In different ways H. J. Massingham, who had embraced guild socialism and had been inspired by the vision of William Morris, explored the inter-connectedness of people and animals on the land.[53] Believing in the 'psychic unity of mankind', he looked to organic farming, wholemeal stone-ground flour and the benign treatment of animals to create a new way of life.[54] Drawing on his earlier interest in birds, he wrote eloquently about the ways in which chemicals destroyed animal life and the soil. Observing that blue-tits went to apple blossom which was infested with maggots and removed the pests he noted:

> Had I sprayed the trees with DDT for the weevils and arsenate of lead for the sawflies, I should have destroyed the insect predators as well as the grubs, poisoned the soil, killed many earthworms, spent a good deal of money and labour and presumably lost the services of the blue-tits.[55]

New spectacles: new tactics

Popular novels and stories which depicted the plight of animals threatened with vivisection continued to be produced, particularly by Gertrude Colmore and Annie Sophie Cory, who wrote under the name of Victoria Cross.[56] In Cross's dramatic story 'Supping with the Devil', the vivisector Sir Charles Smith-Brown receives his nemesis at the hand of his assistant, 'not an educated man . . . but a good man', who locks his employer in the lethal chamber and turns the gas taps full on before sending away the captive dogs to a new home in the country.[57] Even more melodramatically, in Colmore's last novel, *A Brother of the Shadow,* Donnithorne, a professor of physiology, turns

C. L. Hartwell, *Protecting the Defenceless*, a bronze statue dedicated
'To all protectors of the defenceless' and particularly Gertrude Colmore and
Harold Baillie Weaver, St John's Lodge, Regent's Park, London, 1928.

out to be literally the devil, who ritualistically tortures cats, hypno-
tizes young women and men and causes the heroine Jessica to be
almost cremated alive. He too dies a dramatic death, struck as if by
lightning in Richmond Park.[58]

New genres of narrative fiction emerged through the popularity of
the cinema, with some films specifically recalling campaigns waged
on behalf of animals. Opposition to hunting was to receive a boost
when Felix Salten's anti-hunting book was translated into cartoon
form by Walt Disney. *Bambi*, released in 1942, emphasized the
corrupting influence of humans on animals and the deceit they practised towards them. The first English edition of the book had been
published in 1928 with a foreword by John Galsworthy, who recommended it to sportsmen in particular.[59] The 1950 British film critical

of hunting, *Gone to Earth* by Powell and Pressburger, based on Mary Webb's novel of the same name, feautured Sybil Thorndyke, a committee member of the League Against Cruel Sports and of the London and Provincial Anti-Vivisection Society (LAPAVS).[60] But such was the incorporation of animals into cultural life that they became easily read narrative devices in a range of films. In *The Third Man* the black marketeer played by Orson Welles is first revealed to the audience not by human agency but by his cat entwining itself round his feet in a darkened doorway. It is the cat's very loyalty – a far cry from early Victorian sentiment – which betrays his presence. In the 1950s horror film *The Fly*, the audience can easily read the ominous signs when it notes that the family of the mad scientist has a loved pet, a Persian cat. Experimented upon in the home, the cat's 'atoms' disappear – together with the cat – into the great beyond. The children are never told, but we, the audience, know and are horrified.

The London zoo continued to be a site of spectacle, enhanced during the 1930s by the attraction of seeing penguins in apparently naturalistic, open-air settings while parading as exhibits on modernist ramps designed by Lubetkin and Drake.[61] In a similar attempt to suggest that animals were being seeing in 'natural settings' the Whipsnade zoo was designed to promote conservation and allow space for animals to move more freely. Built in the 1930s by the forced labour of men transported from the distressed areas, the new zoo there first opened in 1931.[62] At Regent's Park, meanwhile, ideals of naturalism, conservation and education were set against attendance as a leisure activity. The opening of a children's zoo encouraged children to relate more closely to animals by handling them, but animals were also required to be photographed with children, and chimpanzees were obliged to perform a daily tea party, a ritual that ran from 1926 to 1972. The years after the Second World War saw a decline in attendance, despite the arrival of 'Chi-chi', a giant panda, the endangered species chosen by the World Wildlife Fund in 1962 for its logo.[63] The public preferred 'not to know about' the caging of animals; they preferred to see them on film and television – at once more 'real' and more of a visual treat.

Animals continued to be gawped at as objects of amusement in circuses and rodeos. Although such performances were regulated by Parliament in 1925, campaigns continued through to the 1950s to extend legal coverage to a range of unprotected animals, especially seals, dogs and monkeys.[64] Before the First World War the Nonconformist Liberal MP Henry Chancellor had called for more people to oppose vivisection and vaccination, 'even though you pass through the furnace for it': 'The world wants more Daniels, willing to risk the lions' den, rather than be false to their conditions.'[65] There were nevertheless those still willing to engage in campaigns, as Edith Ward wrote in the late 1920s:

> We do not hear much to-day of the Non-Conformist conscience – prominent in the past in the arena of many social struggles, but the things it represented – the awakening, developing, growing, human corporate soul – is no less, but more alive... [66]

Cruelty towards animals for entirely frivolous purposes was particularly opposed by Methodists and Nonconformists. In the past Methodists had been criticized for opposing cock-fighting – now they (along with the RSPCA and the Our Dumb Friends' League) castigated rodeo exhibitions, especially those held at the Empire Exhibition in 1924. It was entertainment made possible only through the suffering of animals. Congregationalists also criticized dog-racing.[67] Further, Lord Danesfort of the NCDL who was also vice-chair of the RSPCA, tried unsuccessfully on several occasions to persuade Parliament to ban the training of apes and larger carnivores.[68] More successfully, the RSPCA prosecuted Tex Austin for terrifying and ill-treating a steer during a rodeo in the White City stadium in 1934.[69]

War and domestic animals: new icons

When war was declared against Germany in the summer of 1939, dogs were again volunteered for official war work. As Eileen Woods remembered, Rover, her beautiful black Labrador, was volunteered by her mother to sniff for land mines in Belgium and France.[70] But during this war the focus of animal campaigners was upon the plight of animals at home, rather than in combat abroad. During the 1930s, the NCDL and the Our Dumb Friends' League had helped fund refugees from fascist Germany who had managed to escape to Britain with their dogs and cats. The fees were paid for 95 dogs and one cat in quarantine.[71] Even this small act of humanity needed to be justified to detractors:

Although this action has received anonymous criticisms, the
League felt that this country, which prides itself on its love for
animals and seeks to better the lot of animals abroad, could not
lower its prestige in the eyes of so many foreigners by deliberately
killing their pets; not only was it a national, but an international,
duty to save them. When, after the war, these people return to their
homes the remembrance of this kindness on the part of English
men and women would help to improve the lot of animals in their
own countries.[72]

Clearly refugees who had fled oppression at great personal cost to
themselves, and had humanely protected their own animals, would
have been distraught if the first act of the safe haven, Britain, had
been to put their animals down. As one penniless refugee from Vienna
said to the NCDL, once reunited with his St Bernard dog at quarantine kennels, 'I shall always be indebted to you.'[73] Further, as the
anti-vivisectionists surmised, 'refugee dogs' – and those left behind
by evacuees – might fall prey to vivisectors.[74]

The Our Dumb Friends' League also made arrangements with
Scotland Yard to take into its care any pets belonging to fascists
interned under section 18b of the Emergency Powers (Defence) Act.[75]
Fascists, as well as socialists and radicals, cared for animals and had
been attracted to animal politics. By 1939 the London and Provincial
Anti-Vivisection Society was run by Norah Dacre Fox (otherwise
known as Norah Elam) and her elderly husband, Dudley. Both were
members of the British Union of Fascists and the premises were raided
twice.[76] In Parliament Sir John Anderson, the Home Secretary, indicated that one of the officers of the society was an adherent of the BUF
and using the offices for fascist business.[77] The committee of the
LAPAVS was subsequently reorganized and new members included
Lady Tenterden, a former supporter of the BUAV and a manager of
the Battersea Anti-Vivisection Hospital.[78] Dudley Elam continued to
write for the organization and Wilfred Risdon, a former miner, divi-
sional organizer of the ILP in the Midlands and then director of
propaganda for Mosley's fascists, became the group's secretary. He
had parted company with Mosley and later became the national
secretary of the National Anti-Vivisection Society, from 1957 to 67.[79]
Perhaps his most important contribution to the publicity work of the
LAPAVS during the war was to draw up illustrations complete with

instructions on how to make an air raid shelter for pets, which were banned from public air raid shelters.[80]

Within the first four days of declaration of war in 1939, 400,000 pet cats and dogs were destroyed by their owners fearful of imminent invasion and gas attacks, despite protestations of the Battersea Dogs' Home, anti-vivisectionists and the NCDL, which deplored the massacre as the 'September Holocaust'.[81] The National Anti-Vivisection Society was horrified to report that outside the Wood Green animal shelter in north London, an area marked for evacuation, people stood in a queue half a mile long waiting to have their pets destroyed.[82] Bombardments of British cities, bringing the war directly home to people and animals alike, killed thousands of domestic animals, particularly in London.[83] Petrified animals were rescued by animal charities from bombed houses, often being the only member of the family to survive, and the Home Office issued guidelines for the return of animals to their owners.[84] Fears also grew that stray cats and dogs were being trapped by vivisectors – or cat

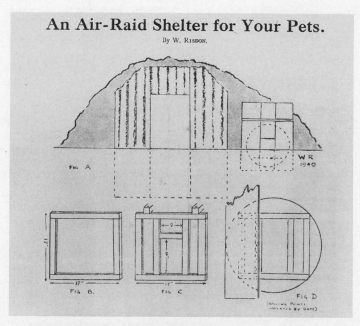

Separate entrances. 'An Air-Raid Shelter for your Pets', by W. Risdon, from the London and Provincial Anti-Vivisection Society *Newssheet* for 4 October 1940.

"FAITH"

OUR DEAR LITTLE CHURCH CAT, OF ST. AUGUSTINE AND ST. FAITH.
THE BRAVEST CAT IN THE WORLD.
ON MONDAY, SEPTEMBER 9th, 1940, SHE ENDURED HORRORS AND PERILS
BEYOND THE POWER OF WORDS TO TELL.
SHIELDING HER KITTEN IN A SORT OF RECESS IN THE HOUSE (A SPOT
SHE SELECTED ONLY THREE DAYS BEFORE THE TRAGEDIES OCCURRED) SHE
SAT THE WHOLE FRIGHTFUL NIGHT OF BOMBING AND FIRE, GUARDING HER
LITTLE KITTEN.
THE ROOFS AND MASONRY EXPLODED, THE WHOLE HOUSE BLAZED, FOUR
FLOORS FELL THROUGH IN FRONT OF HER. FIRE AND WATER AND RUIN
ALL ROUND HER.
YET SHE STAYED CALM AND STEADFAST AND WAITED FOR HELP.
WE RESCUED HER IN THE EARLY MORNING WHILE THE PLACE WAS STILL
BURNING AND

        BY THE MERCY OF ALMIGHTY GOD SHE AND
        HER KITTEN WERE NOT ONLY SAVED BUT UNHURT.

        GOD BE PRAISED AND THANKED FOR HIS GOODNESS
        AND MERCY TO OUR DEAR LITTLE PET.

Faith the cat and the myths of the Blitz.

Egalitarianism in the Second World War.
'BOTH ON SHORE LEAVE: "Minnie" escaped from a torpedoed
ship and was found by an R.S.P.C.A. Inspector, who treated her for
burns and placed her in a safe shore billet.'

skinners – since there were import restrictions on furs.[85] The Board of
Trade added to these fears by refusing to prohibit cat skins for manufacture or export.[86] The NCDL adopted an egalitarian position on the
destruction of dogs. Dog breeders who claimed preferential treatment
were not supported: the lessons of the last war had been learnt, the
League said, and all dogs, irrespective of social origin, should be saved.[87]

With the return of the defeated army from Dunkirk and the
victorious army a few years later, men arrived with their loyal dogs.[88]
This time, as befitted the more egalitarian mythology of the Second
World War, cats too were there, such as Minnie who, on HMS
Argonaut, was one of the first of the Allied cats to arrive at the
Normandy beach-head.[89] Now differential – and fairer – costs were
introduced for quarantine, according to the soldier's rank: the officer
paid £20, the more junior corporal just £5.[90] Stories of dogs who

Loved even after death.
The pet cemetery in Hyde Park (1881–1903).

had rescued their owners from bombed houses or cats who defended their kittens through the Blitz were constructed to complement the myths of resistance.[91] The image of St Paul's Cathedral standing alone amidst swirling smoke was complemented, for instance, by the story of Faith, the cat of St Augustine and St Faith's Church, opposite the cathedral in Watling Street in the City of London. As roofs fell and masonry exploded she remained calm and steadfast, guarding her tiny kitten. Her image alongside a plethora of 'mascots' from the armed forces was published in a special collection after the war to complement similar human stories of heroism. The People's Dispensary for Sick Animals (PDSA) awarded medals named after its founder, Miss Dickin, to animals for their bravery in war.[92]

The death of animals also became memorialized in new forms. The Ilford pet cemetery included the bodies of dogs who had been war heroes; other cemeteries specifically for ordinary pets followed. The NCDL opened a graveyard in Bushey in Hertfordshire in the 1960s, followed by another at Evesham in 1980.[93] The dogs of the wealthy had long enjoyed commemoration after death, either with individual monuments such as that erected in the grounds of the eighteenth-century Chiswick House, or with tombstones as found in the nineteenth-century pet cemetery at Hyde Park which commemorated the much-loved pets of the wealthy who lived nearby.[94] Now this form of memorial was made more widely available.

Post-war challenges

Employing techniques practised decades before, the BUAV hired a shop in Whitehall to expose experimentation: in 1945 a vivisector's lab was labelled 'Animals' Belsen'.[95] The shop later displayed pictures of the atom bomb tests in the Pacific, in which 4,000 animals placed in boats in the explosion area died.[96] The American navy explosions united animal campaigners in opposition. All the anti-vivisectionist groups and the Blue Cross, as the ODFL now called itself, protested against the experiments as cruel, unnecessary and likely to be mis-leading if the results were applied to human beings. Far from leading to peace, as the tests were alleged to do, they increased insecurity and fear.[97] Anti-vivisectionists continued to draw links between atrocities committed on humans and animals in the context of war. In condemning the way in which prisoners in concentration camps had been experimented upon, or in which 'mentally deficient' and 'deformed' people were scientifically slowly starved and poisoned, the LAPAVS made explicit the links between human and animal experimentation, as the Humanitarian League had done so many years before: 'Those who have been prepared to condone the application of such diabolical tortures to animals should now take pause and consider this, the logical outcome of what they have condoned.'[98]

The new Labour government contained nearly twenty supporters of the BUAV, including Peter Newman, a vegetarian and secretary of the Welsh Theosophical Society; George Mathers, president of the National Temperance Federation; and Ernest Thurtle, son-in-law of George Lansbury. But it showed no signs of bucking the trend for experimentation or even of withdrawing the certificate to practice vivisection from an Oxford professor of physiology, Dr Liddell, convicted in the courts of causing unnecessary suffering to cats in the course of his experiments at the university.[99] In the 1950s much parliamentary work in the House of Lords opposing vivisection was undertaken by Lord Dowding, the Air Chief Marshal, who had been

Old tactics, new age. 'Two Years' Shop Campaign in Piccadilly', from an
issue of *The Anti-Vivisection Review*, 1913.

a leader in the Battle of Britain with his strategy of creating the 'fear of
the fighter'.[100] A keen dog-lover and in sympathy with Theosophy, he
became a vegetarian and established a fund for humane research
which still exists and is now named after him.[101] His wife Muriel, a
Theosophist, founded the cosmetic company Beauty without Cruelty,
which still thrives and continues to refuse to test its products on
animals.[102] Dowding's unsuccessful attempt at introducing legislation
in the 1950s was rooted in strong moral beliefs: 'I firmly believe that
painful experiments on animals are morally wrong, and that it is
immoral to do evil in order that good may come – even if it were
proved that mankind benefits from the suffering inflicted on
animals.'[103]

In the mood of optimism which had greeted the end of war and the
election of a Labour government, a plethora of animal organizations
including the Equine Defence League, the Metropolitan Drinking
Fountain and Cattle Trough Association, the RSPB, the PDSA, the

Liberal – but not Labour – Party and the Blue Cross met in a concerted attempt to get the new government to prioritize action and legislation against all forms of animal cruelty, but without success.[104] The Blue Cross adapted its literature for the new times. Its appeal for funds was based on the contrasting fates of animals and people: 'There is no welfare state for animals.' The introduction of the welfare state indicated that Britain had a highly developed social conscience; it was the political expression of a moral responsibility that we are our brothers' and sisters' keepers, and that this should be extended to animals.[105]

But there was no new age for animals. In 1951 a convention was held of British Animal Protection Societies, attended by a plethora of groups including the NCDL and the Metropolitan Drinking Fountain and Cattle Trough Association to discuss dealing with the cruelties of the time. Its sponsoring organizations – and those of a subsequent conference in 1954 – reflected a mix of old and new issues. Still giving cause for concern was the docking of horses' tails, the overloading of draught animals and vivisection. New topics tackled included oil pollution and the extermination of rabbits in Australia.[106] Myxomatosis had been developed by scientists during the war as a way of 'containing' the wild rabbit population. It soon became an issue in Britain, when Parliament discussed introducing myxomatosis in 1951 as a way of dealing with the problem of rabbits eating crops. It was forced to reject this option in the face of public outrage. Farmers were less sanguine. According to protesters, they spread the disease themselves.[107] In the early 1950s Kent, Essex and Sussex were affected. The highly contagious disease which caused a lingering and painful death to rabbits had spread to 47 English counties, nineteen Scottish counties and the whole of Wales by 1954. Farmers organized themselves into Rabbit Clearance Societies, shooting thousands of rabbits and destroying wild pigeon nests, ostensibly to prevent disease on their lands but also to destroy threats to their property.[108] Confronted with public disgust at the way in which rabbits were being treated, the government made it an offence to spread the disease and suggested that rabbits were indeed valuable, particularly in keeping down grass on chalk downland pastures.[109]

The way in which the flora and fauna of rural areas was treated received much attention with the publication of Rachel Carson's book *Silent Spring* in 1963. The work brought strands of ecological thinking together with those on animal welfare. Carson cited foxes dazed, partially blind and dying of thirst through eating chlorinated hydrocarbons and poisons. Birds too were dying in their thousands, poisoned by seed dressings and the herbicides used on verges. These issues affected town and country alike. The movement for allotments had grown through the war and over a million now existed in the cities.[110] The gardening craze had led to the use of pesticides, and these in turn had killed within the cities song thrushes and owls, which before had eaten uncontaminated insects and rodents.[111] Presciently, Carson warned that these practices in the food chain would have a knock-on effect for humans: 'It looks as if we will go on swallowing these chemicals whether we like it or not and their real effect may not be seen for another twenty or thirty years.'[112] Her expression of the relationship between the production of food and the effect on the animal and human environment found practical outcomes. In 1967, Peter Roberts, a small dairy farmer in Hampshire, became increasingly uneasy about his methods of earning a living. Even though he was a humane man, allowing his cows to roam and providing them with clean, straw-bedded shelter, he started to question the factory farming methods flourishing in the countryside.[113] In the face of ridicule, he founded Compassion in World Farming to protest against the abuse of farm animals, particularly as expressed in the increased farming of battery hens. His approach applied the understanding developed towards domestic animals, namely that they had individual characteristics, to animals of the farmyard, usually perceived as an undifferentiated type. The application of individual sensibilities would, he hoped, create a sense of compassion where it had not previously existed: 'Compassion is much more than vegetarianism. It involves a change in consciousness, so that we come to see animals as individuals, each developing its own character, rather than as herds or flocks.'[114]

NINE

Continuing cruelty: unconcluded campaigns

The world is dangerous to live in, not because of those who do evil
but because of those who look on and let them do so.[1]

From the countryside to the sea

The ecological thinking pioneered by H. J. Massingham and later
developed by activists such as Bertram Lloyd who were concerned
with the inter-connectedness of human and animal life found new
outlets in the campaigns of the 1960s and 1970s against the hunting
of whales and seals. In the Edwardian years sealskins had become
a fashion accessory: even the painter so opposed to murderous
millinery, George Watts, sported a sealskin coat.[2] Some had castigated those who wore fur, 'Ruthless women [wearing] odds and ends
torn from thousands of harmless little fur-bearers . . . [are] about as
fascinating, when thus bedizened, as a crude savage embellished with
a necklace of human scalps'[3]

But seals had not become a focus for animal campaigners since
they had not faced extinction – until the 1950s – and the yearly culls
in Canada had taken place away from the gaze of humanitarians.
Now, imagined links with the horrors of human annihilation in the
Second World War and the impact of nuclear weapons apparently
caused new interest in the fate of seals.[4] In the tradition of the need to
see and personally experience animal suffering, several observers
witnessed the 1955 Canadian seal cull, perpetrated with clubs and
pikes. Subsequently the International Fund for Animal Welfare
(IFAW), founded in the 1970s by Brian Davies to oppose all seal hunting, achieved some success. The Canadian government regulated the
annual culls, ensuring the survival of at least some seal herds. With
the backing of Greenpeace and the threats of consumer boycotts of
Canadian fish, the IFAW also succeeded during the 1980s in getting
the EEC to ban the import of sealskins.[5]

There was a surge of interest too in the fate of whales. In the 1930s

Australian and New Zealand whaling stations had obliterated the last
great herds of migrating humpback whales without provoking great
public outrage. Ironically, it was not until a killer whale was captured
alive by the US Air Force in 1964 that attitudes changed, and whales
were perceived as gentle, intelligent and friendly.[6] The attribution
of characteristics more usually applied to domestic animals helped
turn public opinion against the continuing destruction of whole
groups of animals. With support from Spike Milligan and Paul
McCartney, a British section of Greenpeace was established in 1977.
Although over 60 species of whales, dolphins and porpoises became
protected over the following two decades, the regulations of the
International Whaling Commission still allow for exemptions and
hunting continues.[7]

The concern for animals in the wild remained a focus during the
1970s and 1980s. After several unsuccessful attempts the Wild
Mammals [Protection] Act in 1996, drafted by the League Against
Cruel Sports (LACS) and pioneered through Parliament by the Labour
MP for Mansfield, Alan Meale, became the first ever Act to protect all
species of wild mammals in Britain from cruelty.[8] As the LACS
proudly proclaimed, it became 'the most important all-encompassing
animal welfare legislation since the 1911 Protection of Animals Act'.[9]
The protection afforded to domestic animals for over 80 years was
now extended to wild animals, making it illegal to inflict acts of
cruelty such as kicking, eating, mutilation or asphyxiation with intent
to inflict unnecessary suffering.[10] Fox and deer hunting, however, was
exempt from these strictures. Encouraged by these developments, the
LACS, RSPCA and IFAW joined forces within the Campaign for the
Protection of Hunted Animals to lobby Parliament to make hunting
illegal. The British Field Sports Society mounted a vigorous response
by attempting to define rural interests as entirely separate from those
of city dwellers. Humane treatment of animals was caricatured as an
urban quirk promulgated by those who did not see animals in daily
life. The society's establishment of the Countryside Movement has
been an attempt not only to define the countryside as a separate
geographical entity from the town, but one in which different values
pertain. Such a dichotomy has been challenged by the thousands of
people who live outside towns and who have been the main supporters
of the work of the League Against Cruel Sports, which does not even

boast a London branch. Meanwhile towns have started to become an informal sanctuary for foxes and for a wealth of other wildlife.[11]

Vegetarianism: spirituality and consumption

The impact of the Second World War led to renewed pressure for world peace, and, in Britain, the establishment of the Campaign for Nuclear Disarmament in 1958.[12] This same concern had led Donald Watson to found the Vegan Society in 1944. World peace and veganism – the total opposition to any killing of animals or use of their produce – were, he argued, inextricably linked.[13] Like Peter Roberts, who would found Compassion in World Farming, Watson was concerned about growing trends in dairy farming such as the removal of calves prematurely from their mothers to be slaughtered as veal, and the growth of TB in dairy herds. Watson argued that animals should have justice on equal terms with humans, to protect both animals and humanity itself:

> The acceptance of a reformed relationship between man and animals is imperative. The higher animals have feelings like ours, therefore they should have justice on equal terms with ourselves, or not be bred into the world . . . The attitude is one of conceit and selfishness and unless discarded will not confine itself to the treatment of animals. Therefore in man's interest animal exploitation must end.[14]

By the late 1960s there were different currents which adopted vegetarianism and veganism as a way of life that nourished the spirit. In the Moray Firth in Scotland Peter and Eileen Caddy established Findhorn as an alternative community sustained by home-grown fruit and vegetables: 'Through our diet we were absorbing the light that made the vegetables and fruit grow – the light of the sun and the light of our conscious.'[15] There was a fashion for simple macrobiotic foods, which placed emphasis upon the spiritual well-being of the human consumer. The 1971 *Alternative London* listed specialist shops and thirteen restaurants, the names of which indicated their bias towards elements of Eastern spirituality and asceticism: Manna, Raw Deal, Whole Meal, Magic Carpet, Hari Krishna and the London Health Centre.[16] The guide provided vegetarian recipes – for dahl, brown rice and vegetables and cheap chapatis. The emphasis on plain eating had much in common with those vegetarians of the late nineteenth century who had been influenced by Theosophy. As the guide suggested: 'Food could almost go under the mystical section these days as so many people feel that food is not just to fill the belly or titillate the palate, but to feed and heal the body, mind and spirit.'[17]

This turn towards vegetarianism had a different rationale to the surge of the 1990s. By 1997 at least 5 per cent of all Britons were vegetarian and 5,000 people a week were estimated to be moving to a meat-free diet.[18] Organic food sales had increased by 800 per cent between 1988 and 1992.[19] This did not necessarily mean that people were more aware of animal suffering; rather, they were concerned with their own state of well-being, since vegetarians were said to be 40 per cent less likely than their meat-eating counterparts to die of cancer.[20] Indeed the almost daily publicity about farm animals contaminated by disease had, like the scandal of contaminated meat and milk 100 years ago, provided a rationale of self-preservation for the adoption of a lifestyle selected by others on moral and ethical grounds.

The past twenty years, however, has also seen a growth in fast-food outlets arguably antithetical to the well-being of animals and of human health. The McDonald's hamburger chain opened its first outlet in Britain in 1974; by May 1996 there were 674 such premises. Much adverse publicity has been drawn to the chain by the libel action initiated by the company against Helen Steel and David Morris, the so-called McLibel Two. Using the tactics employed by anti-vivisectionists decades before, the pair went to court to challenge and publicize the practices of McDonalds against the animals used in its products, the environment in which they were kept and the human consequences for staff employed in the outlets and those who ate the product. Despite the eventual finding against the campaigners, the Hon. Mr Justice Bell ruled that McDonald's was indeed 'culpably responsible for cruel practices in the rearing and slaughter of some of the animals which are used to produce their food'. It was cruel to keep pigs virtually the whole of their lives in dry sow stalls, with no access to the open air and sunshine and without freedom of movement; it was also a cruel practice to keep broiler chickens cooped up in the last days of their lives with very little room to move, he agreed. Moreover some of the chickens were still fully conscious when their throats were cut.[21] Such publicity, drawing links between the health of humans and the conditions in which animals were kept, mirrored the work undertaken decades before by sanitary experts and food reformers. The plethora of food scares, from contamination of eggs with salmonella to *E. coli* infestation in meat and BSE in a range of animals, which seemed to spread daily in the 1990s, suggest that little has been learnt from the experiences of nineteenth-century campaigners.

New spectacles: new consumers

There has continued to be a close relationship between the cultural representation of animals and particular campaigns. The film *Babe,* about the speaking pig with an identity crisis – it thinks it is a dog – caused public interest at the time of its release since it coincided with protests about the conditions under which farm animals were kept. The relationship between fictional and real animals has continued to be explored imaginatively in film: in *Beethoven* a real dog rescued his canine friends from a vivisecting vet; *101 Dalmatians* was re-made with real Dalmatians doing unreal things, uniting animals against their human persecutors; and *Lost World,* the sequel to *Jurassic Park*, urged its viewers not to meddle with nature.

Within the domestic domain, next to the televisual and video images of animals, most 1990s British households contained an animal as a family pet. By 1995 cats had overtaken dogs as the most popular pets, with a nationally estimated 7.2 million cats compared to 6.6 million dogs.[22] An increasing number of owners have taken out pet insurance,[23] while less fortunate animals continue to be looked after by the Mayhew Trust, the Cats Protection League, the Blue Cross or the National Canine Defence League.[24] Pet therapy has soared and one university offers a diploma in companion animal behaviour.[25] Respondents to a survey run by the makers of Go-Cat dried cat food claimed that if owners could say anything to their cat in its own language it would be, 'I love you'.[26] Memorials to domestic animals have incorporated the latest forms of visualization; on the Internet pet owners have devised their own memorial sites to much-loved animals.[27]

However, whereas dogs in the 1880s became a focus for frenzy about rabies, in the 1980s and early 1990s certain breeds of dog became the object of hysteria, particularly at governmental level. The National Canine Defence League had exposed the imports of Staffordshire bull terriers in the 1930s, and the Kennel Club had refused to recognize them for many years, since such dogs were used for dog-fighting.[28] In the wake of publicity over a number of attacks on people, the Dangerous Dogs Act of 1991 was hastily pushed through Parliament in response to hysteria about pit bulls and other imported 'fighting dogs' which legislators had not thought to clearly define. The NCDL refused to be drawn into castigating the behaviour of dogs by their appearance alone, and with parliamentary action led by the Labour Lord Houghton, a vice-president of the League Against Cruel Sports, and Roger Gale, a Conservative MP, some amendments were introduced: 'Innocent dogs that would have been destroyed because of their appearance will now be safe, while the owners of truly dangerous dogs can still be prosecuted.'[29] Individuals faced with prosecution over ownership of such dogs even took their cases to the European Court of Human Rights. One particular dog, Otis, was seized by the police, who claimed he was an unmuzzled pit bull; his Hackney owner insisted he was a Great Dane cross. After spending four years in police custody the dog was killed when his owner's legal fight to save him failed.[30]

Pets themselves have developed from useful servants of the family into active consumers. In the 1950s and 1960s it was recommended that cats be fed vegetables such as carrots, spinach, broccoli, beans, chives and potatoes alongside raw meat, particularly liver, and cooked fish. Titbits were to be an occasional treat – a peppermint cream or grape was suggested.[31] Recently, however, cats and dogs have been depicted as mirroring their owners' concerns more closely: manufacturers have developed an extensive range of dietary products, including low-calorie dried food to deal with obesity. Dog and cat toothpaste has been developed and cat owners have been advised to spread sunblock on cats with white ears and noses to protect them from harmful ultra-violet rays.[32]

Owning certain pets is seen to be desirable: a sign of being human. Accordingly, for those unable to keep a living pet, there are substitutes. Walking holidays can be taken in southern Ireland in which the

ramblers are accompanied by a 'faithful donkey friend' which acts
as an 'affectionate and loyal companion, who will nuzzle up to you
for attention and treats'.[33] Children, or their parents, can buy 'Kitty
in my pocket', sold in packaging resembling sweet bags. These toys
are collectables of rubbery cats with names and details of their
qualities. Joe, the tortoiseshell, for instance, is given eight marks for
huggability, nine for playfulness and seven for cuteness. At six weeks
old he's 'just started learning to read'.[34] In not much more sophisti-
cated vein the Tamagotchi, an electronic pet devised in Japan,
demands the attention of its owner or dies. The manufacturer
planned to sell 13 million in 1998. In Tokyo those without time to
care for a pet of their own can rent an animal to take it for a walk.[35]

At the British Museum, the very heart of the nation's cultural
centre, images of cats are prized. Two of the most popular postcards
sold here in the early 1990s were of the Egyptian Gayer-Anderson cat
and the same statue photographed against a modern tabby. This
may tell us much about how visitors view a museum experience in
the 1990s; it also tells us that some cats more than others are part
of cultural life. The ferocious semi-wild cats which gather on the
museum's steps in the early morning and are kept to chase away
rodents from the building's basement are not the sort of felines
worthy to be photographed alongside an Egyptian statue.[36] Nor has
the nation itself become a safe place for domestic animals. Cats are
still stolen in huge numbers, apparently for their furs, and used in
laboratories, giving rise to the establishment of a national monitoring
organization, National Petwatch, while establishments such as
Hillgrove Farm in Oxfordshire continue their work as 'the biggest
supplier of cats for vivisection in Britain'.[37]

Seeing animals and hidden cruelty

In 1957 the National Anti-Vivisection Society directed its attention
to cruelty to animals which was not on public view. Like the
Humanitarian League in the 1890s, the Society initiated a petition to
stop live animals being exported, to be slaughtered abroad.[38] Recent
campaigners have likewise been inspired to action by the thought of
what happens to animals at the end of transportation – and by seeing
the way in which they are actually transported along the country's

roads and motorways. Humanitarians in the early nineteenth century
were goaded into action by the sight of animals driven along roads
to Smithfield market. In the 1990s the roads that traverse the land
linking country to town became a site of concern. Whoever travels on
motorways will have seen the huge lorries with slatted sides enclosing
farm animals. We cannot see inside but it is easy to imagine the
animals' discomfort, especially if they are being transported for long
distances without food or water.

Nowadays the Metropolitan Drinking Fountain and Cattle
Trough Association no longer exists to provide aid; instead organizations like Compassion in World Farming (CIWF) have demonstrated
to eradicate such transportation abroad in its entirety. Although the
media made much of the presence of women, especially older women,
at protests at coastal ports, such events received support from men
and women alike.[39] Many interpreted what they were seeing as
images of fascism: 'It makes me think with a shudder of the Nazi
cattle trucks.'[40] This seems a common interpretation of such scenes.
The actor Martin Shaw, for example, suggested, 'People of my generation have grown up on films about Belsen, Auschwitz, and the
Holocaust, and feel horrified . . . In my mind, what I have just seen is
no different, and it's going on every day, all the time, constantly.' For
him there was no distinction between human and animal suffering
and he was again reminded of the Nazis' thinking that 'people of
inferior intellect and ability were the ones who were exterminated'.[41]
As a result of the CIWF campaigns, narrow veal crates and narrow
stalls and tether chains for pregnant pigs were banned in Britain.[42]
The CIWF's campaign, however, did not mean the end of the confinement of young cows. European consumers were less squeamish than
their British counterparts in their desire for white veal. Animals,
including calves, were transported to satisfy the demand in Europe,
entailing neglect on journeys the length and conditions of which
defied the more humane laws on transportation of animals operating
in Britain. Maverick seaports and airports – notably Shoreham,
Brightlingsea and Coventry – continued to export animals. There
were protests in which lorries holding 'tightly packed, terrorized
calves' were attacked.[43]

The CIWF's insistence that animals were sentient beings was
interpreted by some demonstrators to mean that baby animals –

Carrying on the traditions of the Humanitarian League.
Women at Brightlingsea, Essex, from the *Independent*, April 1995.

calves – were just that, babies. Demonstrators included children displaying handmade placards of a calf with the slogan 'I want my mummy'.[44] Groups of animals were not invested with individual characteristics, rather they were perceived as a vulnerable group, like young children, that needed adult protection. Protesters numbered those of all ages, including elderly residents in wheelchairs, as dismayed by the police response to their actions as by the issue itself. Civil liberties became a motivating factor, as much as concern for animal welfare itself.[45] Several participants dramatically taped up their mouths so that they could not be falsely accused of starting a riot or of swearing at police officers.[46] The actions of the protesters recalled earlier events, like that of Miss Revell drenching the policeman to defend a supposedly rabid dog from attack. Here Tilly Merritt, an elderly protester at Brightlingsea, for example, turned a garden hose on policemen who were accompanying a convoy of lorries to the port, encouraged protesters to sit in the road, and had to be restrained from striking a policeman.[47]

The concern for the fate of animals outside Britain, which had certainly attracted the attention of nineteenth-century campaigners such as Ouida, was an implicit feature of the movement against exports. In late twentieth-century Britain, foreigners were substituted for the role previously enacted by cab drivers and drovers. Much of the focus of the BUAV has been on Indonesia, Barbados, and Portugal, from where animals have been imported into Britain for the vivisectors' labs.[48] The British CIWF has campaigned against the way sheep have been killed in Paris by Muslims during the celebrations of the festival of Eid el Kebir. Campaigners here were particularly concerned, since apparently these were not French sheep, but British sheep exported from Dover specifically for the occasion.[49] Wary of allegations of anti-Muslim views, the CIWF circulated its supporters urging them to write letters of protest to the French government pointing out that 'Christian' events like bull-fighting in Spain had also been tackled by the organization.[50]

New laws: old practices

Much as Frances Power Cobbe had predicted in the 1870s, experiments on animals increased up to the 1970s. By 1970 over five million experiments were performed on live animals, dropping to a still staggering three million for 1985 – two-thirds of which were performed without anaesthetics.[51] Experimentation continued, despite the introduction of the Animals (Scientific Procedures) Act of 1986, replacing the equally contentious legislation of 1876. At the time David Mellor, then the Conservative minister responsible for its parliamentary passage, claimed that the reduction in the number of animals used and the reduction in suffering was at the heart of the legislation.[52] But no category of experimentation was banned and the intention that humane alternatives should be found has come to little.[53] The notorious LD50 test, in which animals are routinely poisoned to find the dose of the test substance designed to kill half of them, has continued, with over 160,000 such tests conducted in 1994 – and has not been banned by the Labour government of 1997.[54] Although the Labour government backed the new status for animals under the Treaty of Rome, in which animals were recognized as sentient beings, experimentation has continued. A ban by the new government on the testing of finished cosmetic products on animals ignored the fact that 90 per cent of cosmetic testing takes place on ingredients rather than end products; moreover, such items are increasingly tested outside Britain and the EEC.[55] Indeed the European Union has postponed a ban on the testing of cosmetics on animals to beyond the year 2000 at the earliest.[56]

Campaigners continued to question the rationale of scientists experimenting on animals. As some have emphasized, despite millions of experiments on animals there has not been a massive improvement in human health. The level of chronic sickness has been extremely high and actually rising. The number of prescriptions issued per person is increasing, heart disease has reached epidemic proportions and cancer shows little sign of decline.[57] Experimentation has moved beyond the aim of researching illness into new areas: genetic engineering and the transplanting of organs between different types of animals.[58] By the 1990s over 70,000 transgenic animals had been produced in Britain alone.[59] It was ironic that a cloned sheep was given an individual name, Dolly, when the purpose of the experiment was to move away from individuality towards replication of 'group' characteristics.

The types of experiments have changed: the tactics of anti-vivisectionists have not. Following in Frances Power Cobbe's pioneering steps, publicity has been used to bring 'light into the dark places' of the labs; certainly the work conducted within laboratories is intended to be hidden. Although vivisection continues, such work is not deemed respectable. Those who work in the labs refrain from exposing their means of gaining a livelihood. As a former vivisector explained, 'It was often commented on by the people I worked alongside, that they could not mention what they did in public. For example, if they are out for a drink and someone asks in all innocence what they do for a living, they have to either lie or the evening will almost certainly end in argument.'[60] Much like their predecessor Louise Lind af Hageby, campaigners have entered into laboratories precisely to publicize their activities through the use of photographs and film.

In the spring of 1997 a Channel 4 documentary, *It's a Dog's Life*, exposed the treatment at unnamed laboratories in Huntingdon, where beagle dogs were deprived of bedding, subjected to beatings, and summarily killed.[61] Even the *Guardian* television critic had been moved to declare, 'It wasn't so much the brutality as the hopelessness of the place that made grim viewing . . . This is why animal libbers resort to bolt cutters and petrol bombs.'[62] Organizations including the NAVS, BUAV, and NCDL led a successful delegation to the Home Office to call for an inquiry. £85 million was wiped off the share prices of the firm, Huntingdon Life Sciences, and the Glaxo, Wellcome and Zeneca pharmaceutical companies withdrew business until the outcome of the Home Office investigation. Two former employees were convicted of cruelly terrifying dogs under the powers of the Protection of Animals Act 1911 and sentenced to 60 hours community service. Yet the process of vivisection itself was not the subject of action, merely the way in which it was conducted: a new licence to practise experimentation was granted to the company.[63]

Respectable protesters and 'animal rights' activists

Writing in the radical environmental magazine, *Squall,* Jim Carey has suggested that the phrases 'animal welfare' and 'animal rights' are integral to the public relations war designed to discredit the entire pro-animal movement. The RSPCA has said that the use of the phrase 'animal rights' has become publicly associated with images of 'balaclavas and violence', while acknowledging that such images are largely manufactured.[64] Indeed many protesters have direct ideological links back to the 'respectable' attitudes towards animals of two centuries ago. Nonconformists, albeit in dwindling numbers, have continued to maintain a commitment to the welfare of animals. Echoing the views of Wesley himself some 200 years before, a former secretary of the Methodist conference, the Reverend Dr Kenneth Greet, declared in his monthly column in *The Methodist Recorder,* 'heaven would surely be a bit bare without the presence in some form of our feathered and furry friends'.[65] Lord Soper, the veteran Methodist preacher, is president of the League Against Cruel Sports. Methodists have protested alongside others against the export of animals. The Reverend Gordon Newton, superintendent minister of the Dover and Deal circuit, and his wife, Elaine, were often with other protesters, carrying a placard which read, 'Jesus the Good Shepherd Cares for his Sheep'. As Mrs Newton told *The Methodist Recorder,* 'The church should be about getting out there in the world and sharing the love and compassion of Jesus. Many conversations about God have started up with other protesters.'[66]

Many of the tactics of campaigners are no different from those of their earlier counterparts: petitions, lobbying, parliamentary private members' bills, demonstrations. Of overriding importance still is the need for a personal engagement and witness. A pensioner participating in the Shoreham export protests explained, 'To be honest, I have never thought about the way things were killed and treated until this came up. I buried my head in the sand.'[67] For some, involvement may mean releasing animals from captivity; for others, providing practical sanctuary. Apparently new features on demonstrations, such as dressing up as animals, were first tried before the 1914–18 war. Filming in laboratories has its origins in the work of Louise Lind af Hageby entering the labs at University College in 1903. What is new is the human sacrifice in the cause of animals. In 1991 Mike Hill, a young man of eighteen, was killed trying to stop a truck taking hounds to a hunt meet in Crewe. In January 1995, at the height of the live export protests, Jill Phipps was crushed by a lorry delivering calves for export at Coventry airport. She came from a family committed to animal campaigns. Her mother had raided Unilevers in protest against animal experiments; her father spoke of his daughter's life: 'She was determined to make a difference in life and hated suffering, against humans or animals. She was the most compassionate person you could ever meet.'[68]

Animals have become a full part of political, cultural and social life. New cruelties emerge: ostrich farming, poisoning pigeons on public buildings, slaughtering animals above a certain age to appease European markets in BSE hysteria, the reintroduction of feathers and fur for winter 'fashion'. Whether people act against them depends of course on their understanding of cruelty to animals. For the radical barrister Michael Mansfield, animal campaigns, especially those enacted on the streets of Shoreham, Brightlingsea and Coventry, were 'a political act'. Animal protest has been the latest in a line of demonized and subsequently suppressed movements following, he has argued, the miners, immigrants and teachers. The court ruling that declared the ban on the export of live animals was illegal showed that 'profit knows no morality. Humans and other animals will increasingly be exploited.' Like his barrister predecessor, Lord Erskine, Mansfield drew fierce analogies with the court's ruling, declaring that, 'the court would have upheld slavery and the slave

Sacrifice for the cause.
Jill Phipps, animal campaigner, killed in 1995.

trade at a time when it, too, was regarded as a legitimate part of a lais-sez faire economy'. While referring to rights, Mansfield has been just as concerned with compassion towards animals as towards people, recognizing that 'every living creature has its part to play in maintain-ing the glorious fabric of our world . . . Without compassion there is little hope for any of us.' Actions of animal campaigners reflect 'a clear expression of a belief in a different way of doing things, a different and better kind of world'.[69]

Those who acknowledge that animals need to be recognized as valued participants in a changing world may be out of tune with the times; but those who bring compassion and humanity into their dealings with animals enhance not only the lives of animals but of people too. While some have only eyes for themselves, others do indeed see the world around them with eyes of compassion. In its publicity CIWF uses the words of Albert Einstein, which encapsulate both the importance of seeing cruelty, and of acting upon it: 'The world is dangerous to live in, not because of those who do evil but because of those who look on and let them do so.'[70]

REFERENCES

PREFACE

1 Michael Smith, 'Alan Clark criticises police at veal demo', *Daily Telegraph*,
   22 April 1995; Alan Clark, *Diaries* (London, 1994), pp. 192, 214–6.
2 By the time of his death in 1937 Swansea Jack had apparently rescued 39 people
   from drowning in the Swansea docks and his brave exploits had been rewarded
   by the National Canine Defence League. (NCDL, *The Dogs' Bulletin*, no. 95,
   August/September 1936, p. 1; no. 103.)
3 Mary M. Innes, ed., Ovid, *Metamorphoses*, Book 1 (Harmondsworth, 1955),
   pp. 43, 132.
4 Ibid., pp. 44–6.
5 Bede, 'The life and miracles of St Cuthbert' in Dom Knowles, ed., *Bede,
   Ecclesiastical history of the English Nation* (1910, reprinted London, 1965),
   p. 301.
6 Ibid., p. 304.
7 Ted Benton, *Natural Relations. Ecology, Animal Rights and Social Justice*
   (London, 1993); Roger Scruton, *Animal Rights and Wrongs* (London, 1996);
   Ted Benton and Simon Redfearn, 'The Politics of Animal Rights – Where is the
   Left?', *New Left Review*, no. 215, January/February 1996; Keith Tester, *Animals
   and Society: the Humanity of Animal Rights* (London, 1991); Lynda Birke,
   Feminism, Animals and Science. The Naming of the Shrew (Milton Keynes,
   1994).
8 I do accept that campaigners in the recent past have been influenced by such
   ideas and in particular by the work of Peter Singer and Tom Reagan. Peter
   Singer, *Animal Liberation*, 2nd edn (London, 1990); Tom Reagan, *The Case for
   Animal Rights* (London, 1988).
9 Brian Harrison, *Peaceable Kingdom* (Oxford, 1982), pp. 82–122. Richard D.
   French, *Anti-Vivisection and Medical Science in Victorian Britain* (Princeton,
   1975); Nicolaas A. Rupke, ed., *Vivisection in Historical Perspective* (London,
   1990).
10 Such organizations, however, have been keen to commemorate their own
   histories. Carmen Smith, *The Blue Cross at War 1914–18 and 1939–45*
   (Oxford, 1990); Peter Ballard, *A Dog is for Life. Celebrating the first one
   hundred years of the National Canine Defence League* (London, 1990). The
   Battersea Dogs' Home, *The Dogs' Home, Battersea 1860–1960* (London, 1960);
   Gloria Costelloe, *The Story of the Battersea Dogs' Home* (Newton Abbot,
   1979).
11 Steve Baker, *Picturing the Beast. Animals, identity and representation*
   (Manchester, 1993); John Berger, 'Why look at animals?' in *About Looking*
   (London, 1980); Kenneth Clark, *Animals and Men. Their Relationship as
   Reflected in Western Art from Pre-history to the Present Day* (London, 1977).

ONE RADICALS, METHODISTS AND THE LAW FOR ANIMALS IN
THE STREETS

 1 John Wesley, 'Sermon LX: The general deliverance', *The Works of John Wesley*,
    ed. Thomas Jackson, vol. VI, 3rd edn (London, 1829), p. 248.
 2 Christopher Hill, *Reformation to Industrial Revolution* (London, 1968),
    pp. 221–2.
 3 George Ferguson, *Signs and Symbols in Christian Art* (New York, 1966),
    pp. 11–27.
 4 Constance-Anne Parker, *George Stubbs: Art, Animals and Anatomy*
    (London, 1984); Kenneth Clark, *Animals and Men* (London, 1977).
 5 Hogarth's paintings were removed during 1997 to the Tate Gallery.
 6 In contrast the room containing French paintings of this period is remarkable
    for its absence of animal life.
 7 Thomas Gainsborough, *The Morning Walk*, c.1785; Willem Van Mieris,
    A Woman and a Fish Pedlar, 1713; Jan Steen, *A Peasant Family at Mealtime*,
    c.1660s; Nicolaes Maes, *A Sleeping Maid and her Mistress*, c.1655. All in the
    National Gallery, London.
 8 Keith Thomas, *Man and the Natural World* (London,1983), p. 117.
 9 The subject of a student exhibition, spring 1997; a detailed commentary is also
    provided on the Gallery's CD Rom within its Micro-Gallery.
10 Wright undertook other domestic portraiture with animals. See for example
    Two Girls Decorating a Kitten by Candlelight, c.1768–70 or *Richard
    Sacheverall Bateman as a Boy*, c.1792–4 (with kitten) or *Miss Sally Duesbury
    Feeding a Pigeon*, c.1790–5 in Benedict Nicolson, *Joseph Wright of Derby.
    Painter of Light* (Paul Mellon Foundation,1968), vol. II, pp. 49, 212.
11 Ferguson, *Lectures on Select Subjects in Mechanics, Hydrostatics, Pneumatics
    and Optics* (London, 1760), p. 200, as quoted in Nicolson, *Joseph Wright of
    Derby*, vol. II, p. 114.
12 It is factually true but not the point that travelling lecturers did perform in such
    locations.
13 Stephen Daniels, *Fields of Vision. Landscape imagery and national identity in
    England and the United States* (New Jersey, 1993), p. 55.
14 This replicates images in later nineteenth- and twentieth-century literature and
    the visual culture of vivisectors hiding away in their houses behind locked
    doors. See Chapters 4 and 6.
15 William Schupbach, 'A select iconography of animal experiment' in Rupke,
    Vivisection, pp. 340–7; Daniels, *Fields of Vision*, pp. 50–5; Nicolson, *Joseph
    Wright of Derby*, vol. II, pp. 112–14; Simon Wilson, *Holbein to Hockney.
    A History of British Art* (London, 1979), p. 54; David Fraser, *Joseph Wright of
    Derby* (Derby, 1979), pp. 1–2.
16 An earlier study for the painting did not include the boy waiting to lower the
    cage, suggesting that death was indeed inevitable. Reproduced in Nicolson,
    Joseph Wright of Derby, vol. II, p. 36.
17 See p. 27 re. Gilbert White.
18 Humphry Primatt, *The Duty of Mercy and the Sin of Cruelty to Brute Animals*
    (London, 1776) as published in Richard Ryder, ed., *The Duty of Mercy*
    (Fontwell, 1992).

19 Ibid., pp.22–3.

20 Ibid., pp. 43, 70–9.

21 Ibid., pp. 125–7.

22 John Keane, *Tom Paine: A political life* (London, 1995), p. 47.

23 E. P. Thompson, *The Making of the English Working Class*, 2nd edn (Harmondsworth, 1980), pp. 45–7.

24 Wesley suffered at the hands of bull-baiters who tried to set a bull upon him while he was preaching. Dix Harwood, *Love for Animals and How it Developed in Great Britain* (New York, 1928), p. 269.

25 John Wesley, *The character of a Methodist*, 3rd edn (London, 1766); J. Wesley Bready, *England Before and After Wesley* (London, 1938), p. 200.

26 Harwood, *Love for Animals*, p. 158. See Lewis G. Regenstein, *Replenish the Earth* (London, 1991), for a useful account of the attitude of different religions towards animals. See also Al-Hafiz B. A. Masri, *Animals in Islam* (Petersfield, 1989). Masri, the first Sunni Imam of Shah Jehan mosque in Woking argues that to kill animals for 'inessentials' is a contradiction of Islam (p. 16ff).

27 John Wesley, *A survey of the wisdom of God in the creation or a compendium of natural philosophy*, 3 vols (London, 1770), vol. I, p. 285.

28 'Sermon LX: The general deliverance', *The Works of John Wesley*, ed. Thomas Jackson, vol. VI, 3rd edn (London, 1829), p. 248.

29 'Sermon XCV: On the education of children', *The Works of John Wesley*, vol. VI, p. 95; Henry Salt, *Flesh or Fruit? An Essay on Food Reform* (London, 1888), p. 9.

30 Bready, *England Before and After Wesley*, p. 407.

31 T. Ferrier Hulme, *John Wesley and his Horse* (London, 1933), p. 2.

32 Ibid., diary of 1770 as quoted on unnumbered frontispiece.

33 Rupert Davies and Gordon Rupp, eds, *A History of the Methodist Church in Great Britain* (London, 1965), vol. I, p. 37.

34 Pottery display in 'Museum of Methodism', Wesley's Chapel, City Road, London EC1, summer 1996.

35 John Stuart Mill, *Utilitarianism, On Liberty, Essay on Bentham*, ed. Mary Warnock (Glasgow, 1962), p. 9.

36 Jeremy Bentham, *The Principles of Morals and Legislation* (London, 1789), ch. 18, sec. 1, as quoted in Jeffrey Masson and Susan McCarthy, *When Elephants Weep. The Emotional Lives of Animals* (London, 1994), p. 219.

37 Elie Halevy, *The Growth of Philosophic Radicalism* (London, 1928). In this 500-page tome devoted to the work and influence of Bentham and the Utilitarians there is not one reference to animals. Ross Harrison, *Bentham* (London, 1985), p. 11; Alan Ryan, ed., *Utilitarianism and other essays of J. S. Mill and Jeremy Bentham* (London, 1987), p. 8.

38 Andres-Holger Maehle and Ulrich Trohler, 'Animal experimentation from antiquity to the end of the eighteenth century: attitudes and arguments' in Rupke, *Vivisection*, pp. 37–8.

39 The discourse of slavery would be adopted by those within Parliament arguing for legislative change to benefit animals and slaves alike. The slave trade in Britain was abolished in February 1807; slavery in the dominions in 1833.

James Walvin, *Slavery and British Society 1776–1836* (London, 1982); Clare Midgley, *Women against Slavery, The British Campaigns 1780–1870* (London, 1992).

40   Halevy, *The Growth of Philosophic Radicalism*, pp. 480ff.

41   Jeremy Bentham, *Principles of Penal Law,* ch. xvi, as quoted in Henry Salt, *Animals' Rights Considered in Relation to Social Progress* (1892, reissued Fontwell, 1980), pp. 5–6.

42   Tester, *Animals and Society;* Peter Carruthers, *The Animals Issue. Moral Theory and Practice* (Cambridge, 1992).

43   Joseph Ritson, *An essay on abstinence from animal food* (London, 1802), p. 88.

44   Ibid., p. 85.

45   John Oswald, *The Cry of Nature; or an appeal to mercy and justice, on behalf of the persecuted animals* (London, 1791), p. 17.

46   Ibid., p. 27.

47   Tim Marshall, *Murdering to Dissect. Grave-robbing, Frankenstein and the Anatomy Literature* (Manchester, 1995), p. 291; Georges Lefebvre, *The French Revolution From its Origins to 1793* (Columbia, 1961), pp.109, 133.

48   Stephen Bostock, *Zoos and Animal Rights* (London, 1993), p. 25.

49   E. J. Hobsbawm, *The Age of Revolution* (London, 1962), p. 73.

50   Ibid., pp. 90–1.

51   Thompson, *The Making of the English Working Class*, p. 22ff, 115.

52   Davies and Rupp, *A History of the Methodist Church*, vol. I, pp. 302–4; David Hempton, *Methodism and Politics in British Society 1750–1850* (London, 1987), p. 78.

53   Robert Moore, *Pit-men, Preachers and Politics* (Cambridge, 1974), pp. 142–4; Hempton, *Methodism*, pp. 27, 29.

54   E. Welbourne, *The Miners' Unions of Northumberland and Durham* (Cambridge,1923), p. 57, as quoted in Davies and Rupp, *A History of the Methodist Church*, vol. I, p. 311.

55   E. S. Turner, *All Heaven in a Rage*, 2nd edn (Fontwell, 1992), p. 115. The London Corresponding Society has often been claimed as the first definitively working-class political organization formed in Britain. See Thompson, *The Making of the English Working Class*, 2nd edn (Harmondsworth, 1980), pp. 22, 63.

56   Halevy, *The Growth of Philosophic Radicalism*, pp. 153–77

57   Flora Fraser, *The Unruly Queen. The Life of Queen Caroline* (London, 1997), p. 400.

58   Edward G. Fairholme and Wellesley Pain, *A Century of Work for Animals* (London, 1924), p. 17.

59   Isabella's lover is killed by her brothers. She subsequently retrieves his head which she uses as compost for a cherished pot of basil. The inhumanity and pride of the wealthy brothers is emphasized by their brutalization of the natural world to gain wealth:

> . . . for them in death
> The seal on the cold ice with piteous bark
> Lay full of darts; for them alone did seethe
> A thousand men in troubles wide and dark:

Half-ignorant, they turn'd an easy wheel
That set sharp racks at work, to pinch and peel.

John Keats, 'Isabella', *Poems Published in 1820*, ed. Gerald Bullet (London, 1944), pp. 168–9.

60 John Clare, 'On Cruelty', *The Poems of John Clare*, ed. John Tibble, vol. I, pp. 79–80; 'The badger', *The Poems of John Clare*, vol. II, pp. 333–4.

61 John Clare, 'On seeing a lost greyhound in winter lying upon the snow in the fields', *The Early Poems of John Clare 1804–1822*, ed. Eric Robinson and David Powell (Oxford, 1989), vol. I, pp. 202–4.

62 He wrote a pamphlet on the vegetable system of diet, and translated two of Plutarch's essays on vegetables. Richard Holmes, *Shelley: The Pursuit* (London, 1994), p. 220; Paul Foot, *Red Shelley* (London, 1984).

63 Stanza VIII, *The works of P. B. Shelley* (Ware, 1994), p. 32.

64 Ibid., p. 31.

65 Foot, *Red Shelley*, pp. 237–9. 'The Mask of Anarchy' was not published until 1832.

66 Lynda Nead, 'Mapping the Self. Gender, Space and Modernity in Mid-Victorian London', in Roy Porter, ed., *Rewriting the Self* (London, 1997), pp. 178–9. See also Barbara Maria Stafford, *Body Criticism. Imaging the Unseen in Enlightenment Art and Medicine* (Massachusetts, 1993), p. xvii; Daniel Pick, 'Stories of the Eye,' in Porter, *op. cit.*, p. 197.

67 Seymour Drecher, 'Public Opinion and the Destruction of British Colonial Slavery' in Walvin, *Slavery*, p. 47.

68 Michel Foucault, *Discipline and Punish* (Harmondsworth, 1979), pp. 201–3; Ryan, *Utilitarianism*, p. 8. It also became the model for museum layout during the nineteenth century; Tony Bennet, *Birth of the Museum* (London, 1995), p. 101.

69 Gilbert White, *The Natural History of Selborne* (1788–9, reprinted London, 1987); Raymond Williams, *The Country and the City* (St Albans, 1975), pp. 147–8.

70 Sydenham Teak Edwards, *Cynographia Britannica* (London, 1800).

71 Ibid., pp. 4–5.

72 Bostock, *Zoos and Animal Rights*, pp. 26ff.

73 Turner, *All Heaven in a Rage*, pp. 104–18.

74 Manchester and Birmingham contained populations of over 100,000 and there were twenty towns in England and Wales with populations of over 10,000. S. G. Checkland, *The Rise of Industrial Society in England 1815–1885* (London, 1971), pp. 32–5; Sally Alexander, *Becoming a Woman* (London, 1994), p. 10.

75 John Summerson, *Georgian London* (London, 1947), pp. 140–1, 244–5.

76 Alison Adburgham, *Shopping in Style. London from the Restoration to Edwardian Elegance* (Hampshire,1979), p. 100.

77 Ibid., p. 98.

78 Ibid., pp. 70–1.

79 Robert Trow Smith, *British Livestock. A history of British livestock husbandry 1700–1900* (London, 1959), p. 12.

80 Ibid., pp. 15, 23.

81 Ibid., p. 325.

82 Thomas, *Man and the Natural World*, p. 301.
83 See David Cannadine, ' The present and the past in the English industrial revolution 1880–1980', *Past and Present* , no. 103 (May 1984); Williams, *The Country and the City*.
84 See Baker, *Picturing the Beast*, pp. 20–1, where he criticizes Tester, *(Animals and Society)* and John Berger (' Why look at animals?' in *About Looking*) for almost suggesting that cats are simply less real than cows.
85 Thomas, *Man and the Natural World*, p. 182.
86 S. Maccoby, *English Radicalism* (London, 1955), p. 55; Turner, *All Heaven in a Rage*, pp. 110–17.
87 James Turner, *Animals, Pain and Humanity in the Victorian Mind: Reckoning with the beast* (New York, 1980), pp. 33–5.
88 Journal of the House of Commons, vol. 55, 1799–1800, 2 April 1800, p. 362. See also F. W. Hackwood, *Old English Sports* (London, 1907), pp. 304–18.
89 Peter Bailey, *Leisure and Class in Victorian England* (London, 1978), p. 31.
90 Turner, *All Heaven in a Rage*, p. 112; J. L. and Barbara Hammond, *The Town Labourer 1760–1832*, 2nd edn 1925 (reissued London, 1996), pp. 61–2; John Rule, *The Labouring Classes in Early Industrial England 1750–1850* (Harlow, 1986), pp. 214–15.
91 *Parliamentary History*, vol. XXXVI, p. 851, as quoted in Hugh Cunningham, *Leisure in the Industrial Revolution* (London, 1980), p. 50.
92 Anon., *Observations on some of the amusements of this country, addressed to the higher classes of society* (London, 1827), p. 18.
93 William Youatt, *The obligation and extent of humanity to brutes* (London, 1839), p. 169; Lucinda Lambton, *Beastly Buildings. The National Trust Book of Architecture for Animals* (London, 1985), p. 18; Hackwood, *Old English Sports*, pp. 231–59, 273. *Colonel Mordaunt's cock match* by Johan Zoffany, commissioned by Warren Hastings, the Governor-General of Bengal, in 1784, still hangs in the Tate Gallery. The current notice (autumn 1997) in the Tate describes it as 'lively and humorous'.
94 '. . . there are men who would wish to rank even as gentlemen who drop to the lowest grade in society, by practising such disgraceful modes of what they call amusement and sport [namely acting as] dog-fighters, cat-killers, and badger-baiters.' Anon., *Thoughts on the established church* (London, 1845), p. 33.
95 Lord Erskine, *Cruelty to Animals. The speech of Lord Erskine in the House of Peers, 15 May 1809* (London, 1824), p. 4; Turner, *All Heaven in a Rage*, p. 117; Fairholme and Pain, *A Century of Work*, pp. 17–31.
96 Erskine had also subsequently been employed by Wilberforce's evangelical 'Proclamation Society' to prosecute Paine for publication of *The Age of Reason* in 1797.
97 Albert Goodwin, *The Friends of Liberty. The English Democratic Movement in the Age of the French Revolution* (London, 1979), pp. 271, 346–58.
98 Along with other MPs, including the playwright Richard Sheridan and Charles Grey, he had also been part of the 'Friends of the People Society' in opposition to Pitt in 1792, of which James Mackintosh (see page 35) was treasurer. He had supported the Foxite group against Pitt in the 1790s. Maccoby, *English Radicalism*, p. 54.
99 T. Holcroft, *A Narrative of Facts Relating to a Prosecution for High Treason,*

etc. (London, 1795), p. 124, as quoted in Goodwin, *The Friends of Liberty*, p. 347.

100 Erskine, *Cruelty to Animals*, p. 30

101 Ibid., p. 12.

102 Ibid., pp. 3, 16.

103 Ibid., p. 31 and Turner, *All Heaven in a Rage*, pp. 121–3.

104 Wilberforce introduced the first motion to abolish slavery in 1791; abolition was not achieved until 1834. Peter Fryer, *Staying Power* (London, 1984), pp. 208–13. Midgley, *Women against Slavery*; Kathryn Gleadle, *The Early Feminists. Radical Unitarians and the Emergence of the Women's Rights Movement 1831–51* (Basingstoke, 1995).

105 See Turner, *All Heaven in a Rage*, p. 117, and Fairholme and Pain, *A Century of Work*, pp. 17–31, for accounts of unsuccessful attempts to prevent horses being flogged.

106 Bulls were not covered which meant that, at least for the time being, bull-baiting would continue.

107 Harold Perkin, *The Origins of Modern English Society 1780–1880* (London, 1969), p. 282. Wilberforce was also a friend of Jeremy Bentham. See Halevy, *The Growth of Philosophic Radicalism*, p. 251.

108 Turner, *All Heaven in a Rage*, p. 129.

109 *Hansard*, vol. VII, 24 May 1822, cols. 758–9.

110 In the course of the third reading on 7 June 1822 Martin urged peace and tranquillity in Ireland. *Hansard*, vol. VII, June 1822, col. 869. Born a Roman Catholic but brought up as a Protestant, his father had wanted him to become an MP primarily to work for Catholic Emancipation. As Linda Colley has noted, by the 1820s only a minority of MPs were opposed to this. See Fairholme and Pain, *A Century of Work*, p. 44; Linda Colley, *Britons. Forging the Nation 1707–1837* (London, 1992), pp. 324–9.

111 Buxton's wife, Hannah Gurney, was the daughter of John Gurney and the sister of Elizabeth Fry. See Bready, *England Before and After Wesley*, pp. 408–9; Trevor May, *Gondolas and Growlers. The History of the London Horse Cab* (Stroud, 1995), p. 107.

112 Buxton was associated with the West London Lancastrian Association, the original members of which included James Mackintosh, Francis Place and James Mill. Alice Prochaska, 'The practice of Radicalism: educational reform in Westminster', in John Stevenson, ed., *London in the Age of Reform* (Oxford, 1977), pp. 106–8.

113 *DNB*, vol. XII, pp. 617–21.

114 Maccoby, *English Radicalism*, pp. 41, 328, 369; Joseph O. Baylen and Norbert J. Gossman, eds, *Biographical Dictionary of Modern British Radicals, Vol 1: 1770–1830* (Sussex, 1979), pp. 305–7.

115 Rev. A. Broome, *SPCA Founding Statement* (London, 1824).

116 Ibid., p. 1. The same view about the horror of foreigners is expressed in Henry Curling, *A Lashing for the Lashers; being an exposition of the cruelties practised upon the cab and omnibus horses of London* (London, 1851), p. 13.

117 Broome, *SPCA Founding Statement*, p. 2. It was made after the publication of Thomas Southwood Smith's important article, 'The Uses of the Dead to the Living', *The Westminster Review*, no. 2, 1824, pp. 59–97, in which he

advocated that all unclaimed bodies from hospitals and workhouses should be handed over for dissection. See also Marshall, *Murdering to Dissect*.

118   Broome, *SPCA Founding Statement*, p. 2.

119   Ibid. p. 2.

120   Peter Singer, ed., Lewis Gompertz, *Moral Inquiries on the Situation of Man and of Brutes* (1824, reissued Fontwell, 1992), pp. 115–17.

121   Singer, preface to *Moral Inquiries*, pp. 12, 50.

122   See Chapter 2.

123   Lewis Gompertz, *Objects and Address of the Society for the Prevention of Cruelty to Animals, established 1824* (London, 1829), pp. 8–10.

124   Ibid., p. 9.

125   Ibid., p. 8.

126   Lord Erskine, 'The Liberated Robins' in Florence Horatia Suckling, *The Humane Educator and Reciter* (London, 1891), p. 22.

127   Turner, *All Heaven in a Rage*, p. 128.

128   Ibid., p. 119.

129   Lord Mahon speaking to the annual meeting of 1835, as quoted in Harrison, *Peaceable Kingdom*, p. 120.

130   The 1822 legislation was used against bull-baiters in West Bromwich in 1827, who were then imprisoned in Stafford jail for non-payment of their fines. Bull-running also continued in the Midlands, especially in Stamford. See Hackwood, *Old English Sports*, pp. 304–32; Harrison, *Peaceable Kingdom*, p. 86.

TWO   SIGHT, SPECTACLE AND EDUCATION: FROM REGENT'S PARK ZOO TO SMITHFIELD CATTLE MARKET

1   Letter from F. M. Thompson, *The Voice of Humanity*, vol. I, 1830, p. 37.

2   Carol Duncan, *Civilizing Rituals* (London,1995), p. 40.

3   Tony Bennett, *Birth of the Museum*, p. 6.

4   Bennett, *Birth of the Museum*, p. 6ff; Duncan, *Civilizing Rituals*; Sir Henry Ellis, director of the British Museum, 1835, as quoted in David M. Wilson, *The British Museum and its Public* (London, 1982), p. 4.

5   Wilson, *The British Museum and its Public*, p. 4. See too later comments by Henry Cole of the Victoria and Albert Museum (Bennett, *Birth of the Museum*, p. 20).

6   Londa Schiebinger, 'Gender and Natural History' in Nick Jardine, Jim Secord, Emma Spary, eds, *Cultures of Natural History* (Cambridge, 1996), pp. 172–3.

7   Martin Hoyles, *The Story of Gardening* (London, 1991), pp. 122–55.

8   Philip L. Sclater, secretary of the Zoological Society, *A Record of the Programme of the Zoological Society of London* (London, 1901), p. 147.

9   The original plans did not in fact materialize. Summerson, *Georgian London*, p. 164.

10   Deborah Epstein Nord, *Walking the Victorian Streets. Women, Representation and the City* (New York, 1995), pp. 26–9.

11   Peter Guillery, *The Buildings of London Zoo* (London, 1993), p. 3.

12   *The Mirror*, 6 September 1828, as printed in Gwynne Vevers, ed., *London's*

Zoo. An anthology to celebrate 150 years of the Zoological Society of London
(London, 1976), pp. 20–1.

13 Cunningham, *Leisure in the Industrial Revolution* (1980), pp. 33–6.

14 Oliver Impey and Arthur MacGregor, eds, *The Origins of Museums. The
Cabinets of Curiosities in Sixteenth and Seventeenth Century Europe* (Oxford,
1985).

15 'There is no domesticated animal, quadruped, or fowl, to whom we do not owe
something,' Youatt, *The obligation and extent*, p. 37.

16 Ibid., p. 2.

17 Heralding much future criticism, Youatt castigated the French leading
vivisector, François Magendie, for repeating experiments on the same animals
just to illustrate lectures for students. Ibid., p. 194.

18 The secretary and vice-secretary of the Zoological Society, *The gardens and
menagerie of the Zoological Society delineated 1830–31* (London, 1831), p. v.

19 Minutes of the Zoological Society, 1 July 1835, as printed in Vevers,
London's Zoo, p. 25

20 Leigh Hunt, *The Townsman*, II, III, IV, 1833, as printed in L. H. Houtchens and
C. W. Houtchens, eds, *Leigh Hunt's Political and Occasional Essays* (New
York, 1967), p. 295.

21 Bostock, *Zoos and Animal Rights*, p. 29.

22 Vevers, *London's Zoo*, p. 28.

23 Peter Ackroyd, *Dickens* (London, 1990), pp. 279–80.

24 Sclater, *A Record of the Programme of the Zoological Society of London*.

25 *Daily Telegraph*, 4 January 1880, as printed in Vevers, *London's Zoo*, p. 59.

26 White, *The Natural History of Selborne*.

27 Berger, 'Why look at Animals?', pp. 1, 19–20.

28 Thomas Huxley, 'On the educational value of the natural historical sciences',
1854, in *Lay sermons, addresses and reviews* (London, 1870), p. 101. See too
Jean-Marc Drouin and Bernadette Bensaude-Vincent, ' Nature for the People' in
Jardine et al, *Cultures of Natural History*, pp. 408–25.

29 *The gardens and menagerie.*

30 E. T. Bennett, preface to 'Quadrupeds' in *The gardens and menagerie*, p. v.

31 Ibid., p. vi.

32 *The gardens and menagerie*, pp. 99–100.

33 Ibid., pp. 92–3, 190.

34 Ibid., p. 185; vol. II, p. 288.

35 Ibid., pp. 109, 188, 288.

36 Harwood, *Love for Animals*, p. 249ff.

37 Shows introduced horses, elephants, monkeys, dogs, fencers, tumblers, and
rope dancers. Thompson, *The Making of the English Working Class*, p. 808.
Harwood sees travelling circuses and menageries as evidence of 'a democratizing
of zoological interest'. Harwood, *Love for Animals*, p. 223.

38 Thomas Kelly, *A History of Adult Education in Great Britain* (Liverpool,
1962), pp. 112–33.

39 Ibid., p. 122.

40 Richard Johnson, '"Really Useful Knowledge": radical education and working-
class culture, 1790–1848' in John Clarke, Charles Critcher and Richard
Johnson, eds, *Working-Class Culture* (London, 1979), pp. 75–102.

41 June Purvis, *A History of Women's Education in England* (Buckingham, 1991), pp. 36–8.

42 Major Egerton Leigh, *Pets. A Paper dedicated to all who do not spell pets – pests*. Read at the Mechanics' Institution at the Music Hall, Chester (London, 1859), pp. 6, 61–2.

43 J. F. C. Harrison, *Learning and Living 1790–1960* (London, 1961), pp. 28–9.

44 *The Penny Magazine*, vol. LI, 19 January 1833.

45 'The orang-outang', *The Penny Magazine*, vol. LXVIII, 27 April 1833, pp. 156–9.

46 W. J. Linton, *James Watson: A Memoir*, 1880, p. 2 7, as quoted in Harrison, *Learning and Living*, p. 29.

47 Mary Wollstonecraft, *Original Stories*, 2nd edn (London, 1820), p. 114. My thanks to Carolyn Steedman for drawing my attention to this.

48 Charlotte Brontë, *Jane Eyre* (1847, reprinted Harmondsworth, 1985), pp. 40–1.

49 There are no books listed in the British Library catalogue before 1800 featuring pets in the title. There are 11 between 1821 and 1860, 49 between 1861 and 1880, 45 between 1881 and 1990, 92 between 1941 and 1960 and titles in the hundreds by the 1970s.

50 Jane Webb Loudon, *Domestic Pets: Their Habits and Management* (London, 1851), p. 159. See Leonore Davidoff and Catherine Hall, *Family Fortunes: men and women of the English middle classes 1780–1850* (London, 1987), pp. 188–92.

51 Loudon, *Domestic Pets*, pp. 62–6.

52 Anon., *Beeton's Book of Home Pets* (London, 1862), part XVII, 'The Squirrel', pp. 673–4. Although the work is anonymous many of the phrases are those of Jane Loudon and the drawings are by Harrison Weir, the prolific illustrator and cat-lover who illustrated Loudon's earlier book.

53 W. H. Pyne, *Microcosm, or a picturesque delineation of the arts, agriculture, manufactures of Great Britain*, vol. II (London, 1808), p. 28.

54 Richard Perren, *The Meat Trade in Britain 1840–1914* (London, 1977), p. 43.

55 Metropolitan Sanitary Association, *First Report* (London, 1850), p. 71.

56 William Youatt, *The Horse* (London, 1831), p. 42.

57 J. C. Loudon, *Encyclopaedia of Agriculture* (London, 1831), p. 1122, as quoted in F. M. L. Thompson, 'Horses and Hay in Britain, 1830–1918' in F. M. L. Thompson, ed., *Horses in European Economic History. A preliminary canter* (Reading, 1983), p. 59.

58 George August Sala, *Twice Round the Clock or the Hours of the Day and Night in London* (London, 1859, republished Leicester, 1971), pp. 69, 77, 82. See also Metropolitan Sanitary Association, *First Report*, p. 80; Norman Longmate, *King Cholera*, as quoted in Paul Bailey, *London* (Oxford, 1996), pp. 133–6.

59 Raphael Samuel, 'Comers and Goers' in H. J. Dyos and Michael Wolff, eds, *The Victorian City. Images and Realities*, (London, 1977), vol. I, pp. 123–60; Nord, *Walking the Victorian Streets*; Lynda Nead, 'Mapping the Self' in Porter, *Rewriting the Self*, pp. 167–85; Doreen Massey, *Space, Place, and Gender* (London, 1994).

60 See Pamela Sharpe, *Adapting to Capitalism. Working Women in the English Economy 1700–1850* (Basingstoke, 1996), pp. 151, where she argues that women's work in the cities was characterized by mobility.

61 See James A. Schmieched, *Sweated Industries and Sweated Labour. The London*

Clothing Trades 1860–1914 (Beckenham, 1984); Alexander, *Becoming a Woman*, pp. 3–55.

62 Flora Tristan, *The London Journal of Flora Tristan or the aristocracy and working class of England* (1842, trans. Jean Hawkes and republished London, 1982), p. 18.

63 This grew further to well over 800,000 by 1871. See Philip E. Jones, *The Butchers of London. A History of the Worshipful Company of Butchers of the City of London* (London, 1976), p. 80.

64 *The Animals' Friend or Progress of Humanity*, no. 1 (London, 1833), p. 24.

65 The first legislative attempts to deal with fierce driving of horses had been made by William Garrow, the Attorney-General, in 1816. By 1820 laws had been passed against 'furious driving', although Hackney coaches were exempt. Lord Erskine and Richard Martin personally prosecuted those acting with wanton cruelty to horses, an action supported by the judges, and the offenders were fined. *Hansard*, vol. 1834, 10 June 1816, col. 1040; Turner, *All Heaven in a Rage*, pp. 119, 128.

66 *The Voice of Humanity* (1827), p. 33.

67 Curling, *Lashing*, pp. 3–4.

68 Charles Dickens, *Sketches by Boz* (1839, reissued Dennis Walder, ed., London, 1995), p. 107.

69 Ibid., p. 172.

70 Ibid.

71 Curling, *Lashing*, p. 16.

72 *The Voice of Humanity*, 1827, p. 27.

73 Youatt, *The obligation and extent of humanity*, p. 135.

74 *The Voice of Humanity*, 1827, p. 4.

75 *The National Animals' Friend Society for the protection of the dumb creation against cruelty (which has been so signally efficient in bringing to light the horrors of the knackers' yard)* (London, n. d., 1840s), pp. 10–11.

76 Curling, *Lashing*, p. 15.

77 John Bull, *An enquiry into the present state of Smithfield cattle market etc.*, 2nd edn (London, 1848), p. 18.

78 Charles Dickens, *The Pickwick Papers* (1836–7, republished Harmondsworth, 1972), ch. XIX, p. 335.

79 Richard K. P. Pankhurst, *William Thompson, Pioneer Socialist* (1954, reissued London, 1991), pp. 5, 98. See also William Thompson and Anna Wheeler, *Appeal of one half of the human race, women*, with a new introduction by Michael Foot and Marie Mulvey Roberts (Bristol, 1994).

80 Speech of Joseph Brotherton MP to the ladies and gentlemen of the Vegetarian Conference, 30 September 1847. *The Truth Tester, Temperance Advocate, and Healthian Journal*, vol. II, 1848, supplement of 22 October 1847, p. 2.

81 Lewis Gompertz, 'The Vegetarian Society', in *Fragments in Defence of Animals* (London, 1852), p. 173.

82 Brian Harrison, *Drink and the Victorians. The temperance question in England 1815–1872*, 2nd edn (Staffordshire, 1995), pp. 38–40, 290–2.

83 As quoted in L. D. Schwarz, *London in the Age of Industry* (Cambridge, 1992), p. 235.

84 Metropolitan Drinking Fountain and Cattle Trough Association (MDFCTA),

Eighth Annual Report, 1866–7, p. 8. Metropolitan Sanitary Association *First Report*; Anthony S. Wohl, *Endangered Lives. Public Health in Victorian Britain* (London, 1983).

85 It was originally situated in Snow Hill, which was rebuilt with the Holborn viaduct. *Half a Century of Good Work. A Jubilee History of the Metropolitan Drinking Fountain and Cattle Trough Association 1859–1909* (London, 1909), p. 14.

86 Ibid., p. 32.

87 This also still exists. As a child I remember seeing horses drinking there. Hazel Conway, *People's Parks. The Design and Development of Victorian Parks in Britain* (Cambridge, 1991); *Half a Century of Good Work*, p. 32.

88 He also protested against the brutality of the Smithfield market. Harrison, *Peaceable Kingdom*, pp. 112, 121.

89 *Half a Century of Good Work*, pp. 5–16; *MDFCTA Executive Minutes*, 30 May 1859, 31 May 1860 (Mill gave a donation). *Eighth Annual Report*, 1866–7, p. 38.

90 *Eighth Annual Report* (as above), p. 8.

91 Ibid., p. 6.

92 David Naismith, the founder, appointed a former cabman specifically to undertake missionary work with cab drivers. This followed the tradition established by the Society for the Promotion of Christian Knowledge to produce pamphlets aimed particularly at hackney coachmen who were seen to be in moral jeopardy. May, *Gondolas and Growlers*, p. 107.

93 Jones, *The Butchers of London*, p. 103.

94 K. J. Bonser, *The Drovers: Who they Were and How they Went: an Epic of the English Countryside* (London, 1970), p. 221.

95 Although Newgate Prison, built in the 1770s, was burnt out by the Gordon rioters in 1780, it was rebuilt with minor variations and survived until 1902 when the Old Bailey central criminal court took its place.

96 Jones, *The Butchers of London*, p. 77. See Margaret Forster, *Hidden Lives: A Family Memoir* (London, 1995), pp. 20–35 for a description of the cattle market and shambles in Carlisle in the 1870s.

97 This pre-dates the West End of London as a shopping venue by many years. Adburgham, *Shopping in Style*, p. 13.

98 Chris Philo, 'Animals, Geography, and the City: Notes on Inclusions and Exclusions', *Environment and Planning D: Society and Space,* vol. XIII, 1995, pp. 655–81.

99 Anon., *Cursory remarks on the evil tendency of unrestrained cruelty, particularly on that practiced in Smithfield Market* (London, 1823), pp. 11–14, 23.

100 Ibid., p. 8; Anon.,*Thoughts on the established church and Puseyite clergymen; the voluntary system, etc.* (London, 1845), p. 32.

101 William Drummond, *Rights of animals and man's duty to treat them with humanity* (London, 1838), p. 163.

102 Letter from Frances Maria Thompson, *The Voice of Humanity,* vol. I, 1830–33, p. 37.

103 Ibid., pp. 102–3.

104 *The Voice of Humanity* (1830–33)

105 Proceedings of 5 June 1828, *Hansard*, new series, vol. 19, 1828, cols. 1049–53.

106 *Thoughts on the established church*, pp. 31–2.

107 *The Voice of Humanity,* vol. II, p. 2.

108 James Turner, *Animals, Pain and Humanity*, p. 33.

109 Letter from J. Silverton of Newington Green, *The Voice of Humanity*, vol. II, p. 37. Regulations prevented cattle being driven improperly through Sydney; action was also taken against 'loose dogs'.

110 Jewish slaughter was praised since it used a sharp knife and a single incision. Cattle were not kept for days without food, they were not diseased and were allowed to drink before they were killed. *The Voice of Humanity*, 1827, p. 9 .

111 *The Voice of Humanity*, 1827, p. 10; *Thoughts on the established church*, pp. 32–3. Marshall Berman, *All that is Solid Melts into Air* (London, 1983), pp. 150–2.

112 Ann Morley with Liz Stanley, *The Life and Death of Emily Wilding Davison* (London, 1988), p. 107.

113 Bull, *An enquiry,* p. 23–5.

114 Although the market was supposed to be regulated and patrolled by police, they did not attend at night time since the job had low status and pay: policemen soon moved on to better paid posts. *The Voice of Humanity*, 1827, p. 26.

115 Ibid., p. 27.

116 *Cursory remarks*, p. 5.

117 Bull, *An enquiry*, p. 17.

118 *The Voice of Humanity*, p. 6.

119 Ibid., p. 7.

120 Ibid., pp. 7, 9.

121 Attempts were also made to stop the import of diseased carcasses from abroad through the the Contagious Diseases Prevention Act of 1848, amended in the 1850s. This was introduced against diseased meat with the emphasis on preventing the import of foreign diseased cattle rather than on improving the methods of slaughter at home. Perren, *Meat Trade*, pp. 50–65.

122 Jones, *The Butchers of London*, p. 103. London then developed a thriving deadmeat market, importing carcasses from as far afield as Aberdeen, Edinburgh and Leeds. In other parts of the country such as Leicester and Norwich live markets continued much as before (Jones, *op cit.*, p. 45).

123 Perren, *Meat Trade,* p. 41.

124 Women were employed to clean out the innards of slaughtered animals, a job they apparently preferred to the alternative of being general domestic servants. Concern was expressed upon the specific effects of such a degrading job on the gut girls, as they were known locally. This market finally closed in 1913. Jess Steele, *Turning the Tide. The History of Everyday Deptford* (London, 1993). See Chapter 6.

125 William A. Mackinnon, *On the Rise, Progress and Present State of Public Opinion, in Great Britain, and Other Parts of the World* (London, 1828). Dror Wahrman, *Imagining the Middle Class. The Political Representation of Class in Britain, c.1789–1840* (Cambridge, 1995), p. 299–302.

126 *The Voice of Humanity*, vol. III, 1832, p. 17

127 Ibid., p. 30.

128 Thompson, *The Making of the English Working Class*, pp. 891ff.

129 Nord, *Walking the Victorian Streets*, p. 52; Davidoff and Hall, *Family*

Fortunes, p.19. The Municipal Corporations Act of 1835 increased in different ways middle-class involvement in state institutions. Dissenters and Unitarians became eligible for public office. G. Kitson Clark, *The Making of Victorian England* (London, 1962), pp.159–61.

130　He also castigated followers of the socialist Robert Owen and the popular Radical 'Orator' Hunt. Edward Gibbon Wakefield, *Householders in Danger From the Populace* (London, 1831).

131　Ibid., p. 7.

132　Harrison, *Peaceable Kingdom,* p. 147.

133　Flora Tristan, *London Journal,* p. 162.

134　In Saffron Walden and Bristol respectively, Mrs Webster and Mrs Harford set up local Rational Humanity groups against animal cruelty; in London Frances Thompson gave donations and wrote letters to the press. The specific contribution of 'several respectable female friends [. . .] at the expense of many personal sacrifices' was acknowledged at the annual general meeting of *The Voice of Humanity* in 1832. *The Voice of Humanity*, vol. III, 1832, p. 24.

135　Report of meeting of 15 June 1831, *The Voice of Humanity*, vol. II, 1831, p. 22.

136　*The Animals' Friend*, no. 1, 1833, p. 6. Reference is also made to the role of clergy and dissenting ministers in giving sermons on the treatment of animals, *The National Animals' Friend Society*, pp. 24–5.

137　Joan Wallach Scott, *Gender and the Politics of History* (New York, 1988), p. 84.

138　Midgley, *Women against Slavery,* p. 5.

139　*The Voice of Humanity,* vol. I, 1830, p. 109.

140　*The Voice of Humanity,* vol. III, 1832, pp. 44–5.

141　Evidence of Charles Underwood and John Brow, *The Voice of Humanity,* vol. III, 1832, pp. 51–2.

142　Ibid., p. 42.

143　Ibid.

144　Fairholme and Pain, *A Century of Work,* p. 85.

145　RSPCA, *Domestic Animals and their Treatment* (London, 1857), pp. 11ff.

146　*Claims of Animals. A Lecture* (London, 1875), pp. 22–3.

147　Thomas W. Cowan, *British Beekeepers' Association Jubilee: A History of the Association – Representing fifty years of bee-keeping progress* (London, 1928), p. 1. My thanks to Eva Barnes for information on the nature of bee-keeping.

148　*The Voice of Humanity* ,1831, vol. II, pp. 13–15.

149　William Wilberforce, *A Practical View of the Prevailing Religious System of Professed Christians, in the Higher and Middle Classes in This Country, Contrasted with Real Christianity,* 17th edn (London, 1829), p. 135.

150　*The Voice of Humanity,* vol. I, p. 28.

151　Youatt, *The obligation and extent; The Voice of Humanity,* 1827, 1830–33

152　Youatt, *The obligation and extent,* p. 111.

153　*The Animals' Friend,* no. 7, 1839, pp. 16–17.

THREE CONTINUITY AND CHANGE: FALLEN DOGS AND
VICTORIAN TALES

1　George R. Sims, 'Told to the Missionary', in Suckling, ed., *The Humane Educator*, pp. 308–10.

2   Tester, *Animals and Society*, pp. 88ff.
3   Stephen R. L. Clark, *Animals and Their Moral Standing* (London, 1997), p. 117.
4   Charles Darwin, *Life and Letters*, vol. II, p. 5, as quoted in Francis Darwin, *The life of Charles Darwin* (1902, reprinted London, 1995), p. 170.
5   Peter Marshall, *Nature's Web. An exploration of ecological thinking* (New York, 1992), p. 325.
6   Charles Darwin, *On the Origin of Species by means of Natural Selection* (1859, reprinted Harmondsworth, 1968), pp. 124–5.
7   Francis Darwin, *The life of Charles Darwin*, pp. 69–71.
8   Charles Darwin, *The Expression of Emotions in Man and Animals* (1872, reprinted London, 1998) as quoted in Masson and McCarthy, *When Elephants Weep*, p. 14.
9   He also believed that the lower races had to be wiped out by higher civilized (sic) races. Darwin, *The Descent of Man* (Watts, 1930), pp. 243–4, as quoted in Marshall, *Nature's Web*, p. 327.
10 Subsidies were also given for a book by Joseph Hooker on the botany of the Antarctic voyage of *Discovery*. Janet Browne, 'Biogeography and empire' in Jardine *et al.*, *Cultures of Natural History*, p. 310.
11 *Life and Letters of T. H. Huxley* (1901), p. 217, as quoted in Misia Landau, *Narratives of Human Evolution* (New Haven, 1991), p. 21.
12 Notes of Rev. W. H. Fremantle as quoted in Francis Darwin, *The Life of Charles Darwin*, pp. 238–9.
13 Ibid., p. 239.
14 T. H. Huxley, 'On the Study of Zoology', 1861, in Huxley, *Lay sermons* , p. 129.
15 T. H. Huxley, 'On the Educational Value of the Natural History Sciences', in *Lay Sermons*, p. 102.
16 David Allen, 'Tastes and Crazes', in Jardine *et al.*, *Cultures of Natural History*, p. 405. Edmund Gosse, a member of the Plymouth Brethren, attempted to reconcile Darwin's ideas with those of the power of God and declared, 'This was the great moment in the history of thought when the theory of the mutability of species was preparing to throw a flood of light upon all departments of human speculation and action.' Edmund Gosse, *Father and Son* (1907, reprinted Harmondsworth, 1983), p. 102.
17 Mary Ward, *The Microscope*, 3rd edn (London, 1869); Lydia Becker, *Botany for Novices* (London, 1864); Women and Natural History Exhibition, Bodleian Library, Oxford, April 1996.
18 *Mayhew's London. Being Selections from London Labour and the London Poor* (London, 1861).
19 Alfred Rosling Bennett, *London and Londoners in the 1850s and 1860s* (London, 1924), p. 58.
20 Andrew Mearns, *The Bitter Cry of Outcast London* (London, 1883), p. 5. See too Mearns, *London and its Teeming Toilers* (London, 1887), p. 17.
21 Ibid., p. 18.
22 Evidence from ordnance survey map for Bermondsey 1871 (Greater London Record Office).
23 *Mayhew's London*, p. 306.
24 *Dickens's Dictionary of London, 1879. An Unconventional Handbook* (1879, reissued London, 1972), p. 19.

25 Charles Booth, *Life and Labour of the People in London* (London, 1889).

26 Rev. Charles Maurice Davies, *Mystic London* (London, 1875), pp. 85–90.

27 J. C. Hotten, *A Dictionary of Modern Slang*, 2nd edn (London, 1860), p. 122 as quoted in Gareth Stedman Jones, 'The Cockney and the Nation 1780–1988', p. 294, in David Feldman and Gareth Stedman Jones, eds, *Metropolis London* (London, 1989). See also William Gilbert, *James Duke, Costermonger. A Tale of the Social Deposits* (London, 1879).

28 *Mayhew's London*, p. 75.

29 *The Leisure Hour* (London, 1873), pp. 492–3.

30 *Mayhew's London*, p. 75.

31 *The Leisure Hour*, pp. 492–3.

32 Deborah Weiner, 'The People's Palace' in Feldman and Stedman Jones, *Metropolis London*, pp. 40–55.

33 *Animals' Guardian*, vol. I, 9 June 1891, p. 106; vol II, 11 August 1892, p. 137.

34 Our Dumb Friends' League, *Programme of Costers' and Street Traders' Donkey Show, People's Palace May 24th 1909* (London, 1909); *Programme of Costers' and Street Traders' Donkey Show, Victoria Park, July 5th 1922* (London, 1922). Blue Cross Archive, Burford.

35 G. Holden Pike, *Golden Lane. Quaint Adventures and Life Pictures* (London, 1875), p. 14.

36 *The Cabman*, monthly journal of the London Cabmen's Mission Hall, King's Cross, vol. I, 1 September 1874, pp. 2–4.

37 *The Cabman*, vol. I, pp. 4ff; vol II, 6 February 1876, pp. 88–90. The notorious drinking habits of cab drivers dated back to the eighteenth century. See Harrison, *Drink and the Victorians*, pp. 50–1.

38 Cab Drivers' Benevolent Association, established 1870 (*The Cabman*, vol. I, 11 July 1875, pp. 129–30; *Cab Trade Record*, June 1903, p. 8). The first licensed Cab Driver's Trade Union Society was founded at the same period, in 1867.

39 General Booth, *In Darkest England and the Way Out* (London, 1890), p. 19.

40 For example W. J. Gordon, *The Horse-World of London* (London, 1893) issued by the Religious Tract Society.

41 Statement made by Colonel Colville. Also present at the meeting of the Horse Accident Prevention Society was the ubiquitous Angela Burdett-Coutts. *Animals' Guardian*, vol II, 9 June 1892, p. 106; *Cab Trade Record*, December 1902, p. 10; Our Dumb Friends' League, *Second Annual Report 1898–9*, p. 17 for a report of a protest meeting held at Westminster Town Hall on 17 April 1898 against the use of asphalt.

42 Susan Chitty, *The Woman who wrote Black Beauty* (London, 1971), pp. 220–5.

43 Anna Sewell, *Black Beauty* (1877, reissued London, 1994), p. 109; Chitty, *The Woman who wrote Black Beauty*, p. 232; Moira Ferguson, 'Breaking in Englishness: Black Beauty and the Politics of Race and Class', *Women, a Cultural Review*, vol. V, no. 1, Spring 1994, p. 35. Thanks to Marie Mulvey Roberts for drawing my attention to this article.

44 Gordon, *The Horse-World of London*, pp. 142–4.

45 Sewell, *Black Beauty*, pp. 109ff; 172.

46 William Secord, *Dog Painting 1840–1940: A social history of the dog in art* (Woodbridge, 1992), pp. 231ff.

47 Although he loved painting animals, he also enjoyed killing them. In the course of his life he accumulated 30 trophies of murdered animals: stags' heads and antlers, bull's horns, rams' heads and a stuffed swan. Nevertheless his visual representation of animals helped to create a milieu in which affection towards animals and admiration for their qualities were prominent.

48 Kenneth Clark, *Animals and Men*, p. 193.

49 Loudon, *Domestic Pets*, p. 1.

50 The first trials of field dogs took place some six years later in Bedfordshire.

51 See Chapter 1, note 70.

52 Secord, *Dog Painting*, p. 14.

53 J. H. Walsh, *The Dogs of the British Isles*, 5th edn (London, 1886).

54 Secord, *Dog Painting*, p. 251.

55 Sylvia Pankhurst, *The Suffragette Movement* (1931, reissued London, 1978), pp. 516–17. See Chapter 6.

56 *The Kennel Review*, vol. IV, no. 41, December 1885, p. 212, records her favourites as Noble, a grand collie – always downstairs when they ate – a Skye terrier called Corran, and Flo, a fox terrier; Secord, *Dog Painting*, p. 251.

57 *Notable dogs of the year and their owners*, reprinted from *The Ladies' Kennel Journal* (London, 1896). Advert in Walsh, *The Dogs of the British Isles*.

58 One example was the breeding of 'noseless' spaniels. See Judith Lytton, *Toy Dogs and their Ancestors* (London, 1911); *Animals' Guardian*, vol. II, 11 August 1892, p. 137.

59 Secord, *Dog Painting*, pp. 251, 500. The ears of dogs bred for the fighting ring were originally cropped to prevent dogs having bits of the other dog to grasp. Victoria's stance was also endorsed by Edward, Prince of Wales, who wrote to the Kennel Club expressing his abhorrence at this particular maltreatment of dogs. When Edward became king he also abolished the royal bloodhounds and the hunting of tame deer – but continued hunting.

60 *Notable dogs*.

61 *Notable dogs*, p. 184.

62 Charles Lamb, 'A complaint on the decay of beggars in the metropolis', *The Essays of Elia* (London, 1883), p. 159.

63 *Mayhew's London*, p. 230.

64 George Augustus Sala, *Twice Round the Clock* (London, 1859), pp. 160–1. Dogs were often sent to France until a sufficient reward was raised for their return (Youatt, *The obligation and extent*, p. 170).

65 Dog carts had been abolished in the London area before the rest of the country through a clause in the Metropolitan Police Act of 1839. *Thoughts on the established church*, p. 33; *The Voice of Humanity*, vol. III, 1833, pp. 184–5; Turner, *All Heaven in a Rage*, pp. 149–51.

66 *Mayhew's London*, pp. 239–40; Ouida, *Puck* (London, 1870), vol. I, pp. 168ff.

67 *The Leisure Hour*, p. 593. Bulldogs continued to be kept for rat-killing matches. *Mayhew's London*, p. 417.

68 Samuel Smiles, *Duty with Illustrations of Courage, Patience, and Endurance* (London, 1880), pp. 366ff.

69 Gelert was the dog and Beddgelert the place, meaning Gelert's grave.

70 For example, *The Grave of Gelert* (London, 1849), p. 36.

71 Ibid., p. 36.

72 William Robert Spencer, 'Beth Gêlert or the grave of the greyhound', *Poems* (London, 1811), p. 85.

73 David E. Jenkins, *Bedd Gelert. Its facts, fairies and folk-lore* (Portmadoc, 1899), p. 71.

74 Rt Hon. W. R. Spencer, *Gelert's grave or Llewelyn's Rashness – a ballad* (Carnarvon, 1840).

75 Jenkins, *Bedd Gelert*, p. 71.

76 Dogs of miners in South Yorkshire, for example, were being sold cheaply or given away as their owners could not afford the dog tax. *The Sportsman's Journal and Fanciers Guide*, 25 January 1879, p. 8.

77 RSPCA, *Claims of Animals* (London, 1875) p. 46. See too the work of George Watts, including his bronze sculpture of Tennyson and his wolfhound Kerenina outside Lincoln Cathedral. A plaster cast is also on show at the wonderful Watts gallery at Compton near Guildford. Elizabeth Hutchings, *Discovering the Sculptures of George Frederick Watts* (Hunnyhill, 1994], pp. 9ff; Hester Thackeray Fuller, *Three Freshwater Friends. Tennyson, Watts, and Mrs Cameron* (Newport, Isle of Wight, 1992), p. 24.

78 Henry T. Hutton, *The True Story of Greyfriars Bobby* (Edinburgh, 1903).

79 Thanks to Brenda Duddington for this information and photographs of his grave and statue.

80 'Dogs at funerals', *Animals' Guardian*, vol. III, no. 12, September 1893, p. 203.

81 Sims, 'Told to the Missionary' in Suckling, *The Humane Educator*, pp. 308–10.

82 *An appeal for the home for lost and starving dogs by a member of the society* (London, 1861), p. 6. The home had started in Holloway in north London, the up-and-coming suburb where the fictional Pooters lived, before moving to Battersea.

83 Costelloe, *Battersea Dogs' Home*, pp. 18–19; subscription list in RSPCA pamphlet; Earl of Harrowby, *Our Moral Relation to the Animal Kingdom* (London, 1862).

84 Costelloe, *Battersea Dogs' Home*, pp. 21–2.

85 See in particular the publications of Jane Webb Loudon on women's role in maintaining family pets – and the garden.

86 Robert Humphreys, *Sin, Organized Charity and the Poor Law in Victorian England* (Basingstoke, 1995). By the late nineteenth century Louisa Hubbard estimated that at least 20,000 salaried and half a million women volunteers were at work with the homeless rootless and 'handicapped'. Judith Walkowitz, *City of Dreadful Delight. Narratives of Sexual Danger in Late Victorian London* (London, 1992) pp. 53–4.

87 Humphreys, *Sin, Organized Charity*, pp. 57–8.

88 Ibid., p. 54.

89 Costelloe, *Battersea Dogs' Home*, p. 19.

90 Frances Power Cobbe, *The Confessions of a Lost Dog Reported by her Mistress* (London, 1867).

91 Charles Dickens, 'Two dog shows' in *All the year round*, 2 August 1862, as quoted in Costelloe, *Battersea Dogs' Home*, p. 29.

92 Ibid., p. 31.

93 Costelloe, *Battersea Dogs' Home*, p. 50.

94 Battersea Dogs' Home, *The Dogs' Home*, p. 8.

95 Gareth Stedman Jones, *Outcast London*, 2nd edn (Harmondsworth, 1984), p. 12.

96 *Hydrophobia of 1889, its cause and cure: a plea to commute the sentences of six months written by a dog with a sore nose* (London, 1889), p. 3.

97 Legislation was enacted against dogs first under the Metropolitan Streets Act of 1867, which gave the Commissioner of Police power to muzzle dogs in the capital and then nationally in the case of rabies, then under the Dogs Act of 1871 and subsequently in the rabies orders of 1886 and 1887. Harriet Ritvo, *The Animal Estate: the English and other creatures in the Victorian age* (Harmondsworth, 1990), p. 190; John K. Walton, 'Mad dogs and Englishmen: the conflict over rabies in late Victorian England', *Journal of Social History*, vol. XIII, no. 2, 1979, pp. 227–9.

98 Walton, 'Mad dogs', p. 233.

99 In London alone there were over 830,000 dogs in 1867, rising to over 1,300,000 by 1878. Many, of course, were untaxed. Walton, 'Mad dogs', p. 220.

100 Perren, *Meat Trade*, pp. 65, 85-6. Perren estimates that from 1870 to 1873 12, 894 diseased and 9,146 healthy animals were killed as a result.

101 Judith Walkowitz, *Prostitution and Victorian Society: Women, Class, and the State* (Cambridge, 1980), pp. 71–2.

102 Surgeon-General C. A. Gordon MD CB, *Comments on the report of the Committee on M Pasteur's treatment of rabies and hydrophobia* (London, 1888), p. 92.

103 Walton, 'Mad dogs', p. 227; E. Douglas Hume, *Hydrophobia and the mad dog scare. Resumé of lecture to London and Provincial Anti-Vivisection Society* (London, 1919), p. 5; *Animals' Guardian*, vol. I, 12 September 1891, p. 133.

104 Walton, 'Mad dogs', p. 233.

105 Costelloe, *Battersea Dogs' Home*, pp. 55–7.

106 Letter of Charles Warren to Home Secretary Godfrey Lushington, 1886, as printed in Costelloe, *Battersea Dogs' Home*.

107 *The Voice of Humanity*, vol. I, 1830, p. 30; George Jesse, *Association for the protection of dogs and prevention of hydrophobia* (Macclesfield, n. d., c.1880s), leaflet re dogs bred for the pit most likely to have rabies and those who lived in captivity in kennels without exercise.

108 Letter to *The Morning Post*, 8 January 1886, as reprinted in *The Kennel Review*, vol. V, no. 44, March 1886, pp. 73–4; Elizabeth Lee, *Ouida: A Memoir* (London, 1914), p. 138.

109 *Hydrophobia of 1889*, p. 4.

110 It initially supported muzzling as it assumed packs of hounds and sporting dogs belonging to the rural aristocracy would be exempted, which indeed they were. Walton, 'Mad dogs', p. 231.

111 Editorial, *The Kennel Review*, vol. IV, no. 40, December 1885, p. 191.

112 National Canine Defence League, *Annual Report 1899–1900*, p. 11.

FOUR BRINGING LIGHT INTO DARK PLACES: ANTI-VIVISECTION AND
THE ANIMALS OF THE HOME

1   John Simon, *Experiments on Life. Address at the International Medical
    Conference, State Medicine Section* (London, 1882), pp. 17–18.
2   Much recent work on anti-vivisection has focused solely on analysing this
    within scientific parameters. Richard D. French, *Anti-vivisection and Medical
    Science*; Rupke, *Vivisection*.
3   Broome, *SPCA Founding Statement*, 1824
4   *London Medical Gazette*, vol. XX, 1837, pp. 804–8, as quoted in Diana
    Manuel, 'Marshall Hall (1790–1857): Vivisection and the Development of
    Experimental Physiology' in Rupke, *Vivisection*, p. 95.
5   *The Voice of Humanity*, 1827, pp. 13–14. See also Youatt's castigation of
    Magendie's experiments in *The obligation and extent*, p. 196.
6   Youatt (as above), p. 194–6.
7   Sharpey was disgusted, for example, to see Magendie make repeated incisions
    in the skins of an animal simply to demonstrate that pain was caused, which,
    Sharpey observed, scientists already knew. W. J. O'Connor, *Founders of
    British Physiology. A Biographical Dictionary, 1820–1885* (Manchester,
    1988), pp. 23, 78–85.
8   Patrizia Guarnieri, 'Moritz Schiff (1823 – 96): Experimental Physiology and
    Noble Sentiment in Florence' in Rupke, *Vivisection*, p. 105–24. Opposition
    was not exclusively British. Although the founding committee of the Societa
    Protettrice Degli Animali in Firenze included Richard Digby Beste, Misses
    Annie Powers and Bianca Light on its committee, many of its supporters
    were Italian countesses and *marchese* and its honorary president was Victor
    Emanuel, King of Italy (*Societa Protettrice Degli Animali in Firenze Resoconto
    dell' Assemblea Generale*, Florence, 1874).
9   Marshall Hall, 'On experiments in physiology, as a question of medical
    ethics', *The Lancet*, 1847, pp. 58–60, as printed in O'Connor, *Founders of
    British Physiology*, p. 18. See also Manuel, 'Marshall Hall' in Rupke,
    Vivisection, pp. 78–104.
10 Arthur Salusbury MacNulty, *A Biography of Sir Benjamin Ward Richardson*
    (London, 1950], pp. 35–42.
11 Ward Richardson's work in the interests of animals was recognized by the
    RSPCA; his opposition to capital punishment, and promotion of model abattoirs,
    healthy food, temperance and cycling was publicly acknowledged by his knight-
    hood in 1893 for services to humanitarian causes. But he took no part in the
    meetings of the Physiological Society which was set up in 1876, though invited
    to be a founder member. MacNulty, *A Biography*, pp. 35, 39, 58; O'Connor,
    Founders of British Physiology, pp. 66–7; Lady Burdon Sanderson and J. S. and
    E. S. Haldane, *Sir John Burdon Sanderson: a Memoir* (Oxford, 1911], p. 104.
12 Marshall, *Nature's Web*, pp. 319–32; Coral Lansbury, *The Old Brown
    Dog. Women, Workers, and Vivisection in Edwardian England* (Wisconsin,
    1985), pp. 155ff.
13 Much of Marshal Hall's work, for example, was upon frogs. O'Connor,
    Founders of British Physiology, p.17; Manuel, 'Marshal Hall' in Rupke,
    Vivisection, pp. 91ff.

14 RSPCA , *Domestic Animals*, p. vii.
15 Ibid., p. 60.
16 They often pushed the skewers of cooked horsemeat through the letter boxes of regular customers. C. H. Rolph, *London Particulars* (London, 1980), pp. 48–9.
17 *Mayhew's London*, pp. 127–8.
18 Fairholme and Pain, *A Century of Work*, p. 94.
19 Turner, *All Heaven in a Rage*, p. 220.
20 Frances Powers Cobbe, preface to Benjamin Bryan, ed., *Vivisectors' Directory* (London, 1884), p. iv.
21 Arthur de Noe Walker, *Address on Vivisection to the International Congress for the Prevention of Cruelty to Animals held in London 1874* (London, 1875), pp. 4–5; *The Zoophilist*, 1 December 1893, p. 194.
22 John Purcell Fitzgerald, *Barbarous Cruelty to Living Animals Made Legal in Great Britain* (London, 1877), p. 27.
23 Ouida, *Puck*, vols I–III. Also see Ouida's tome on the loyal Patrasche who follows the starving boy Nello to Antwerp Cathedral to die with him in another of her melodramas. Ouida, *A Dog of Flanders* (London, 1872).
24 W. Gordon Stables, *Sable and White: the autobiography of a show dog* (London, 1893), p. 263.
25 Frances Power Cobbe, *Mr Lowe and the Vivisection Act* (London, 1877) reprinted from *The Contemporary Review*, February 1877, p. 17.
26 Jonathan Crary, *Techniques of the Observer. On Vision and Modernity in the Nineteenth Century* (London, 1990), p. 76.
27 See Mary Ann Elston, *Gender, Medicine and Morality in the Late Nineteenth Century: a Study of the Anti-Vivisection Movement*, MA University of Essex, 1984, p.10. A recent visual depiction of the effect of this change of approach can be seen in the film *The Madness of King George*.
28 Julia Wedgwood, *Why Am I an Anti-Vivisectionist?* (London, 1910).
29 Louise Lind af Hageby and Liesa K. Schartau, *The Shambles of Science*, 5th edn (London, 1913), p. ix.
30 Lucy Bland, *Banishing the Beast* (London, 1995), pp. 53ff.
31 Sarah Grand, *The Beth Book* (1897, reprinted with introduction by Sally Mitchell, Bristol, 1994), p. 441–2. A later novel by Gertrude Colmore, *Priests of Progress*, (London, 1908) had the same narrative device of the quasi-Bluebeard motif. See Chapter 6.
32 Wilkie Collins, *Heart and Science* (1883, reprinted Gloucester, 1990), pp. 291, 324.
33 Jardine *et al.*, *Cultures of Natural History*; Linda E. Marshall, 'Astronomy of the invisible: contexts for Christina Rossetti's Heavenly Parables', *Women's Writing*, vol. II, no. 2, 1995, p. 175.
34 See Ch 1, pp. 15–17.
35 Turner, *All Heaven in a Rage*, p. 202. According to Mark Cartmill the animals were actually dissected in the cellar. Mark Cartmill, *A view to a death in the morning: hunting and nature through history* (Cambridge, MA, 1993).
36 George Eliot, letter to Lewes's son in 1859, as quoted in O'Connor, *Founders of British Physiology*, p.123. She also endowed a fellowship in physiology in Cambridge after Lewes's death. (Lansbury, *The Old Brown Dog*, p.153).
37 O'Connor, *Founders of British Physiology*, p. 216.

38 Convocation at Oxford passed by only 85 to 82 votes the expenditure of
    £10,000 on the erection of a physiological laboratory. O'Connor, *Founders of
    British Physiology*, pp. 144–5.

39 'I called on him in his house in Gordon Square. Our interview took place in the
    dining room, and when he realised that I thought of trying to do a little
    physiological work of an advanced kind, his response was prompt and singularly
    to the point. It consisted in leading me into a small back room full of apparatus,
    where a gentleman unknown to me was seated in what seemed to be an
    impenetrable jungle of wires.' F. Gotch, a fellow physiologist at University
    College, on his first meeting with Burdon Sanderson, as quoted in O'Connor,
    Founders of British Physiology, p. 143.

40 Presidential address of the Rt Rev. Bishop of Southwell, Dr Ridding, at 1893
    NAVS conference, *The Zoophilist*, 1 December 1893, p. 182.

41 Joseph H. Levy, *Vivisection and personal rights* (London, 1902), p. 19. See too
    Elizabeth Lee, *Ouida*, p. 324; George Bernard Shaw, 'Preface to *The Doctor's
    Dilemma*', *Prefaces* (London, 1934), pp. 261–2.

42 O'Connor, *Founders of British Physiology*, pp. 190–4; Sir James Crichton-
    Browne, *The Doctor Remembers* (London, 1938).

43 Edward Maitland, 'Public Control of Hospitals', *The Voice of Humanity*,
    June 1895, p. 31.

44 Ibid., pp. 5, 29–31.

45 Fitzgerald, *Barbarous Cruelty*, p. 47.

46 Levy, *Vivisection*, p. 19, cites an example of an experiment on a poor woman
    with breast cancer. The doctor performed a mastectomy and then transferred
    the cancer to the other breast.

47 Lee, *Ouida*, p. 324; Anna Davin, 'Imperialism and Motherhood', *History
    Workshop Journal*, 5, 1978, pp. 28–31, 50–1; Joanna Bourke,
    Dismembering the Male. Men's Bodies, Britain and the Great War (London,
    1996), pp. 171–6; Tim Marshall, *Murdering to Dissect*; V. A. C. Gattrell,
    The Hanging Tree. Execution and the English People 1770–1868 (Oxford,
    1994). This macabre practice still continues. See Derek Brown, 'Head case
    rights and wrongs', *Guardian*, 7 June 1997, p. 5, for information on
    experiments on the brain of Ronnie Kray.

48 Marion Lee, 'A woman to woman', *The Animals' Friend*, no. 1, June 1894, p. 6.

49 Mark Thornhill, *Experiments on Hospital Patients*. Speech to East Kent Anti-
    Vivisectionist Society, 1 May 1889 (London, 1889), p. 11.

50 Anna Kingsford, *Dreams and Dream Stories*, 2nd edn (London, 1888), pp. 44–5.

51 Frances Power Cobbe, *Light in Dark Places* (London, 1885), pp. 8–9. See Hilda
    Kean, '"The Smooth Cool Men of Science": the feminist and socialist response
    to vivisection', *History Workshop Journal*, 40, 1995, pp. 16–38.

52 Lind af Hageby and Schartau, *The Shambles of Science*, p. xii.

53 Frances Power Cobbe, *A Controversy in a Nutshell* (London, 1889), p. 1. The
    reference to horses is not an exaggeration; Burdon Sanderson vivisected horses
    in the Brown Institute in Battersea.

54 Frances Power Cobbe, *The Right of Tormenting. A Meeting of the Scottish
    Society for the Total Suppression of Vivisection* (London, 1881), p. 8.

55 Walkowitz, *City of Dreadful Delight*, pp. 73–6. Humphreys, *Sin, Organized
    Charity*; Nord, *Walking the Victorian Streets*.

56 Lind af Hageby and Schartau, *The Shambles of Science*, p. xii. See Chapter 6.

57 *Statement of the Society for the Protection of Animals Liable to Vivisection*, The
Royal Commission on Vivisection (London, 1876), pp. 5–7.

58 Turner, *All Heaven in a Rage*, pp. 207ff.

59 Ibid.

60 Victoria Street Society for Protection of Animals from Vivisection, *Memorial to
the Right Hon. W. E. Gladstone* (London, 1879), p. 1.

61 Nicolaas Rupke, 'Pro-Vivisection in England in the Early 1880s: Argument and
Motives' in Rupke, *Vivisection*, p. 188.

62 There was a crossover of individuals involved in a number of organizations
campaigning in the interests of animals which included Sidney Trist of the
London Anti-Vivisection Society and later the Battersea Dogs' Home
Committee, and Lord Llangattock, a supporter of the Metropolitan Drinking
Fountain and Cattle Trough Association and vice-president of the British Union
for the Abolition of Vivisection.

63 Lee Holcombe, *Wives and Property. Reform of the Married Women's Property
Law in Nineteenth-century England* (Toronto, 1983), p. 139.

64 Ibid., p. 123; Mary Anne Elston, 'Women and Anti-vivisection' in Rupke,
Vivisection, p. 263.

65 Josephine Butler, ed., *Woman's Work and Woman's Culture* (London, 1869).

66 Georgina Weldon, *The Ghastly Consequences of Living in Charles Dickens'
House* (London, 1880); Georgina Weldon, *How I escaped the Mad Doctors*
(London, 1879) ; Edward Greirson, *Storm Bird. The strange life of Georgina
Weldon* (London, 1959), pp. 123, 232; Judith Walkowitz, 'Science and the
Seance; Transgressions of Gender and Genre in Late Victorian London',
Representations, 22, Spring 1988, p. 8; Helen Nicolson, 'Urban Spectacle and
Street Theatre: Georgina Weldon's Campaigns for Lunacy Reforms', unpublished
paper presented to Women's History Network Conference, 1996.

67 Sandra Stanley Holton, *Suffrage Days. Stories from the Women's Suffrage
Movement* (London, 1996), pp. 28–9.

68 William Young, *Vaccination Tracts* (London, 1879), p. 29.

69 Simon, *Experiments on Life*, p. 18; See also Simon, *Report on the Contagious
Diseases Act* (Nottingham, 1871); Walkowitz, *Prostitution and Victorian
Society*, p. 86.

70 *Vaccination Inquirer*, vol. II, no.13, April 1880, p. 2.

71 Barbara Caine, *Victorian Feminists* (Oxford, 1993), p. 139; for Dr Mary
Scharlieb, the campaigner for women doctors, the issue was simply that she
found dissection difficult to do. Dr Mary Scharlieb, *Reminiscences* (1924),
pp. 61–2.

72 At a time when the government was starting to submit to pressure to relent on
its line on compulsory vaccination she called on it to admit it was wrong in this
regard, to continue with compulsion and to employ 'vaccination missionaries',
preferably women, who would teach others about the benefits of vaccination.
Letter from Mrs Garrett Anderson on vaccination, reprinted from *The Times* ,
10 January 1899.

73 Lansbury, *Old Brown Dog*, pp. 89–90.

74 She was also a committed opponent of racism in America, which she visited
several times, and was the first Welsh woman to qualify as a doctor. Onfel

Thomas, *Frances Elizabeth Hoggan 1843–1927* (Newport, 1971);
Elston, 'Women and Anti-vivisection' in Rupke, *Vivisection*, pp. 263, 277.

75   *Food Reform Magazine*, 5:1, July 1885, p. 9. In her pamphlet *On the advantages
of a vegetarian diet in workhouses and prisons* (London, 1883) Frances
Hoggan argues against the expensive luxury of animal flesh for the pauper who
typically is a sensual, self-indulgent creature [sic]: pp. 4, 7.

76   From letter of Robert Browning to Frances Power Cobbe as published in
Friends' Anti-Vivisection Association, *Quotes from Great Thinkers* (London,
1895), p. 8. For an account of Christina Rossetti's opposition to vivisection and
a poem written for an anti-vivisection bazaar, 'Pity the Sorrows of a Poor Dog',
see Frances Thomas, *Christina Rossetti* (London, 1994), pp. 300, 344–5.

77   Robert Browning, 'Old Tray', as published in Suckling, *The Humane
Educator*, p. 113.

78   See too Tennyson's opposition to vivisection as expressed in his poem 'The
Children's Hospital', critical of knife-wielding surgeons and vivisectors alike.
Anti-Vivisection Review, April–June 1914, p. 65.

79   Radical MPs signing the petition included P. A. Taylor, James Stansfeld, and
Jacob Bright. Victoria Street Society, *Memorial to W. E. Gladstone,* p. 2.

80   John Davidson, *The Testament of a Vivisector* (London, 1901), p. 18.

81   RSPCA, *Annual Report*, 1885, p. 5.

82   Fitzgerald, *Barbarous Cruelty.*

83   Simon, *Experiments on Life*, p. 12. He believed, erroneously, that the legislation
would lead either to the cessation of experiments in their entirety or to
clandestine activities.

84   Evidence to the Royal Commission, 1875, as printed in Simon, *Experiments on
Life*, note b, p.27.

85   Review of Ouida's *The New Priesthood* in *Shafts*, December 1893, p. 173.

86   Collins's preface to *Heart and Science*, pp. 2–3. Similar castigation was made of
those compulsorily vaccinating children: that they were not medical men, but
literally butchers. Women 'carried their babes to the vaccinator's *shambles* with
horror and detestation.' Young, *Vaccination Tracts*, p. 23.

87   Kean, '"The Smooth Cool Men of Science"'.

88   These included the London Anti-Vivisection Society, the Animal Defence and
Anti-Vivisection Society and various religious pressure groups such as the
Church Anti-Vivisection League.

89   Stephen Coleridge, *Memories* (London, 1914), pp. 234–5.

90   Church Anti-Vivisection League, *First Report* (London, 1890), p. 4.

91   'Against vivisection: verbatim report' (London, 1899), p. 25; Mrs Henry Lee,
London Anti-Vivisection Society, *AGM Report* (London, 1898), p. 25;
Charlotte Despard, speech at AGM of BUAV, *The Abolitionist*, 1 August 1917,
p. 203.

92   Collins's preface to *Heart and Science*, p. 2.

93   Stephen Paget, *The case against anti-vivisection* (London, 1904), p. 14.

94   *The Lancet*, 15 April 1882, as quoted in George Jesse, *Comments made by the
society for the abolition of vivisection at the Birmingham Medical Institute,*
9 March 1882, 5th edn (London, n. d.).

95   Henry Salt, *A Lover of Animals*, as printed in George Hendrick, *Henry Salt,
Humanitarian reformer and Man of Letters* (Illinois, 1977), p. 181.

96 Levy was the secretary of the Personal Rights Asociation and editor of its journal, *The Individualist*. The PRA was the successor to the feminist organization which had campaigned against the Contagious Diseases Acts. See Walkowitz, *Prostitution and Victorian Society*, p. 252; *Animals' Guardian*, vol. VI: 7, 14 July 1904, p. 89. The Battersea Hospital was founded in 1901.

FIVE DEAD ANIMALS: SPECTACLE AND FOOD

 1 Smiles, *Duty*, p. 355.
 2 Lord Erskine, 'The Liberated Robins' in Suckling, *The Humane Educator*, p. 22. See Chapter one.
 3 Pyne, *Microcosm*, p. 6, for a description and illustrations of songbirds caught in the environs of London using call birds and nets.
 4 'By the author of Domestic Pets' [Jane Loudon?] in *Bird-Keeping. A Practical Guide for the Management of Caged Birds* (London, 1869), p. 1; Loudon, *Domestic Pets*, p. 68. See too one of the first manuals of pigeon breeding: Anon., *How to Manage Pigeons* (London, 1890).
 5 Loudon, *Domestic Pets*, pp. 79, 83, 107–11.
 6 Harrison, *Peaceable Kingdom*, p. 88.
 7 Zoological Society Annual Report, 1890, as quoted in Vevers, *London's Zoo*, p. 129.
 8 Bostock, *Zoos*, pp. 37ff.
 9 J. R. V. Marchant, *Wild Birds Protection Acts 1880–1896* (London, 1897), pp. 23–6.
10 John Stuart Mill, *Programme of the Land Tenure Reform Association* (London, 1871), pp. 4–6.
11 William Thomson Hill, *Octavia Hill. Pioneer of the National Trust and Housing Reformer* (London, 1956), p. 148.
12 For the RSPB, reserves or sanctuaries for birds would be seen as more important than access to land for people. Anthony Taylor, '"Common stealers", Land Grabbers, and Jerry Builders. Space, Popular Radicalism and the Politics of Public Access in London 1848–80', *International Review of Social History*, LX, no. 3, December 1995, p. 402. See too Stephen Coleman, *Stilled Tongues. From Soapbox to Soundbite* (London, 1997).
13 Edward Abelson, ed., *A Mirror of England. An Anthology of the Writings of H. J. Massingham* (Devon, 1988); Patrick Wright, *The Village that died for England* (London, 1995), pp. 106–17.
14 Harrison Weir, 'Birds in the country and town', *Animals' Guardian*, vol. I: 11, August 1891, p. 121.
15 Turner, *All Heaven in a Rage*, p. 189; Smiles, *Duty*, p. 355.
16 H. E. Waring, 'A Girl's Confession to a Friend' in Suckling, *The Humane Educator*, pp. 321–2.
17 Letter from 'English Ladies', *The Times*, 28 December 1897.
18 Rev. H. Greene MA, *'As in a mirror.' An appeal to the ladies of England against the use of birds in millinery*, RSPB pamphlet no. 2, 1894, p. 8.
19 Booth, *Life and Labour. First series: Poverty. Trades of East London connected with poverty* (London, 1902), p. 373.

20 Ibid., p. 287.
21 Alexander, *Becoming a Woman*, pp. 27–33; Mearns, *London and its Teaming Toilers*, p. 17. It became a particular employment in the late nineteenth century for Jewish women. Indeed Booth argues that ostrich feather curling was one of the few jobs 'Jewesses' were employed to do (*Life and Labour*, p. 294).
22 SPB, *Feathered Women*, leaflet no. 10 (London, 1893); *Animals' Guardian*, vol. II: 12, September 1892, pp. 155–6.
23 SPB, *Feathered Women*.
24 Ibid.
25 (Mrs) E. Phillips, *Destruction of Ornamental Plumaged Birds* (London, 1894); see also Edith Carrington, 'Workers Without Wage', *Shafts*, August 1893, p. 117. In this article she also criticizes writers for always using the masculine pronoun to describe living creatures.
26 Edith Carrington, *The Extermination of Birds* (London, 1894), pp. 7–8.
27 Reginald Abbott, 'Birds don't sing in Greek: Virginia Woolf and "the Plumage Bill"' in Carol J. Adams and Josephine Donovan, eds, *Animals and Women* (North Carolina, 1995); Stephen Winsten, *Salt and his Circle* (London, 1951), p. 86.
28 Sydney Buxton, letter to *The Times,* 30 December 1897, p. 8.
29 His empathy towards birds apparently stemmed from a childhood incident when he had inadvertently killed a pet sparrow. The first painting he exhibited at the Royal Academy in 1837 was of a 'Wounded Heron' based on one such bird bought in a poulterers' shop. Wilfred Blunt, *England's Michelangelo* (London, 1975), p. 7; Ronald Chapman, *The Laurel and the Thorn* (London, 1945), p. 17.
30 Blunt, *England's Michelangelo*, p. 215.
31 Ibid. His concern for other animals included opposition to the docking of horses' tails on aesthetic and cruelty grounds, but he also wore a sealskin coat. Hutchings, *Discovering the Sculptures of George Frederick Watts*, p. 27.
32 Henry Salt, *Humanitarianism: Its general principles and progress* (London, 1893), pp. 21–2.
33 Fairholme and Pain, *A Century of Work*, p. 95.
34 The secretary was Mrs F. E. Lemon of Redhill in Surrey; the treasurer, Miss C. V. Hall of Croydon. *Occasional paper for circulation among fellow workers* [of the SPB], no. 1, 1893.
35 Marchant, *Wild Birds Protection Acts,* p. 33.
36 Ibid., pp. 26–33.
37 SPB, *Proceedings of the Second Annual Meeting* (n. d., 1894?), p. 3.
38 Lee, *Ouida*, p. 323.
39 In 1883, for example, Lord Randolph Churchill similarly declared that he found pigeon shooting the most repulsive and horrible sight possible to imagine. House of Commons Debates, 7 March 1883, col. 1684, as quoted in Harrison, *Peaceable Kingdom*, p. 90; *Food Reformers' Year Book*, 1907, p. 14.
40 SPB leaflets as discussed in *The Times*, 20 December 1894.
41 W. H. Hudson, *Lost British Birds* (London, 1894), p. 32.
42 Norman Gale, 'A Thrush in Seven Dials' in Bertram Lloyd, ed., *The Great Kinship. An Anthology of Humanitarian Poetry* (London, 1921), pp. 204–6.

43 Ernest Bell, *The Other Side of the Bars. The Case against the Caged Bird* (London, 1911), pp. 8–9.

44 Royal Commission on Handloom Weavers, Reports of Assistant Commissioners, part II, 1840, p. 216–7 as quoted in Kelly, *A History of Adult Education*, p. 105.

45 Anon., *How to Manage Pigeons* (London, 1890), pp. 1–9.

46 *Animals' Guardian*, vol. II: 4, January 1892, p. 43.

47 Raphael Samuel, '"Quarry roughs": life and labour in Headington Quarry, 1860–1920' in Raphael Samuel, ed., *Village Life and Labour* (London, 1975), p. 226.

48 *Mayhew's London*, p. 241–6; SPB, *Second Annual Meeting*, pamphlet no. 15, p. 2.

49 'Author of Domestic Pets', *Bird-Keeping*, p. 149.

50 *Animals' Guardian*, vol. III: 3, December 1892, p. 41.

51 Ibid.; Bell, *The Other Side of the Bars*, p. 9. Mayhew, pp. 228–9, 241, 246, 251.

52 Mayhew, pp. 251–4.

53 Booth, *In Darkest England*, p. 239.

54 John Mackenzie, *The Empire of Nature. Hunting, Conservation and British Imperialism* (Manchester, 1988), p. 41; Giles Waterfield, 'Art for the People' in Giles Waterfield, ed., *Art for the People: Culture in the Slums of Late Victorian Britain* (London, 1994), pp. 38ff.

55 Colonel Coulson speaking at meeting of SPB. *Second Annual Meeting*, p. 4.

56 See Jane Grigson, *Good Things* (Harmondsworth, 1973), pp. 114–15, for an account of the process of pigeon and lark plucking involving paper bags, water and much mess.

57 Fiona McCarthy, *William Morris* (London, 1994), pp. 402, 444–5.

58 Ralph Hodgson, 'Stupidity Street' in Lloyd, *The Great Kinship*, p. 222; *Mayhew's London*, p. 241; Smiles, *Duty*, pp. 358–9.

59 *Mayhew's London*, p. 246.

60 SPB, *Occasional Paper for circulation among fellow workers*.

61 'English Ladies', letter to *The Times*, 28 December 1897.

62 Wohl, *Endangered Lives*, p. 49.

63 Salt, *Flesh or Fruit?*, p. 9; Edmond J. Hunt, *The Necessity for Food Reform* (London, 1910), p. 18. The proprietors of the Wesley House Museum in City Road, London, seem unaware of his position, with their proud display of 'plastic' meat in Wesley's kitchen. See Chapter 1.

64 Colin Spencer, *The Heretic's Feast. A History of Vegetarianism* (London, 1994), p. 285.

65 F. Pierce, 'The Bitter Cry Answered', *Food Reform Magazine*, vol. III: no. 3, January–March 1884, pp. 85–8. The title imitated Andrew Mearn's *The Bitter Cry of Outcast London*.

66 Presidential address to the Vegetarian Society, Henry Amos, ed., *Food Reformers' Year Book [and Health Annual]*(London, 1909), p. 18.

67 Anna Kingsford, preface to *Dreams and Dream Stories*.

68 *Food Reform Magazine*, vol. I: no. 1, July 1881, p. 21.

69 *Shafts*, April 1895, p. 9. *Shafts*, the progressive journal 'for women and working-class men', identified itself explicitly with a range of animal – and human – issues, committing itself against slaughterhouses, inoculation, prison treatment, stag and fox hunting, prostitution, dangerous trades and all acts of

cruelty against 'women, children, the poor, every helpless human being, every animal that breathes and moves, every bird, fish and reptile'. *Shafts*, January 1897, p. 1. See too Kean, '"The Smooth Cool Men of Science"'.

70 Henry Amos, ed., *Vegetarian Year Book*, 1905.

71 Frances Hoggan, *On the advantages of a vegetarian diet in workhouses and prisons*, talk to Vegetarian Society (Norwich, 1883), p. 4; C. Delolme [sic] 'Poor children's dinners and school boards', *Food Reform Magazine*, vol. IV, no. 1, July–September 1884, p. 14.

72 *Food Reform Magazine*, vol. V, no. 1, July–September 1885, p. 3.

73 Walkowitz, *City of Dreadful Delight*, pp. 46ff. The first ABC tea shops opened in 1880 (Adburgham, *Shopping in Style*, p. 152).

74 Spencer, *Heretic's Feast*, p. 275.

75 Henry S. Salt, *Company I have Kept* (London, 1930), p. 136; Spencer, *Heretic's Feast*, pp. 291–2.

76 Advertisement in *Food Reformers' Year Book*, 1908, p. 10.

77 Advertisements in *Vegetarian Year Book*, 1906; and in *Shafts*, 28 January 1893, p. 207.

78 Charles W. Forward, *Food of the Future* (London, 1904), pp. 84–9; *Vegetarian Year Book*, 1907; Henry Light, *Vegetarian Athletics (What They Prove and Disprove)* (Manchester, n. d.).

79 Colin Spencer's assertion that the movement gave rise to Fabianism is too simple. Although Fabians were involved in food reform, the movement included those with a wide range of beliefs (Spencer, *Heretic's Feast*, p. 278).

80 Kingsford and Maitland were also influenced by Theosophy and supported the Humanitarian League. Newman was prominent in a number of causes including the Anti-Tobacco Society, anti-vivisection, temperance, anti-vaccination and opposition 'to all women's wrongs'. *Food Reform Magazine*, vol. IV, no. 2, October 1884, p. 35.

81 Florence was married to Charles Bramwell Booth, the son of the Salvation Army founder and subsequently the Salvation Army general. The Salvation Army promoted allotments and market gardens to produce a vegetable diet to complement their temperance regime. Bramwell Booth, *Echoes and Memories*, 2nd edn (London, 1928), pp. 117ff; Booth, *In Darkest England*, pp. 248–9; *Food Reformers' Year Book*, 1907, p. 11; Harrison, *Drink and the Victorians*, p. 152.

82 *Food Reformers' Year Book*, 1906, p. 11; 1909, p. 44.

83 National Food Reform Association, *Reasons for Food Reform. An Account of a Private Meeting Held at 54 Mount St, Grosvenor Square, London, February 26th 1908* (London, n. d., 1908?), pp. 23–5.

84 Edith Ward, 'The food question and Theosophy', *Food Reformers' Year Book*, 1907, p. 17.

85 *Food Reform Magazine*, vol. IV, no. 4, April–June 1885, pp. 97–9.

86 *Food Reform Magazine*, vol. II, no. 4, April–June 1883, p. 127; *Food Reform Magazine*, vol. I, no. 1, July–September 1881, p. 25.

87 *Food Reform Magazine*, vol. IV, no. 4, April–June 1885, p. 131.

88 Forward, *Food of the Future*, p. 97.

89 *Food Reformers' Year Book*, 1906, p. 6; *Humane Review*, April, 1905.

90 Rev. Charles Maurice Davies, *Heterodox London*, vol. II, 1874, pp. 285, 304.

91 H. G. Wells, *Ann Veronica* (1909, reissued London, 1984), p. 109.
92 Ibid., pp. 110–11.
93 Ibid., p. 111.
94 Winsten, *Salt and his Circle*, p. 94.
95 McCarthy, *William Morris*, p. 492.
96 Ella Wheeler Wilcox, 'The Voice of the Voiceless' in *Poems of Experience*, as printed in *Poems* (London n. d., 1913?), pp. 108–9.
97 Thomas Hardy, *The Mayor of Casterbridge* (1886, reprinted Harmondsworth, 1978), pp. 398–405. See also *Tess of the D'Urbevilles*, especially the scenes at Talbothay's dairy; and *The Return of the Native*, in particular the role of the reddleman, Diggory Venn.
98 Thomas Hardy, *Jude the Obscure* (1895, reprinted Oxford, 1985), p. 9. Such scenes are used to great effect in the recent film *Jude*. See contemporary enthusiastic review in *Shafts*, February 1896, p. 12. Apparently Hardy, who would be a supporter of the Slaughterhouse Reform Society, offered a copy of the pig-butchering scene to an animal rights journal for publication. Jonathan Rose, *The Edwardian Temperament 1895–1919* (Ohio, 1986), p. 64.
99 Julia Twigg, 'Vegetarianism and the meanings of meat' in Anne Murcott, ed., *The Sociology of Food* (Aldershot, 1983), p. 20.
100 *The Friend of the People*, 21 June 1851, p. 240; 5 July 1851, pp. 256–7; 12 July 1851, p. 266; 19 July 1851, p. 272–3; 26 July 1851, p. 282.
101 Editorial, *The Friend of the People*, 21 June 1851, p. 248.
102 Diana Orton, *Made of Gold: A biography of Angela Burdett-Coutts* (London, 1980), p. 210.
103 Wohl, *Endangered Lives*, p. 21.
104 Ibid., p. 33.
105 B. Boecker, 'Poisons of the Kitchen', *Food Reform Magazine*, vol. II, no. 3, December 1882, pp. 72–5; Harrison, *Drink and the Victorians*, p. 293.
106 Thomas Mansell, *Vegetarianism and Manual Labour* (London, 1907), p. 5.
107 Mary Dawtrey, 'Women as Food Reformers', *Food Reform Magazine*, vol. I, no. 3, January 1882, p. 89.
108 Booth, *Life and Labour*, p. 203. Sausages of this nature were particularly sold in Charterhouse Street near Smithfield.
109 Anne Hardy, *The Epidemic Streets. Infectious disease and the rise of preventive medicine 1856–1900* (Oxford, 1993), p. 287.
110 D. J. Oddy, 'Working-class diets in late nineteenth-century Britain', *Economic History Review*, Second series, no. 23, 1990, p. 321.
111 In 1872 Dr Hassall, a pioneer investigator in food adulteration, had noted that 50 per cent of bread he examined had been thus polluted, which both inhibited digestion and lowered the nutritional value of other food. Wohl, *Endangered Lives*, p. 53.
112 *Food Reform Magazine*, vol. IV, no. 1, July–September 1884, p. 13; Mansell, *Vegetarianism*, p. 5.
113 Richardson also drew attention to the practice of working long hours in heat with lack of sleep. Benjamin Ward Richardson, *On the Healthy Manufacture of Bread* (London, 1884), pp. 14, 77.
114 Spencer, *Heretic's Feast*, p. 278.
115 Dawtrey, 'Women as Food Reformers', p. 134.

116 Perren, *Meat Trade*, pp. 85, 95.

117 Ibid., p. 217; Salt, *Flesh or Fruit?*, p. 25.

118 I. M. Greg and S. H. Towes, *Cattle Ships and our Meat Supply* (London, 1894).

119 A very long-handled hammer with a heavy head which ended in a hollow steel spike.

120 Rev. John Verschoyle, *Slaughterhouse Reform* (London, n.d.), p. 6.

121 Ibid.

122 Ernest Bell, *The Humane Slaughtering of Animals* (London, 1904), p. 5.

123 Humanitarian League, *Second Annual Report*, 1892. A petition had been presented by the Humanitarian League to the LCC to this effect.

124 By 1895 there were still 700 slaughterhouses in London alone. Perren, *Meat Trade*, p. 151; Bell, *Humane Slaughtering*; MacNulty, *Ward Richardson*, p. 58.

125 Salt, *Flesh or Fruit?*, p. 20; MacNulty, *Ward Richardson*, p. 58.

126 Interview with Joseph Oldfield, *The Animals' Friend*, November 1894, p. 62.

127 Thomas Hardy, 'Compassion', 1924, in *The Collected Poems* (London, 1930), p. 783. Correspondence of Thomas Hardy to Florence Henniker, 22 August 1911, in Michael Millgate, ed., *Thomas Hardy. Selected Letters* (Oxford, 1990), pp. 91–2, 244; John Galsworthy, *For Love of Beasts* (London, 1912); Galsworthy, *Treatment of Animals* (London, 1913).

128 Charles Reinhardt, *A plea for the humane slaughter of animals for food*, Council of Justice for Animals (London, n. d.), 1911.

129 Chairman of the Admiralty Committee on the Humane Slaughtering of Animals, as quoted in Bell, *Humane Slaughtering* (opposite title page).

130 Charles W. Forward, *The Reform of the Slaughterhouse* (London, 1913), p. 13.

131 Appendix by Ernest Bell, 'A Visit to Deptford' in Forward, *Reform of the Slaughterhouse*, p. 18; Verschoyle, *Slaughterhouse Reform*, p. 5. See pp. 139ff.

132 Galsworthy, *Treatment*, p. 7.

133 Gertrude Colmore, *The Angel and the Outcast* (London, 1907), pp. 98–103; 207–11.

134 Booth, *Life and Labour*, p. 196.

135 Bell, *Humane Slaughtering*, p. 6.

136 Steele, *Turning the Tide*, pp. 97–8.

137 As quoted in *The Voice of Humanity*, vol. II, no. 32, October 1897, p. 74.

138 Steele, *Turning the Tide*, p. 97.

139 Margaret McMillan, *The Life of Rachel McMillan* (London, 1927), pp. 103–4, as quoted in Carolyn Steedman, *Childhood, Culture and Class in Britain. Margaret McMillan 1860–1931* (London, 1990), p. 115.

140 McCarthy, *William Morris*, p. 475.

141 Winsten, *Salt and his Circle*, p. 65; Aveling took over the translation on Joynes's death. Warren Sylvester Smith, *The London Heretics 1870–1914* (London, 1967), p. 76.

142 J. L. Joynes, 'Law for the People', *Food Reform Magazine*, vol. II, no. 3, December 1882, pp. 84–6.

143 Ibid., p. 86.

144 *Food Reform Magazine*, vol. III, no. 3, January–March 1884, pp. 68–70.

145 SDF, *Conference Report* (London, 1895); ILP, *Annual Conference Report* (London, 1895), p. 23.

146 Winsten, *Salt and his Circle*, p. 64.

147 Obituary of Isabella Ford, *The Animals' Defender and Zoophilist*, vol. XLIV, no, 5, September 1924; June Hannam, *Isabella Ford* (Oxford, 1989), p. 73.
148 Isabella Ford, *Women and Socialism* (ILP, 1907), pp. 7, 11.
149 Bill Lancaster, *Radicalism Co-operation and Socialism, Leicester working-class politics 1860–1906* (Leicester, 1987) p. 77.
150 Salt, *Humanitarianism*, p. 15.
151 Ibid., p. 3.
152 Edward Carpenter, *My Days and Dreams* (London, 1916), p. 240.
153 *The Voice of Humanity*, no. 13, March 1896, p. 101.
154 Ibid.
155 Other signatories included the feminist Elizabeth Wolstenholme Elmy; William Morris's daughter, May Morris Starling; Mrs Bramwell Booth; Thomas Burt, the Northumberland miners' MP and anti-vaccinationist campaigner; Joseph Levy of the PRA; and G. W. Foote, the president of the Secular Society.

SIX NEW CENTURY: NEW CAMPAIGNS

1 Salt, *Humanitarianism* (London, 1893), p. 26.
2 Carpenter, *Days and Dreams* , p. 240.
3 Edward Carpenter, ed., *Forecasts of the coming century by a decade of writers* (London, 1897).
4 Alfred Russell Wallace, *My Life* (London, 1905), vol. II, pp. 351–3; Edward Carpenter and Edward Maitland, *Vivisection* (London, 1893).
5 J. Howard Moore, *The Universal Kinship* (London, 1906), p. 329; Henry S. Salt, *Seventy Years among Savages*, (London, 1921), p. 133.
6 Annie Besant, *The Changing World* (London, 1909), pp. 122–3.
7 Rolph, *London Particulars*, pp. 160–1.
8 The organization still exists, now called the Blue Cross. Our Dumb Friends' League (ODFL), *Second Annual Report*, 1898–99, p. 5. In 1902 it lobbied successfully on behalf of a driver sacked by Carter Patterson for watering his horse at a trough against company regulations. (ODFL, *Sixth Annual Report*, 1902–03, p. 25).
9 ODFL, *Second Annual Report*, p.18; *Fourth Annual Report*, 1900–01, p. 14.
10 It also rewarded organizations such as the Metropolitan Drinking Fountain and Cattle Trough Association and the Animals' Branch of the Humanitarian League.
11 ODFL, *Second Annual Report*, p. 5.
12 Obituary for John Rickwood, *Cab Trade Record*, September 1901, p. 5; story of closure of water troughs, *Cab Trade Record*, October 1903, p. 11; Ned Dyke, 'Labour Day', *Cab Trade Record*, May 1902, p. 6.
13 NCDL, *Annual Report*, 1911, p. 39.
14 *Animals' Guardian*, vol. V, no. 11, November, 1903.
15 Battersea Dogs' Home, *The Dogs' Home*, p. 3.
16 See a print of the Webbs at home with their dog at their feet. Original in the LSE, copy in Ruskin Hall, Ruskin College, Oxford. Costelloe, *Battersea Dogs' Home*, p. 92; National Food Reform Association, *Reasons for Food Reform* (London, 1908). See too Angela V. John, *Elizabeth Robins: Staging a Life*

(London, 1995), p. 198, and Marie Mulvey Roberts, 'Militancy, Masochism or Martyrdom? The Public and Private Prisons of Constance Lytton' in Sandra Stanley Holton and Jane Purvis, eds, *Votes for Women* (London, forthcoming).

17 Sylvia Pankhurst, *Suffragette Movement*, pp. 189–200.

18 Christabel Pankhurst, *Unshackled* (1959, reissued London, 1987), p. 43.

19 O'Connor, *Founders of British Physiology*, p. 79.

20 The women had registered to study at the London School of Medicine for women and because women were unable to receive training in vivisection at the women's college they attended the prestigious UCL. Catriona Blake, *The Charge of the Parasols: Women's Entry to the Medical Profession* (London, 1990), p. 174.

21 She also wrote an ironically titled pamphlet for the WFL after the vote was partially won. Louise Lind af Hageby, *Unbounded Gratitude! Women's Right to Work* (London, 1920).

22 Louise Lind af Hageby, 'Women as Humanitarians', address given to Humanitarian League AGM, *The Humanitarian*, vol. V., June 1910, p. 45.

23 Louise Lind af Hageby, *The New Morality. An inquiry into the ethics of anti-vivisection* (London, 1911), p. 14.

24 Ibid., p. 12.

25 Shaw, *Prefaces*, p. 257. *The Doctor's Dilemma*, originally published in 1913, contains specific criticism of vivisection, p. 99.

26 See for example the work of Frances Power Cobbe and Josephine Butler against vaccination and the Contagious Diseases Acts. Holton, *Suffrage Days*, p. 46.

27 Hageby Trial Papers. Box 1, Day 5, p. 85.

28 *The Voice of Humanity*, 1827, pp. 8, 42.

29 Hageby and Schartau, *The Shambles of Science*, p. 19.

30 *Animals' Guardian*, vol. V, no. 12, December 1903, p. 144; *The Animals' Defender and Zoophilist*, vol. XLI, no. 1, May 1921, pp. 1–2. The original libel action was against Stephen Coleridge of the NAVS who read out from the account with Hageby and Schartau's permission at a public meeting, with the full knowledge that this was likely to lead to such action.

31 Hageby and Schartau, *The Shambles of Science*, p. 19.

32 Ernest Starling, 'On the use of dogs in scientific experiments', Wellcome Institute Archives, n.d., SA/RDS G1/21–36.

33 Hageby Trial Papers. Box 4, Day 4; Church Anti-Vivisection League, *The Royal Commission on Vivisection 1906–8* (London, 1910). Hageby won in a further libel action, against Stephen Paget, in 1911 who had stated erroneously that *The Shambles of Science* had been impounded by the court. He was obliged to apologize and pay a sum into the court (*Anti-Vivisection Review*, vol. II, 1911, p. 139).

34 *The Animals' Defender and Zoophilist*, vol. XLI, no. 1, May 1921, pp. 1–2.

35 Minutes of Research Defence Society, 31 March 1908, Wellcome Institute Archives SA/RDS C1.

36 Letter to Florence Henniker, 13 September 1903, in Millgate, *Thomas Hardy*, p. 160.

37 *Animals' Guardian*, vol. VI, no. 18, August 1904, p. 97.

38 Sir Edward Sharpey-Schafer, *History of the Physiological Society during its first fifty years 1876–1926* (London, 1927), pp. 40, 64.

39 Research Defence Society, *Minutes Book*, first meeting 27 January 1908ff. Wellcome Institute, SA/RDS C1.

40   *The Young Socialist*, August 1906, March 1910. For further information on the
     Socialist Sunday Schools see Hilda Kean, *Challenging the State? The socialist
     and feminist educational experience 1900–1930* (Brighton, 1990), pp. 54–77.
41   Julia Goddard, 'The Animals on Strike' in Suckling, *The Humane Educator*,
     p. 247. By 1885 nearly a hundred RSPCA Bands of Mercy for children existed
     nationally (Kean, '"The smooth cool men of science"', p. 21).
42   Edith Carrington, *The Animals on Strike* (London, 1895), pp. 28ff.
43   Stephen Coleridge, *Step by Step. A Reply to Frances Power Cobbe* (London,
     1898), p. 4.
44   *The Animals' Defender and Zoophilist*, vol. LVI, no. 1, March 1936; Minutes
     Book of RDS, 5 January 1909, Wellcome Institute Archives SA/RDS C1.
45   *Animals' Guardian*, vol. II, 10 July 1892, p. 121.
46   *The Anti-Vivisection Review*, vol. IV, nos 3 and 4, 1913, p. 298; *The Anti-
     Vivisection Review*, vol. II, November–December 1911, p. 60; Minutes of the
     Animal Defence and Anti-Vivisection Society, 24 January 1912; George
     Greenwood, *Sport*, a paper read before the Animal Protection Congress at the
     Caxton Hall, London, 9 July 1909 (London, 1910). He also introduced a
     Humane Slaughter Bill in 1911.
47   The legislation made it an offence to cruelly beat, kick, ill-treat, override, overload,
     torture, infuriate or terrify an animal. Fines were increased to up to £25 and
     prison sentences to 6 months. Those guilty of a second offence risked having
     the animal they owned confiscated. Horses specifically benefited. No longer
     could a knacker act as a horse dealer and thereby sell on horses sold to him for
     slaughter. Horses were forbidden to be killed within sight of another horse (*The
     Anti-Vivisection Review*, vol. II, November–December 1911, p. 60).
48   A number of private members' bills to exempt dogs were initiated from 1905.
     See Ballard, *A Dog is for Life*, pp. 10–15. Supporters of the bill included
     Thomas Burt, Henry Chancellor, Will Crooks, Keir Hardie, Arthur Henderson,
     Frederick Jowett, J. Ramsay MacDonald and Philip Snowden. *The Anti-
     Vivisection Review*, vol. V, April–June 1914, pp. 56–7.
49   Letter to Florence Henniker, 17 December 1912, in Millgate, *Thomas Hardy*,
     pp. 261–2.
50   *Cab Trade Record*, October 1901, p. 2.
51   Leonard Petts, *The Story of Nipper and the His Master's Voice Picture Painted
     by Francis Barraud* (Christchurch, 1973). The painting was undertaken around
     1899 and first used in an amended form (the original has the dog looking at a
     phonograph instead of a gramophone) from January 1900.
52   Postcard in possession of author. Lisa Tickner, *A Spectacle of Women. Imagery
     of the Suffrage Campaign 1907–14* (London, 1987).
53   *Sunday Times*, 19 June 1910, as quoted in Tickner, *Spectacle*, pp. 297, 112.
54   Tickner, *Spectacle*, pp. 209–11.
55   A. J. R., ed., *The Suffrage Annual and Women's Who's Who* (1913), p. 145.
56   Tickner, *Spectacle*, pp. 138–40.
57   *Animals' Guardian*, vol. V, no. 12, December 1903.
58   *Animals' Guardian*, vol. V, no. 10, October 1903. For a discussion of this
     popular image see William Schupbach, 'A select iconography of animal
     experiment' in Rupke, *Vivisection*, pp. 351–3.
59   As reproduced in Ballard, *A Dog is for Life*, pp. 4, 9–11.

60   Minutes of the RDS, 17 February 1914.

61   Ballard, *A Dog is for Life*, pp. 1–3.

62   Hageby Trial Papers, Day 3, p. 47.

63   Ibid., p. 50. The same story seems to have been used by PRA comparing patients pleading with doctors. See Levy, *Vivisection*, p. 20.

64   NCDL, *Annual Report*, 1910, p. 105. The engraving was by Charles John Tomkins after an original painting by John McLure Hamilton. See William Schupbach, 'Select Iconography' in Rupke, *Vivisection*, pp. 350–1.

65   Hageby Trial Papers, Day 3, p. 3; Minutes of RDS, 21 February 1910, 23 December 1912. Wellcome Institute.

66   RDS, *The facts of the case* (London, May 1912). Wellcome Institute.

67   Minutes of RDS, 22.3.1909; 14.6.1909; 5.7.1909; 27.2.1911. Wellcome Institute.

68   *The Anti-Vivisection Review*, vol. I, pp. 48–9.

69   Statement made in particular about the visual cartoons in *The Anti-Vivisection Review*. Hageby Trial Papers, Day 5, p. 55.

70   *The Anti-Vivisection Review*, vol. I, p. 5.

71   Minutes of RDS, 20.2.1911. Wellcome Institute.

72   Louise Lind af Hageby, ed., *The Animals' Cause. International Anti-Vivisection Congress 6–10 July 1909* (London, 1909).

73   *The Voice of Humanity*, vol. V, no. 99, May 1910, pp. 33–40.

74   Stephen Paget, *Sir Victor Horsley* (London, 1919), p. 205.

75   Sylvia Pankhurst, *Suffragette Movement*, pp. 341.

76   Paget, *Horsley*, p. 195; *The Anti-Vivisection Review*, vol. II, 1910, pp. 116–7.

77   *The Anti-Vivisection Review*, vol. II, 1910, p. 139.

78   Ibid., image on opposite page. Horsley was defeated by Philip Magnus who was himself a supporter of the RDS, though not personally engaged in such acts.

79   Frances Power Cobbe, 'Report of NAVS conference', *The Animals' Defender and Zoophilist,* Supplement 1, December 1893, p. 199.

80   Ballard, *A Dog is for Life*, p. 13.

81   Lansbury, *Old Brown Dog*, pp. 14ff.

82   By the time the statue was erected Burns had changed his position. He became the local government minister in the Liberal Government of 1905 and opposed vivisection. Lansbury, *Old Brown Dog*, pp. 13ff.

83   Ibid., p. 42.

84   Ibid, pp. 16, 17–22.

85   *The Anti-Vivisection Review*, vol. I, pp. 275, 284–90; Lansbury, *Old Brown Dog*, p. 21. A new statue with the same inscription is now in the Woodland Walk in Battersea Park.

86   Named after Thomas Brown who had bequeathed money for the study and treatment of animals and birds (not in memory of the animals who would die there). O'Connor, *Founders of British Physiology*, p. 136.

87   A vegetarian cottage hospital was also set up in Loughton, on the outskirts of east London, run by Joseph Oldfield, in which 'no member of the fellowship of higher animals' was destroyed (*The Voice of Humanity*, April 1896, p. 112). St Francis Hospital, New Kent Road, was also an anti-vivisection hospital (see Lansbury, *Old Brown Dog*, p. 19).

88   The hospital refused to employ anyone who practised vivisection; it prohibited

anti-toxic serums for treating diphtheria, and discouraged the use of vaccines on the grounds that they originated from Pasteur's experiments on animals. Report of Sir Cooper Perry and Sir Frederick Fry, July 1922, *Records of Battersea General Hospital.*

89 These included Lord Llangattock, Viscount Harberton, Countess de Noailles and a number of women including Miss Bell, Miss Vernon Wentworth and Miss Grove Grady. (King Edward Fund leaflet, 1903, in *Records of Battersea General Hospital.*

90 Minutes of the Management Committee, 1905–1914, *Records of Battersea General Hospital*; Colmore, *Priests of Progress*, pp. 99, 382, 386.

91 Funding Leaflet issued 1903, in *Records of Battersea General Hospital.*

92 *The Anti-Vivisection Review*, vol. V, 2, April–June 1914, pp. 82–3.

93 Stephen Coleridge, *Vivisection. A Heartless Science* (London, 1916), p. 15.

94 Lady Augusta Fane, 'Hunting from a woman's point of view' in Alfred E. T. Watson, ed., *English Sport* (London, 1903), p. 33.

95 *The Animals' Friend*, no. 7, 1839, pp. 16–17

96 Greenwood, *Sport*, p. 6. See too Linda Colley, *Britons*, pp. 170–3.

97 Cunningham, *Leisure*, p. 48; Mackenzie, *Empire of Nature*, p. 22.

98 *New Sporting Magazine*, May 1831, as quoted in Cunningham, *Leisure*, p. 48.

99 Anthony Vandervell and Charles Coles, *Game and the English Landscape. The influence of the chase on sporting art and scenery* (London, 1980), pp. 96–7.

100 See pp. 121ff. Mackenzie, *Empire of Nature*, p. 18.

101 Humanitarian League, *Memorial promoted by the Humanitarian League Sports Department 27 January 1900* (London, 1900).

102 Humanitarian League, *Savage Sport at Eton* (London, 1909), p. 7. Henry Salt was a former master at Eton.

103 Arthur E. T. Watson, *King Edward VII as a Sportsman* (London, 1911), pp. v, 321.

104 Kenneth Clark, *Animals and Men*, p. 194.

105 Elizabeth Mavor, *The Ladies of Llangollen. A study in romantic friendship* (London, 1971); Lillian Faderman, *Surpassing the Love of Men* (London, 1985), pp. 74–7.

106 Stephen Kern, *Eyes of Love* (London, 1996), pp. 134, 263.

107 Controller of the Money Order Office, London, September 1868, as reproduced in Post Office Archives, *Cats on the Payroll*, Information Sheet no. 4, p. 1. Thanks to Nick Baxter for this reference. A similar practice continues today at the British Museum.

108 W. Gordon Stables, *Cats, Their Points and Characteristics* (London, 1876), p. 340; advertisement for Spratt's cat food in Stables, *Cats*, p. viii.

109 Stables, *Cats*, p. 125.

110 *The Voice of Humanity*, vol. II, 1830, p. 47. See Chapter 2.

111 Bennett, *London and Londoners*, p. 39.

112 Fairholme and Pain, *A Century of Work*, pp. 84–5.

113 Stables, *Cats*, p. 348.

114 Fairholme and Pain, *A Century of Work*, p. 60.

115 Booth, *Life and Labour*, p. 83. C. H. Rolph, *London Particulars*, pp. 48–9.

116 Llewellyn Smith and Vaughan Nash, *The Story of the Dockers' Strike* (London, 1896), p. 84, as quoted in Ken Coates and Tony Topham, *The Making of the Labour Movement* (Nottingham, 1994), p. 57.

117   The (modern) windows are designed by John Hayward. See too Tracey
        Trimmer, *Always Ready, Always Willing. A History of the Oxford City Fire
        Brigade*, unpublished thesis, Ruskin College (Oxford, 1996), for an account of
        animals in the Royal Navy, specially Wunpound 'the able seacat', buried with
        full military honours at sea, and of dogs in the Fire Service.

118   Robert Tressell, *The Ragged-Trousered Philanthropists* (1955, reissued
        London, 1967, with introduction by Alan Sillitoe), p. 68. Contrast this
        behaviour with that in Mary Gaskell's *North and South*, 1855, in which an
        elderly parishioner in Helston describes the burning alive of a cat according to
        country superstitions (Lansbury, *Old Brown Dog*, pp. 35–6).

119   Hageby and Schartau, *The Shambles of Science*, pp. 109ff.

120   Edith Carrington, *The Cat. Her place in society and treatment* (London,
        1896), p. 70.

121   *Animals' Guardian*, vol. VI, no. 7, 14 July 1904; Carrington, *The Cat*, back
        cover. There was also a home for lost and starving cats in Haverstock Hill: see
        pp. 175–6.

122   ODFL, *Fifth Annual Report*, 1901–2, p. 39.

123   ODFL, *Eighth Annual Report*, 1904–5, p. 104. Committee members included
        the cat artist Louis Wain.

124   *Cab Trade Record*, February 1903, p. 9.

125   Bessie Rayner Parkes, *The History of our Cat, Aspasia* (London, 1856), p. 5.

126   Anon., *Autobiography of a Cat; of the Cream of Cats, too* (London, 1864),
        p. 27 The cat flees from a vivisector and is saved by a carter.

127   Margaret and Mary Thompson, *They couldn't stop us! Experiences of Two
        (Usually Law-Abiding) Women in the Years 1909–1913* (Ipswich, 1957),
        pp. 16, 22. On her return home from hunger strike she received an enthusiastic
        welcome from the same cat.

128   Letter to Millicent Fawcett, 30 November 1906, in Millgate, *Thomas
        Hardy*, p. 197. Fawcett, of the constitutionalist wing of the suffrage
        movement, declined to publish his statement on the grounds that the public
        was not ready for it.

129   It centred on an article written by Saleeby referring to the earlier *The Shambles
        of Science*. See GC 89 Box 1 in the Wellcome Institute for a full transcript of
        the file.

130   *The Anti-Vivisection Review*, vol. IV, nos 5 and 6, p. 326.

131   NCDL, *Annual Report*, 1910, p. 22.

132   *Vaccination Inquirer*, vol. XVIII, no. 210, September 1896, p. 77.

133   Liberal Party Publicity Department, *The government's record 1906–7.
        Two years of Liberal administration and Liberal legislation* (London, 1907),
        p. 85. Moreover, the new Liberal government had also introduced legislation
        to counter food contamination and strengthen the law on the sanitation of
        buildings and infectious diseases under the Public Health Act of 1907.
        Arthur Sherwell, *Two years of Liberal government 1906–7* (London, 1908),
        p. 30.

SEVEN GREYFRIARS BOBBY AND BLACK BEAUTY GO TO WAR

1   Annette Joyce, ' The gunner's story' in Lady Smith-Dorrien, ed., *A Book of Poems for the Blue Cross Fund* (London, 1917), pp. 53–6.
2   Sydney Galvayne, *War Horses Present and Future* (London, 1902).
3   The effects of transportation upon horses outside war had also been pursued by the RSPCA and ODFL in their respective campaigns against the export of live horses in poor conditions to the Continent for meat. See E. G. Fairholme, *The RSPCA and the Decrepit Horse Traffic to the Continent* (London, 1910); ODFL, *Thirteenth Annual Report*, 1910, pp. 30–1, *Twelfth Annual Report* 1909, p. 34. The *Daily Mail* also publicized the traffic in horses.
4   Ernest Bell and Harold Baillie Weaver, *Horses in Warfare* (London, 1912), pp. 4–6.
5   67 per cent of the horses and 35 per cent of the mules died. Death was frequently due to glanders, epizootic lymphangitis and mange. Brigadier J. Clabbyd, *A History of the Royal Army Veterinary Corps 1919–1961* (London, 1963), pp. 13–14. See too F. M. L. Thompson, 'Horses and Hay in Britain 1830–1918' in Thompson, *Horses in European Economic History.*
6   Clabbyd, *History of the RAVC*, p. 13.
7   Ibid., p. 14.
8   Kean, *Challenging the State?*, p. 8; Bourke, *Dismembering the Male*, pp. 13–14.
9   Edgar Preston, *Half a Century of Good Work: A jubilee history of the Metropolitan Drinking Fountain and Cattle Trough Association 1859–1909*, (London, 1909), photograph opposite p. 64.
10 *Animals' Guardian*, vol. V, no. 11, November 1903, p. 130.
11 Adrian Gregory, *The Silence of Memory* (Oxford, 1994); Geoff Dyer, *The Missing of the Somme* (Harmondsworth, 1995); Michael Heffernan, 'For Ever England: the Western Front and the politics of remembrance in Britain', *Ecumene*, vol. II, no. 3, July 1995; Bob Bushaway, 'Name Upon Name: the Great War and remembrance' in Roy Porter, ed., *Myths of the English* (Cambridge, 1992); Jay Winter, *Sites of Memory. Sites of Mourning* (Cambridge, 1995), p. 1.
12 John Singleton, 'Britain's Military Use of Horses 1914–1918', *Past and Present*, 139, May 1993, p. 178.
13 Thompson, 'Horses and Hay', p. 56.
14 Singleton, 'Britain's Military Use of Horses', p. 178.
15 J. M. Brereton, *The Horse in War* (Devon, 1976), pp. 125–6.
16 Singleton, 'Britain's Military Use of Horses', p. 191.
17 Clabbyd, *History of the RAVC*, p. 17·
18 Siegfried Sassoon, *Memoirs of a Fox-hunting Man* (London, 1928), p. 136.
19 Clabbyd, *History of the* RAVC, p. 16. The commanders who were keen to maintain pre-war standards of groomed horses in fact facilitated their animals' deaths. Those who prevented soldiers grooming the animals so that they were covered in grease ensured some protection against the harsh environment and increased resistance to viruses. Brereton, *Horse in War*, pp. 127–8.
20 NCDL, *Annual Report*, 1914, p. 23.
21 Lt Col E. H. Richardson, *British War Dogs: Their training and psychology* (London, 1920), p. 57.
22 Richardson, *British War Dogs*, pp. 52–60.

23 Ibid., p. 60.

24 Lt Col A. H. Osman, *Pigeons in the Great War. A Complete History of the Carrier Pigeon Service During the Great War 1914–18* (London, 1929), pp. 5–6.

25 The Germans used similar strategies, although the man responsible for the British initiative declared, 'the quality of the German pigeons was not equal to those used by our forces'. Osman, *Pigeons in the Great War*, p. 56.

26 Salt, *Seventy Years*, p. 227.

27 Ibid., p. 243.

28 Salt argued that all human and animal life had been indefinitely retarded by war. *Seventy Years*, p. 229.

29 ODFL, *Annual Report*, 1914, p. 123. The Blue Cross came into being during the Balkan War of 1912.

30 Major-General Sir L. J. Blenkinsop and Lt Col J. W. Rainey, eds, *History of the Great War based on Official documents: Veterinary Services* (London, 1925), p. 87.

31 Winter, *Sites of Memory*, p. 5.

32 Bell and Ballie Weaver, *Horses in Warfare*, pp. 10–11.

33 Preface by Lady Smith-Dorrien in Charles W. Forward, *Under the Blue Cross. A Story of Two Horses in the War* (London, 1915).

34 ODFL, *Annual Report*, 1917, pp. 124–6.

35 ODFL, *Annual Report*, 1915, pp. 116–24; 1917, p. 124.

36 *Humanitarian*, vol. VIII, no. 193, January 1919; vol. VIII, no. 194, April 1919; vol. VIII, no. 195, September 1919.

37 The Quaker Oats company, manufacturers of porridge, had put in a bid to supply horses with cakes of oats and molasses which had been rejected on the grounds of expense. Still, horses in the British army fared better than other war horses. Their ration of ten pounds of oats a day was still three pounds more than their French counterparts and seven pounds more than that given to Italian horses. Singleton, 'Britain's Military Use of Horses', pp. 197–8.

38 *Humanitarian*, vol. VII, no. 162, June 1916, p. 154; vol. VII, no. 163, July 1916, p. 162; vol. VIII, no. 184, April 1918, pp. 100ff; vol. VIII, no. 189, September 1918, pp. 129ff.

39 William and Ernest Axon, *Seventy-five years of the Vegetarian Society* (London, 1923), p. 9; Spencer, *Heretic's Feast*, p. 309.

40 Henry Amos, *Economical Nourishing Dishes for Times of Stress and How to Cook Them* (London, 1916), p. 4.

41 Anon., *How to Manage Pigeons*.

42 George Gardner, *Cavies or Guinea Pigs* (London, 1913), p. 21.

43 C. J. Davies, *Rabbit-Keeping in War Time* (London, 1917). The practice continued in the post-war Depression as the following publications indicate: Lady Rachel Byng, *How to make money by Angora rabbit breeding and wool farming* (London, 1926); Elsie L. Winter, *How to Make £5 a Week from Angora Rabbits in your Spare Time* (London, 1928).

44 John Sheial, *Rabbits and Their History* (1971), p. 182, as quoted in Caroline Arscott, 'Sentimentality in Victorian Paintings' in Waterfield, ed., *Art for the People*, p. 81.

45 Minutes Book of Executive Committee of ADAVS, 2 September 1914, Wellcome Institute; Louise Lind af Hageby, *Woman's Function: Social Development* (London, 1915), paper read at a conference on the pacifist

philosophy of life in Caxton House, 8/9 July 1915, and published by the League of Peace and Freedom.

46 Letter from Stella Browne to Margaret Sanger, 8 June 1916, Sophia Smith Collection of Sanger papers. My thanks to Lesley Hall for this reference.
47 RDS minutes, SA/RDS C1 Minute book, 17 October 1916. Wellcome Institute.
48 RDS Quarterly Report, October 1914, p. 1. Wellcome Institute.
49 RDS minutes, SA/RDS C1 Minute book, 17 October 1916. Wellcome Institute.
50 Arthur Mee, *Letters to Girls* (London, 1915), p. 117. My thanks to John Kain for this reference. Saleeby was a regular contributor to Mee's better known *Children's Encyclopaedia*.
51 *Illustrated London News*, 27 October 1917, front page.
52 *Illustrated London News*, 29 December 1917, p. 823.
53 Conscription for men was not introduced until 1916. Unpublished war diary entry for 1915 by Ethel Bilbrough, Elmstead Grange, Chislehurst (Blue Cross Archive, Burford).
54 Sassoon, *Memoirs*, p. 40. Animals too were decorated for war effort and bravery, a practice which was repeated in the 1939–45 war. Osman, *Pigeons in the Great War*; Smith, *The Blue Cross at War*, p. 32; Arthur Moss and Elizabeth Kirby, *Animals Were There. A record of the RSPCA during the war of 1939–45* (London, 1947), pp. 133ff.
55 Brereton, *Horse in War*, p. 129; Singleton, 'Britain's Military Use of Horses', p. 199; Percy V. Bradshaw, *The Art of the Illustrator: Fortunino Matania* (Forest Hill, n. d.).
56 Smith, *The Blue Cross at War*, p. 15.
57 Lucy Laurence, 'Goodbye Old Man' in Smith-Dorrien, *A Book of Poems*, pp. 73–4.
58 NCDL, *Annual Report*, 1917, p. 11.
59 Ballard, *A Dog is for Life*, p. 32.
60 Richardson, *British War Dogs*, p. 61.
61 Bourke, *Dismembering the Male*, pp. 124–70.
62 Leonard Fleming, lieutenant in the Queen Victoria's Rifles, 'The silent volunteers' in Smith-Dorrien, *A Book of Poems*, p. 3.
63 See note 1.
64 Harvey J. Greenaway, 'Old Bill of the RFA' in Smith-Dorrien, pp. 86–7.
65 Geoffrey Dearmer, 'The Turkish Trench Dog' in Lloyd, *The Great Kinship*, p. 225.
66 Smith Ely Jelliffe and Louise Brink, 'The role of animals in the unconscious, with some remarks on theriomorphic symbolism as seen in Ovid', *Psychoanalytic Review*, vol. IV, no. 3, 1917, p. 271. See preface.
67 Ballard, *A Dog is for Life*, p. 78.
68 NCDL, *Annual Report*, 1914, pp. 17, 20–23; 1915, p. 11; 1916, p. 12.
69 'Keep the home fires burning', words: Lena Guilbert Ford; music: Ivor Novello (London, 1914).
70 NCDL, *Annual Report*, 1916, p. 14.
71 Ballard, *A Dog is for Life*, p. 27.
72 Letter from an ex-serviceman in Bolton, 12 October 1919, ODFL, Blue Cross Fund, *Sixth Annual Report*, 1919, pp. 116–17.
73 Despite the practice of US servicemen to adopt dogs the US government has

never permitted any dogs used in war to be brought back to America, although
Rin Tin Tin, a German mascot puppy smuggled back to the States, became a
matinée idol. Michael G. Lemish, *War Dogs. Canines in Combat* (Washington,
1996), p. 25.

74 London Institute for lost and starving cats and dogs, *Urgent Appeal* (London,
     1920), p. 3.

75 *St Pancras Chronicle, Hampstead Record and Finsbury Guardian*, 25 March
     1919, as reproduced in London Institute for lost and starving cats and dogs,
     Urgent Appeal, p. 13.

76 Blenkinsop and Rainey, *History of the Great War*, p. 546.

77 Smith, *The Blue Cross at War*, p. 30.

78 ODFL, Blue Cross Fund, *Sixth Annual Report*, 1919, p. 112.

79 Battersea Dogs' Home, *The Dogs' Home*, p. 16; NCDL, *Annual Report*, 1914,
     p. 17.

80 NCDL, *Annual Report*, 1916, p. 15.

81 Ballard, *A Dog is for Life*, p. 28.

82 *The Times*, 19 February 1917, letter from A. E. Shipley, Christ's College,
     Cambridge.

83 At the start of the war the NCDL had issued dog biscuit supplies to poor people
     unable to provide for their dogs in order to prevent them being put down.
     NCDL, *Annual Report*, 1914, pp. 20–1; *Annual Report*, 1915, p. 11.

84 Report of Parliamentary proceedings of 27 April 1917. Captain Bathurst in
     reply to Mr Wiles, Liberal MP for Islington South, *The Times*, 28 April 1917;
     The Times, 9 May 1917.

85 Ethel Bilbrough, war dairy, April 1917 (Blue Cross Archive).

86 Fund initiated by The *Daily Telegraph*. Ernest Protheroe, *A Noble Woman. The
     life story of Edith Cavell* (London, 1916), pp. 26–7, 85.

87 Phillip McFayen, *Edith Cavell 1865–1915, A Norfolk Heroine* (Norfolk, 1982).
     There is a photograph of Cavell with her nurses in Brussels with her dog at her
     feet. Apparently the dog was donated to the museum by the Red Cross. The
     Imperial War Museum however has refused to disclose the nature of the
     deposition.

88 It is still there, opposite Kilburn Park underground.

89 Minutes of the RDS, 5 May 1925. Wellcome Institute.

90 Other animal charities such as the Blue Cross were specifically banned by the
     British army from providing services for animals on battle fronts. Blenkinsop
     and Rainey, *History of the Great War*, p. 58; Smith, *The Blue Cross at War*,
     pp. 7, 13. The Blue Cross then opened hospitals in France and became *de facto*
     official veterinary surgeons in Italy (Smith, *The Blue Cross at War*, p. 13).

91 There is a metal camel and man on the top of the plinth and a frieze at the side
     depicting a camel seated with an officer alongside, by Cecil Brown, 1920, in
     Embankment Gardens, London. See Blenkinsop and Rainey, *History of the
     Great War*, for an account of animals at Gallipoli: the legendary coming of age
     of the ANZAC forces, pp. 109–12.

92 Lemish, *War Dogs*, pp. 176, 234.

93 Glenda Spooner, ed., *For Love of Horses: the diaries of Mrs Geoffrey Brooke*
     (London, 1968), pp. 3ff; Brereton, *The Horse in War*, p. 139.

94 June 1934. See Brereton, *The Horse in War*, p. 141.

95 *Humanitarian*, vol. VIII, no. 193, January 1919; vol. VIII, no. 194, April 1919;
    vol. VIII, no. 195, September 1919.

EIGHT   A MEETING OF THE COUNTRY AND THE TOWN

 1 Edith Ward writing in special Women's Number of *Cruel Sports*, vol. I, no. 7,
    July 1927, p. 84.
 2 *Humanitarian*, vol. VIII, no. 193, January 1919, p.154. The Humanitarian
    League wound itself up in September 1919 after a vote at a special general
    meeting of 150 to 15 votes (*Humanitarian*, vol. VIII, no. 195 , September
    1919 , p. 165); Kean, '"Smooth cool men of science"', p. 31.
 3 ADAVS, *A survey of the case against vivisection* (London, 1930), p. 39; ADAVS,
    Annual Report, 1922, p. 11.
 4 London and Provincial Anti-Vivisection Society(LAPAVS), *Newssheet*,VI,
    no. 1, January 1946, p. 2.
 5 Church Anti-Vivisection League, *Annual Report*, 1938, p. 15.
 6 ADAVS, *A survey of the case against vivisection*, p. 19.
 7 RDS, *Parliamentary Returns: experiments on animals*, 1919. Wellcome
    Institute.
 8 RDS, *Quarterly Report*, January 1918, pp. 3, 6. Wellcome Institute.
 9 RDS, *Quarterly Report*, April 1919, p. 5. Wellcome Institute.
10 BUAV, *Annual Report*, 1930, in which 62 MPs are listed as supporters; with the
    election of the National Government in 1931 and the decimation of the Labour
    Party, numbers were down to 26 (BUAV, *Annual Report*, 1932).
11 A protest meeting of 10,000 was held at the Albert Hall in 1921 against the
    traffic in worn-out horses. Smith, *The Blue Cross at War*, p. 34. ADAVS, *Annual
    Report*, 1922, p. 11; 1924, pp. 55–6.
12 BUAV, *Annual Report*, 1919, pp. 33ff; Minutes of RDS, 1 November 1923.
    Wellcome Institute.
13 Minutes of RDS, 10 March 1923; 5 November 1924; 26 May 1926, 23
    November 1926, SA/RDS C2 Box 2. Wellcome Institute.
14 Deirdre Beddoe, *Back to Home and Duty* (London, 1989); Hilda Kean,
    'Searching for the past in present defeat: the construction of historical and
    political identity in British feminism in the 1920s and 1930s', *Women's History
    Review*, vol. III, no. 1, 1994, pp. 57–80.
15 Judith Lytton, *Toy Dogs and Their Ancestors*, p. 11.
16 Charlotte Haldane, *Motherhood and its Enemies*, 1927, p. 156, as quoted in
    Sheila Jeffreys, *The Spinster and her Enemies: Feminism and Sexuality
    1880–1930* (London, 1985), p. 175.
17 RDS, *Quarterly Review*, July 1918, pp. 1–2. Wellcome Institute.
18 Correspondence from Mr J. F. Peart to secretary of the King Edward's Hospital
    Fund, 28 February 1927. *Records of Battersea General Hospital*.
19 Winifred Holtby, 'Let's abolish the dear animals!', *Time and Tide*, 30 January
    1932, p. 118.
20 The Humane Treatment of Animals Committee became a full sectional
    committee in 1930. Dame Maria Ogilvie Gordon, *Historical Sketch of the
    National Council of Women of Great Britain* (London, 1937), p. 44; National
    Council of Women, *Report of Council Meeting and Conference* (London,

1938), p. 149; ODFL, *Annual Report*, 1937, p. 27; *Minutes of the Political Committee*, 1936ff, Box 24, ODFL Blue Cross Archive.

21   League for the Prohibition of Cruel Sports, *Cruel Sports*, vol. I, no. 7, July 1927, pp. 81ff.

22   A. H. Stokes, *The Treatment of Pit Ponies*, Coal Trade Pamphlet no. 5 (London, 1910).

23   R. Page Arnot, *The Miners: Years of Struggle. A History of the Miners' Federation of Great Britain* (London, 1953), p. 301.

24   Ibid., pp. 301–03.

25   This was despite the previous existence of an Equine Defence League that advocated machinery as a substitute for ponies in pits. Gertrude Colmore, *Trades that Transgress* (London, 1918), p. 24; Stokes, *Treatment of Pit Ponies*, p. 22; Turner, *All Heaven in a Rage,* p. 261.

26   Caroline Benn, *Keir Hardie* (London, 1992), pp. 9–10.

27   Appendix to Colmore, *Trades that Transgress*, p. 45.

28   B. L. Coombes, *These Poor Hands* (London, 1939), pp. 55–8.

29   Thanks to Bob Purdie for passing on this story to me which was related to him by the late Paddy Bergin, former president of the Irish Labour History Society.

30   Thanks to Tim Brennan for this information.

31   NCDL, *Annual Report*, 1933, p. 16.

32   PDSA, *A Commemorative Brochure Documenting 80 Years of the People's Dispensary for Sick Animals* (Telford, 1997).

33   Fairholme and Pain, *A Century of Work,* p. 288.

34   ODFL, *Annual Report*, 1937, pp. 19–20 and leaflet.

35   Sassoon, *Memoirs*, p. 105; letter to *The Times* from A. E. Shipley, 19 February 1917; *Hansard*, vol. 92, col. 282, 25 April 1917.

36   *Humanitarian*, vol. VIII, no. 184, April 1918, p. 100.

37   First editorial, *Cruel Sports*, vol. I, no. 1, January 1927, p. 1.

38   Ibid.

39   NAVS, *The Animals' Defender and Zoophilist*, vol. LVI, no. 8, December 1936, p. 66.

40   ODFL, *Animals in Politics*, no. 5, July 1937.

41   ODFL, *Animals in Politics*, no. 6, August 1937.

42   *John Bull*, July 1937, as quoted in ODFL, *Animals in Politics*, no. 6.

43   Poll conducted of 5,000 people taken from local rating polls with attention paid to different jobs and incomes. Air Commodore L. E. O. Charlton, *This Cruelty Called Sport!* (London, 1939), p. 11.

44   ODFL, *Animals in Politics*, no. 11, January 1938; no 12, February 1938.

45   *League Doings. Bulletin of the League for the Prohibition of Cruel Sports*, January–March 1946; *Cruel Sports*, vol. X, no. 5, May 1936, p. 37.

46   *League Doings*, November–December 1948, January–March 1949, April–June 1949.

47   Tom Stephenson, *Forbidden Land. The Struggle for Access to Mountain and Moorland* (Manchester, 1989); Benny Rothman, *The 1932 Kinder Trespass* (Altrincham, 1982).

48   Stephenson, *Forbidden Land*.

49   Derek Jarman, *Derek Jarman's Garden* (London, 1995), p. 14. Jim Glover, 'Dungeness', RSPB *Birds*, vol. XV, no. 2, Summer 1994, pp. 33–6.

50 Simon Barnes, *Flying in the Face of Nature: A Year on Minsmere* (London, 1992), pp. 46–51, as quoted in Raphael Samuel, *Theatres of Memory* (London, 1994), p. 171.

51 Mike Everett, 'Peter Conder, a Personal Memoir', RSPB *Birds*, vol. XIV, no. 8, Winter 1993, p. 16. Membership reached 1,010,042 by winter 1997 (RSPB *Birds*, vol. XVI, no. 7, Winter 1997, p. 1).

52 Samuel J. Looker, *Bertram Lloyd. Humanitarian and Pioneer* (Leicester, 1960); Lloyd, *The Great Kinship*.

53 Wright, *The Village that died for England*, p. 115.

54 Abelson, *A Mirror of England*, p. 185; Wright, *The Village that died for England*, p. 111.

55 H. J. Massingham, *An Englishman's Year* (London, 1948], pp. 182–3, as printed in Abelson, *A Mirror of England*, p. 157.

56 Shosnana Milgram Knapp, '"Real passion and the reverence for life": sexuality and anti-vivisection in the fiction of Victoria Cross' in Angela Ingram and Daphne Patai, eds, *Rediscovering Forgotten Radicals. British Women Writers 1889–1939* (London, 1993), pp. 156–71.

57 Victoria Cross, *The Beating Heart* (London, 1924), pp. 189–280.

58 Gertrude Colmore, *A Brother of the Shadow* (London, 1926).

59 Mark Cartmill, *A view to a death*, pp. 163–6.

60 Michael Powell, *A Life in Movies* (London, 1986), p. 684; LAPAVS *Newssheet*, VI, no. 6, June 1946. The LAPAVS was a continuation of the LAVS.

61 Opened in 1934. Guillery, *The Buildings of London Zoo*, p. 83.

62 Vevers, *London's Zoo*, p. 150.

63 Guillery, *The Buildings of London Zoo*, pp. 86, 152; Timothy W. Luke, 'The World Wildlife Fund: Ecocolonialism as Founding the Worldwide "Wise Use" of Nature', *Capitalism, Nature, Socialism. A Journal of Socialist Ecology*, vol. VIII, no. 2, June 1997, p. 34.

64 ODFL, *Animals in Politics*, no. 9, November 1937.

65 Henry G. Chancellor, *How to Win* (London, 1912), pp. 58–60.

66 Special Women's Number, *Cruel Sports*, vol. I, no. 7, July 1927, p. 84. 5,000 copies of this issue had been printed of which 1,300 had been sent to the local secretaries of the Women's Co-Operative Guild.

67 Davies and Rupp, *A History of the Methodist Church*, vol. I, p. 311; vol. IV, p. 643; see for example Albert Peel, 'Clapton Park Congregational Church as seen in its minutes 1804–1929', *Transactions of the Congregational History Society*, 1929, p. 24.

68 ODFL, *Annual Report*, 1924, p. 23; Turner, *All Heaven in a Rage*, p. 275–7;

69 The *Star*, 30 June 1934, p. 1; re RSPCA prosecution of Tex Austin's rodeo show; for attempts made by Danesfort in 1925, 1930 and 1933, see Turner, *All Heaven in a Rage*, pp. 272–4.

70 The dog survived and was offered back, but since rationing still existed it was decided to leave him with the army, the family being sent a photograph and certificate with his army number. Pam Schweitzer, ed., *Goodnight Children Everywhere* (Greenwich, 1990), pp. 246–9. My thanks to Val Horsfield for this reference.

71 Ballard, *A Dog is for Life*, p. 76; Smith, *The Blue Cross at War*, p. 46.

72 Blue Cross, *Annual Report*, 1940, p. 30.

73 Ballard, *A Dog is for Life*, p. 77. See further accounts in NCDL *Dogs' Bulletin*, no. 111, April–May 1939; no. 112, June–July 1939. Tales include that of a whole family with their dog being sent to a concentration camp, later released and fleeing to Britain.

74 LAPAVS, 'Dog Refugees', *Newssheet* no. 2, August 1940, p. 4.

75 ODFL, Minutes of the Executive Committee for Political Purposes, 12 June 1940, p. 478 (Burford archive).

76 File on raid on LAPAVS, SA/RDS B 11, Box 2, Wellcome Institute; A. W. Brian Simpson, *In the Highest Degree Odious* (Oxford, 1992), pp. 137, 177–8.

77 *Hansard*, vol. 361, cols. 652–3, 30 May 1940.

78 LAPAVS *Newssheet* no. 16, October 1941. Lady Tenterden was also a supporter of the Council for Justice for Animals.

79 Robert Benewick, *The Fascist Movement in Britain* (London, 1972), pp. 113–4; Richard Thurlow, *Fascism in Britain. A History 1918–1985* (Oxford, 1987), p. 212; LAPAVS *Newssheet*, vol. II, no. 2, February 1942; Muriel, Lady Dowding, *Beauty, not the Beast* (Jersey, 1980), p. 159. Thurlow is wrong in defining the group merely as a front organization. The *Newssheet* for members indicates clearly that whatever positions members may have had on Fascism or Socialism they were totally committed to anti-vivisection.

80 W. Risdon, 'An Air-Raid Shelter for Your Pets', LAPAVS *Newssheet*, no. 4, October 1940.

81 Moss and Kirby, *Animals Were There*, p. 18; Costelloe, *Battersea Dogs' Home*, p. 125; NCDL, *Dogs' Bulletin*, no. 109, December 1938, p. 6; no. 114, December 1939, p. 2; *The Animals' Defender and Zoophilist*, November 1939, vol. LIX, no 7, p. 57; vol. LX, no. 2, June 1940, p. 11.

82 *The Animals' Defender and Zoophilist*, November 1939, vol. LIX, no. 7, p. 57.

83 Moss and Kirby, *Animals Were There*, p. 55.

84 Simpson, *Highest Degree Odious*, p. 193; NCDL, *Dogs' Bulletin*, no. 119, Summer 1941, pp. 2–3; Moss and Kirby, *Animals Were There*, p. 19.

85 *Hansard*, vol. 377, 8 January 1942 col. 69; *Daily Sketch*, 2 April 1941, as quoted in LAPAVS *Newssheet*, no. 11, May 1941; *Newssheet*, vol III, no. 6, June 1943.

86 Blue Cross, *Annual Report*, 1944, p. 27.

87 NCDL, *Dogs' Bulletin*, no 116, Summer 1940, p. 5.

88 Moss and Kirby, *Animals Were There*, pp. 113–15. This includes a photograph of 'the last dog from Dunkirk'; Ballard, *A Dog is for Life*, p. 78; Blue Cross, *Annual Report*, 1940, p. 29.

89 Dorothea St Hill Bourne, *They also Serve* (London, 1947), p. 43.

90 Ballard, *A Dog is for Life*, p. 78.

91 Angus Calder, *The Myth of the Blitz* (London, 1991).

92 Bourne, *They Also Serve*.

93 Ballard, *A Dog is for Life*, pp. 102, 106; Lucinda Lambton, *Beastly Buildings*, p. 180.

94 The pet cemetery, established in Hyde Park in 1881 and officially closed in 1903 when it contained 300 graves, is near Lancaster Gate underground. It is open only once a year to the public as part of the annual open house scheme.

95 BUAV, *Annual Report*, 1946, pp. 11ff.

96 Ibid.

97 LAPAVS *Newssheet*, vol. VI, no. 7, July 1946; Smith, *The Blue Cross at War*, p. 67; BUAV, *Annual Report*, 1946.

98 LAPAVS *Newssheet*, vol. IV, no. 2, February 1944, p. 5; vol. V: 8 August 1945, p. 29.

99 LAPAVS *Newssheet*, vol. VI, no. 1, January 1946, p. 2; *Hansard*, 30 October 1946, as quoted in LAPAVS *Newssheet*, vol. VI, no. 12, December 1946, p. 45.

100 Peter Flint, *Dowding and Headquarters Fighter Command* (Shrewsbury, 1996), pp. 170–8; Lady Dowding, *Beauty, not the Beast*.

101 Lady Dowding, *Beauty, not the Beast* (as above); Lord Dowding, *The Dark Star* (London, 1951), p.177.

102 Sylvia Cranston, *HPB. The extraordinary life and influence of Helena Blavatsky, founder of the modern Theosophical movement* (New York, 1993), p. 290

103 Lord Dowding, speech to House of Lords, 18 July 1957, as quoted in Scottish Society for the Prevention of Vivisection, *In the Company of Anti-Vivisectionists* [1966]

104 Smith, *The Blue Cross at War*, pp. 66–7.

105 Blue Cross, *There is no welfare state for animals*, leaflet issued in 1956.

106 Various correspondence from R. Harvey Johns to the Metropolitan Drinking Fountain and Cattle Trough Association (*Records of MDFCTA*, GLRO).

107 See for example *Brighton and Hove Gazette*, 10 November 1961, p. 3; Turner, *All Heaven in a Rage*, pp. 310ff.

108 *Sussex Express and County Herald*, 15 December 1961, p. 7; Ministry of Agriculture and Fisheries, *Myxomatosis. Second Report of the Advisory Committee on Myxomatosis* (London, 1955), pp. 1–2.

109 Ministry of Agriculture and Fisheries (as above). An amendment was passed to the Pests Act 1954.

110 David Crouch and Colin Ward, *The Allotment. Its Landscape and Culture*, (London, 1988), p. 73.

111 Rachel Carson, *Silent Spring*, introduction by Lord Shackleton (1963, reprinted Harmondsworth, 1982), pp. 11–14.

112 Ibid., p. 15.

113 CIWF, *Agscene*, no. 102, 1991 as quoted in Spencer, *Heretic's Feast*, p. 328.

114 Peter Roberts, 'Reflection', CIWF, *Agscene*, no. 116, Winter 1994, p. 15.

NINE CONTINUING CRUELTY: UNCONCLUDED CAMPAIGNS

1 Albert Einstein, quoted in CIWF, *Act Now*, Summer 1997.

2 See p. 117.

3 Our Animal Brothers' Guild, *Fashionable Furs – and How They Are Obtained* (Bristol, n. d.), p. 24.

4 George Wenzel, *Animal Rights, Human Rights. Ecology, Economy, and Ideology in the Canadian Arctic* (London, 1991), p. 46.

5 Ibid., pp. 4, 178–9.

6 David Day, *The Whale War* (London, 1987), pp. 18ff.

7 Ibid., pp. 69, 172ff.

8 Previous similar attempts in recent years had achieved the support of individual MPs from all parties, including Simon Hughes of the Liberal Democrats, Tony Banks and Elliot Morley of the Labour Party, SNP Margaret

Ewing and Conservative Sir Teddy Taylor, but failed due to manoeuvres of supporters of the British Field Sports Society or lack of time for a private member's bill. Kevin McNamara promoted a Wild Mammals (Protection) Bill in 1992, John McFall promoted a similar bill in March 1995. LACS, *Wildlife Guardian*, special edition, January 1995.

9 LACS, *Annual Report*, 1996–7, p. 6.
10 LACS, *Wildlife Guardian*, issue 33, Spring 1996, p. 1.
11 According to Elizabeth Wilson, the larger the city the more plants and animals it will shelter. Wilson, 'The Rhetoric of Urban Space', *New Left Review*, no. 209, January–February 1995, p. 146.
12 See James Hinton, *Protests and Visions. Peace politics in twentieth-century Britain* (London, 1989), pp. 153–70.
13 William V. Collier, 'Veganism and World Peace', *The Vegan*, vol. III, no. 4, Winter 1947, p. 10.
14 Editorial by Donald Watson, 'The case for veganism', *The Vegan*, vol. II, no. 1, Spring 1946, p. 2.
15 Peter and Eileen Caddy, *The Findhorn Garden* (Wildwood House, 1976) as quoted in Spencer, *Heretic's Feast*, p. 321.
16 Nicholas Saunders, *Alternative London*, 2nd edn (London, 1971), pp. 36–41.
17 Ibid., p. 36.
18 Realeat and Oxford surveys in 1994 of 11,000 people, as quoted in Emma Haughton, 'The fruit and nut case', *Guardian*, 3 June 1997, p. 13.
19 CIWF, *Agscene*, no. 113, Winter 1993, p. 10.
20 See note 18.
21 Summary of the judgement read in open court, 19 June 1997, pp. 18–20; John Vidal, 'Long, slow battle in a fast food war', *Guardian*, 20 June 1997, p. 7.
22 'Cats reign in more homes than dogs', *Guardian*, 30 January 1997, p. 10. Report of Social Trends Survey 27 published by the Office for National Statistics.
23 The total spend is £168 million a year, but still only about 13 per cent of dogs and 4 per cent of cats have insurance. Lindsay Mackie, 'Man's Best Friend', *Guardian*, 17 June 1997, pp. 2–3.
24 See Chapter 6. The RSPCA took over the Mayhew Home in 1925 as a clinic until 1982. It reopened in 1983 as an animal home and humane education centre with a non-destruction policy. *Living without Cruelty*, exhibition brochure, June 1992.
25 Lynne Wallis, 'My family and other animals', *Guardian*, 23 March 1996.
26 'File of facts', *All About Cats*, vol. III: no. 4, April 1996, p. 10. 76 per cent of cats owned were 'moggies'; 82 per cent of owners questioned stated that they would spend their last 40 pence on food for their cat rather than on themselves.
27 See for example http//www.duke.edu/dm11/maxhome.htm, a memorial to Max, a Doberman pinscher who died of cancer in 1996. My thanks to Alan Cameron for drawing my attention to this web site.
28 R. H. Johns, *Smash Dog Fighting and Badgering* (NCDL, 1939), pp. 7, 28–9.
29 Clarissa Baldwin, '(Not so) Dangerous Dogs', NCDL, *Wag!*, Summer 1997, p. 5.
30 *Hackney Gazette*, 15 February 1996, p. 7.
31 Brian Vesey-Fitzgerald, *Cats* (Harmondsworth, 1957), pp. 200–13.

32 *Your Cat*, July 1997, p. 13.
33 Slattery's Ireland, *Holiday Brochure*, 1997, p. 6.
34 'Kitty in my pocket' manufactured by Vivid Imaginations Ltd. Also available: ponies in my pocket.
35 Richard Lloyd Parry, 'Virtual poo in the handbag becomes a fashion accessory that no girl can do without', *Independent*, 7, 18 March 1997. My thanks to Chris Sladen for these references.
36 The Egyptian card sold 11,600 and the statue plus tabby sold 9,500 between 1989 and 1900. The Egyptian statues continued to sell well (10,800) between 1990 and 91. Mary Beard, 'Souvenirs of Culture: Deciphering (in) the Museum', *Art History*, vol. XV, no. 4, December 1992, pp. 505–32.
37 Jane Cassidy, 'Animal Rights', *The Big Issue*, no. 271, 16–22 February 1998, p. 5. See also *Turning Point*, no. 12, January–March 1989, pp. 21–3. 'Hill Grove Farm Cats', *Arkangel*, no. 17, 1997.
38 *The Animals' Defender and Zoophilist*, vol. I, no. 9, September 1957.
39 Alun Howkins and Linda Merricks, 'Dewy-Eyed Veal Calves. Live animal exports and middle-class opinion, 1980–1995', unpublished paper, 1997.
40 A 52-year-old woman from Brighton, as quoted in Howkins and Merricks, 'Dewy-Eyed Veal Calves'.
41 Interview with Martin Shaw. CIWF, *Agscene*, no. 116, Winter 1994, p. 8.
42 CIWF, *Agscene*, Summer 1997, p. 3.
43 Paul Binding, 'Alive and Kicking', *New Statesman and Society*, 13 January 1995, pp.16–17.
44 *Independent*, 22 April 1995, p. 1.
45 Benton and Redfearn, 'The Politics of Animal Rights', p. 54.
46 *Independent*, 19 April 1995, p. 1.
47 *Daily Telegraph*, 27 February 1995, p. 4.
48 BUAV, *Campaign Report*, Spring 1994.
49 CIWF, *Agscene*, no. 126, Summer 1997, pp. 10–11. Similar actions performed in Britain's Asian communities have not received this attention.
50 For such opposition Brigitte Bardot, a supporter of the National Front in France, was charged with inciting racial hatred. Writing that France was invaded by an over-population of foreigners, notably Muslims, she was found not guilty on the grounds that such comments were a reaction to the distress suffered by animals. *Guardian*, 24 January 1997, p. 14.
51 BUAV, 'Insight into the Animals (Scientific Procedures) Act 1986', *Campaign Report*, Autumn 1996; Richard D. Ryder, *Victims of Science, The Use of Animals in Research*, 2nd edition (London, 1983), p. 17.
52 As quoted in BUAV, 'Insight into the Animals (Scientific Procedures) Act'.
53 NAVS, *The Good Charities Guide* (London, 1994).
54 BUAV, 'Insight into the Animals (Scientific Procedures) Act'.
55 BUAV, *Campaign Report*, Winter 1997 /8, pp. 1–2.
56 BUAV, *Annual Report*, 1996–7, p. 16.
57 Robert Sharpe, *The Cruel Deception. The Use of Animals in Medical Research* (Wellingborough, 1988), pp. 15–17; Gill Langley, *Faith, Hope and Charity? An Enquiry into Charity-Funded Research* (London, 1988)
58 BUAV, *Annual Report*, 1996–7, p. 9; BUAV, 'Insight into Xenotransplantation', *Campaign Report*, Winter 1994.

59 BUAV, 'Insight into Animal Genetic Engineering – Causes for Concern',
    Campaign Report, Autumn 1994.
60 Consort Beagle Campaign, *The Consort Group Factsheet* (Birmingham, 1996).
61 A somewhat contradictory act. When I rang Channel 4 to discover the name of
    the company I was told this could not be issued on safety grounds.
62 Adam Sweeting, *Guardian*, 27 March 1997; BUAV, *Campaign Report*,
    Summer 1997; Animal Liberation Front Supporters' Group, *Newsletter*, 1997.
63 BUAV, *Campaign Report*, Winter 1997.
64 Jim Carey, 'Animal Warfare', *Squall*, no. 13, Summer 1996, p. 23.
65 Kenneth Greet, 'Wesley and Animal Rights', *The Methodist Recorder*, 4 April
    1996, p. 3.
66 'Port Vigil', *The Methodist Recorder*, 18 April, 1996, p. 12.
67 Benton and Redfearn, 'The Politics of Animal Rights', p. 54.
68 *Guardian*, 3 February 1995, p. 2.
69 Michael Mansfield, 'Case without Compassion', *Guardian*, 14 April 1995, p. 20.
70 See note 1.

SELECT BIBLIOGRAPHY

Reginald Abbott, 'Birds don't sing in Greek: Virginia Woolf and "the Plumage Bill"', in Carol J. Adams and Josephine Donovan, ed, *Animals and Women* (North Carolina, 1995).

Edward Abelson, ed., *A Mirror of England. An Anthology of the Writings of H. J. Massingham* (Devon, 1988).

Alison Adburgham, *Shopping in Style. London from the Restoration to Edwardian Elegance* (Hampshire, 1979).

A. J. R., ed., *The Suffrage Annual and Women's Who's Who* (London, 1913).

Sally Alexander, *Becoming a Woman* (London, 1994).

Henry Amos, ed., *Food Reformers' Year Book* (London, 1909ff).

R. Page Arnot, *The Miners: Years of Struggle. A History of the Miners' Federation of Great Britain* (London, 1953).

Steve Baker, *Picturing the Beast. Animals, identity and representation* (Manchester, 1993).

Peter Ballard, *A Dog is for Life. Celebrating the first one hundred years of the National Canine Defence League* (London, 1990).

The Battersea Dogs' Home, *The Dogs' Home, Battersea 1860–1960* (London, 1960).

Joseph O. Baylen and Norbert J. Gossman, eds, *Biographical Dictionary of Modern British Radicals, Vol I: 1770–1830* (Sussex, 1979).

Beeton's Book of Home Pets (London, 1862).

Ernest Bell, *The Humane Slaughtering of Animals* (London, 1904).

—, *The Other Side of the Bars. The Case against the Caged Bird* (London, 1911).

Ernest Bell and Harold Baillie Weaver, *Horses in Warfare* (London, 1912).

Caroline Benn, *Keir Hardie* (London, 1992).

Alfred Rosling Bennett, *London and Londoners in the 1850s and 1860s* (London, 1924).

Tony Bennett, *Birth of the Museum* (London, 1995).

Ted Benton and Simon Redfearn, 'The Politics of Animal Rights – Where is the Left?', *New Left Review,* no. 215, January/February 1996.

John Berger, 'Why look at animals?', *About Looking* (London, 1980).

Lucy Bland, *Banishing the Beast* (Harmondsworth, 1995).

Major-General Sir L. J. Blenkinsop and Lt Col J. W. Rainey, eds, *History of the Great War based on Official documents: Veterinary Services* (London, 1925).

Wilfrid Blunt, *England's Michelangelo* (London, 1975).

Charles Booth, *Life and Labour of the People in London* (London, 1889).

General Booth, *In Darkest England and the Way Out* (London, 1890).

Stephen Bostock, *Zoos and Animal Rights* (London, 1993).

Joanna Bourke, *Dismembering the Male. Men's Bodies, Britain and the Great War* (London, 1996).

Dorothea St Hill Bourne, *They also Serve* (London, 1947).

J. Wesley Bready, *England Before and After Wesley* (London, 1938).

J. M. Brereton, *The Horse in War* (Devon, 1976).

Rev. A. Broome, *SPCA Founding Statement* (London, 1824).

John Bull, *An enquiry into the present state of Smithfield cattle market etc,* 2nd edn (London, 1848).

Angus Calder, *The Myth of the Blitz* (London, 1991).

Edward Carpenter, *My Days and Dreams* (London, 1916).

Edward Carpenter and Edward Maitland, *Vivisection* (London, 1893).

Edith Carrington, *The Cat. Her place in society and treatment* (London, 1896).

—, *The Animals on Strike* (London, 1895).
—, *The Extermination of Birds* (London, 1894).
Rachel Carson, *Silent Spring*, introduction by Lord Shackleton (Harmondsworth, 1963, reprinted 1988)
Mark Cartmill, *A view to a death in the morning: hunting and nature through history* (Cambridge, MA, 1993).
Ronald Chapman, *The Laurel and the Thorn* (London, 1945).
Susan Chitty, *The Woman who wrote Black Beauty* (London, 1971).
Brigadier J. Clabbyd, *A History of the Royal Army Veterinary Corps 1919–1961* (London, 1963).
Kenneth Clark, *Animals and Men. Their Relationship as Reflected in Western Art from Pre-History to the Present Day* (London, 1977).
Stephen R. L. Clark, *Animals and Their Moral Standing* (London, 1997).
Frances Power Cobbe, *The Confessions of a Lost Dog Reported by her Mistress* (London, 1867).
—, *A Controversy in a Nutshell* (London, 1889).
—, *Light in Dark Places* (London, 1885).
Stephen Coleridge, *Memories* (London, 1914).
—, *Vivisection. A Heartless Science* (London, 1916).
Linda Colley, *Britons. Forging the Nation 1707–1837* (London, 1992).
Wilkie Collins, *Heart and Science* (1883, reprinted Gloucester, 1990).
Gertrude Colmore, *The Angel and the Outcast* (London, 1907)
—, *Priests of Progress* (London, 1908).
Hazel Conway, *People's Parks. The Design and Development of Victorian Parks in Britain* (Cambridge, 1991).
Gloria Costelloe, *The Story of the Battersea Dogs' Home* (Newton Abbot, 1979).
Jonathan Crary, *Techniques of the Observer. On Vision and Modernity in the Nineteenth Century* (London, 1990).
Sir James Crichton-Browne, *The Doctor Remembers* (London, 1938).
Victoria Cross, *The Beating Heart* (London, 1924).
Hugh Cunningham, *Leisure in the Industrial Revolution* (London, 1980).
Henry Curling, *A Lashing for the Lashers; being an exposition of the cruelties practised upon the cab and omnibus horses of London* (London, 1851).
Stephen Daniels, *Fields of Vision. Landscape imagery and national identity in England and the United States* (New Jersey, 1993).
Francis Darwin, *The life of Charles Darwin* (1902, reprinted London, 1995).
Leonore Davidoff and Catherine Hall, *Family Fortunes: men and women of the English middle classes 1780–1880* (London, 1987).
Rev. Charles Maurice Davies, *Heterodox London* (London, 1874).
—, *Mystic London* (London, 1875).
Rupert Davies and Gordon Rupp, eds, *A History of the Methodist Church in Great Britain* (London, 1965).
David Day, *The Whale War* (London, 1987).
Charles Dickens, *Sketches by Boz* (1836–7, reissued Dennis Walder, ed., London, 1995).
Muriel, Lady Dowding, *Beauty, not the Beast* (Jersey, 1980).
William Drummond, *Rights of animals and man's duty to treat them with humanity* (London, 1838).
Carol Duncan, *Civilizing Rituals* (London, 1995).
Sydenham Teak Edwards, *Cynographia Britannica* (London, 1800–05).
Mary Ann Elston, 'Women and Anti-vivisection in Victorian England' in Nicolaas A. Rupke, *Vivisection in Historical Perspective* (London, 1990).
Lord Erskine, *Cruelty to Animals. The speech of Lord Erskine in the House of Peers, 15 May 1809* (London, 1824).
E. G. Fairholme, *The RSPCA and the Decrepit Horse Traffic to the Continent* (London, 1910).
Edward G. Fairholme and Wellesley Pain, *A Century of Work for Animals* (London, 1924).
David Feldman and Gareth Stedman Jones, eds, *Metropolis London* (London, 1989).
John Purcell Fitzgerald, *Barbarous Cruelty to Living Animals Made Legal in Great Britain* (London, 1877).
Paul Foot, *Red Shelley* (London, 1984).

Charles W. Forward, *Food of the Future* (London, 1904).
—, *The Reform of the Slaughterhouse* (London, 1913).
—, *Under the Blue Cross. A Story of Two Horses in the War* (London, 1915).
Michel Foucault, *Discipline and Punish* (Harmondsworth, 1979).
Richard D. French, *Anti-Vivisection and Medical Science in Victorian Britain* (Princeton, 1975).
John Galsworthy, *Treatment of Animals* (London, 1913).
Sydney Galvayne, *War Horses Present and Future* (London, 1902).
Kathryn Gleadle, *The Early Feminists. Radical Unitarians and the Emergence of the Women's Rights Movement 1831–51* (Basingstoke, 1995).
Lewis Gompertz, *Fragments in Defence of Animals* (London, 1852).
—, *Moral Inquiries on the Situation of Man and of Brutes*, ed. Peter Singer (1824, reprinted Fontwell, 1992).
—, *Objects and Address of the Society for the Prevention of Cruelty to Animals, established 1824* (London, 1829).
Albert Goodwin, *The Friends of Liberty. The English Democratic Movement in the Age of the French Revolution* (London, 1979).
W. J. Gordon, *The Horse-World of London* (London, 1893).
Sarah Grand, *The Beth Book* (1897, reprinted with introduction by Sally Mitchell, Bristol, 1994).
I. M. Greg and S. H. Towes, *Cattle Ships and our Meat Supply* (London, 1894).
Peter Guillery, *The Buildings of London Zoo* (London, 1993).
F. W. Hackwood, *Old English Sports* (London, 1907).
Elie Halevy, *The Growth of Philosophic Radicalism* (London, 1928).
Anne Hardy, *The Epidemic Streets. Infectious disease and the rise of preventive medicine 1856–1900* (Oxford, 1993).
Brian Harrison, *Peaceable Kingdom* (Oxford, 1982).
—, *Drink and the Victorians. The temperance question in England 1815–1872,* 2nd edn (Staffordshire, 1995).
Dix Harwood, *Love for Animals and How it Developed in Great Britain* (New York, 1928).
David Hempton, *Methodism and Politics in British Society 1750–1850* (London, 1987).
George Hendrick, *Henry Salt, Humanitarian reformer and Man of Letters* (Illinois, 1977).
Frances Hoggan, *On the advantages of a vegetarian diet in workhouses and prisons* (Norwich, 1883).
Lee Holcombe, *Wives and Property. Reform of the Married Women's Property Law in Nineteenth-century England* (Toronto, 1983).
Sandra Stanley Holton, *Suffrage Days. Stories from the Women's Suffrage Movement* (London, 1996).
Martin Hoyles, *The Story of Gardening* (London, 1991).
W. H. Hudson, *Lost British Birds* (London, 1894).
T. Ferrier Hulme, *John Wesley and his Horse* (London, 1933).
Humanitarian League, *Savage Sport at Eton* (London, 1909).
Robert Humphreys, *Sin, Organized Charity and the Poor Law in Victorian England* (Basingstoke, 1995).
Edmond J. Hunt, *The Necessity for Food Reform* (London, 1910).
Elizabeth Hutchings, *Discovering the Sculptures of George Frederick Watts* (Hunnyhill, 1994).
Henry T. Hutton, *The True Story of Greyfriars Bobby* (Edinburgh, 1903).
Thomas Huxley, *Lay sermons*, addresses and reviews (London, 1870).
Thomas Jackson, ed., *The Works of John Wesley*, 3rd edn (London, 1829).
Nick Jardine, Jim Secord, Emma Spary, eds, *Cultures of Natural History* (Cambridge, 1996).
David E. Jenkins, *Bedd Gelert. Its facts, fairies and folk-lore* (Portmadoc, 1899).
Gareth Stedman Jones, *Outcast London*, 2nd edn (Harmondsworth, 1984).
Philip E. Jones, *The Butchers of London. A History of the Worshipful Company of Butchers of the City of London* (London, 1976).
Hilda Kean, *Challenging the State? The socialist and feminist educational experience 1900–1930* (London, 1990).
—, '"The Smooth Cool Men of Science": the feminist and socialist response to vivisection', *History Workshop Journal*, 40, Autumn 1995.

John Keane, *Tom Paine: A political life* (London, 1995).

Thomas Kelly, *A History of Adult Education in Great Britain* (Liverpool, 1962).

Anna Kingsford, *Dreams and Dream Stories*, 2nd edn (London, 1888).

Ladies' Kennel Club, '*Notable dogs of the year and their owners*' reprinted from *The Ladies' Kennel Journal* (London, 1896).

Lucinda Lambton, *Beastly Buildings. The National Trust Book of Architecture for Animals* (London, 1985).

Coral Lansbury, *The Old Brown Dog. Women, Workers, and Vivisection in Edwardian England* (Wisconsin, 1985).

Elizabeth Lee, *Ouida: A Memoir* (London, 1914).

Joseph H. Levy, *Vivisection and personal rights* (London, 1902).

Louise Lind af Hageby, ed., *The Animals' Cause. International Anti-Vivisection Congress 6–10 July 1909* (London, 1909).

—, *The New Morality. An inquiry into the ethics of anti-vivisection* (London, 1911).

Louise Lind af Hageby and Liesa Schartau, *The Shambles of Science*, 5th edn (London, 1910).

Bertram Lloyd, ed., *The Great Kinship. An Anthology of Humanitarian Poetry* (London, 1921).

Jane Webb Loudon, *Domestic Pets: Their Habits and Management* (London, 1851).

Timothy W. Luke, 'The World Wildlife Fund: Ecocolonialism as Founding the Worldwide "Wise Use" of Nature', *Capitalism, Nature, Socialism. A Journal of Socialist Ecology*, vol. VIII (2), June 1997.

Judith Lytton, *Toy Dogs and their Ancestors* (London, 1911).

Fiona McCarthy, *William Morris* (London, 1994).

S. Maccoby, *English Radicalism* (London, 1955).

John Mackenzie, *The Empire of Nature. Hunting, Conservation and British Imperialism* (Manchester, 1988).

Arthur Salusbury MacNulty, *A Biography of Sir Benjamin Ward Richardson* (London, 1950).

J. R. V. Marchant, *Wild Birds Protection Acts 1880–1896* (London, 1897).

Peter Marshall, *Nature's Web. An exploration of ecological thinking* (USA, 1992).

Tim Marshall, *Murdering to Dissect. Grave-robbing, Frankenstein and the Anatomy Literature* (Manchester, 1995).

Jeffrey Masson and Susan McCarthy, *When Elephants Weep. The Emotional Lives of Animals* (London, 1994).

Trevor May, *Gondolas and Growlers. The History of the London Horse Cab* (Stroud, 1995).

Mayhew's London. Being Selections from London Labour and the London Poor (London, 1851).

Andrew Mearns, *The Bitter Cry of Outcast London* (London, 1883).

Clare Midgley, *Women against Slavery, The British Campaigns 1780–1870* (London, 1992).

Michael Millgate, ed., *Thomas Hardy. Selected Letters* (Oxford, 1990).

Arthur Moss and Elizabeth Kirby, *Animals Were There. A record of the RSPCA during the war of 1939–45* (London, 1947).

Benedict Nicolson, *Joseph Wright of Derby. Painter of Light* (Paul Mellon Foundation, 1968).

Deborah Epstein Nord, *Walking the Victorian Streets. Women, Representation and the City* (New York, 1995).

W. J. O'Connor, *Founders of British Physiology. A Biographical Dictionary, 1820–1885* (Manchester, 1988).

Diana Orton, *Made of Gold: A biography of Angela Burdett-Coutts* (London, 1980).

Lt Col A. H. Osman, *Pigeons in the Great War. A Complete History of the Carrier Pigeon Service During the Great War 1914–18* (London, 1929).

Ouida, *A Dog of Flanders* (London, 1872).

—, *Puck*, vols I–III (London, 1870).

Stephen Paget, *The case against anti-vivisection* (London, 1904).

—, *Sir Victor Horsley* (London, 1919).

Richard K. P. Pankhurst, *William Thompson, Pioneer Socialist* (1954, reissued London, 1991).

Sylvia Pankhurst, *The Suffragette Movement* (1931, reissued London, 1978).

Constance-Anne Parker, *George Stubbs: Art, Animals and Anatomy* (London, 1984).

Bessie Rayner Parkes, *The History of our Cat, Aspasia* (London, 1856).

Richard Perren, *The Meat Trade in Britain 1840–1914* (London, 1977).

Roy Porter, ed., *Rewriting the Self* (London, 1997).

Edgar Preston, *Half a Century of Good Work: A jubilee history of the Metropolitan Drinking Fountain and Cattle Trough Association 1859–1909* (London, 1909).

Humphry Primatt, *The Duty of Mercy and the Sin of Cruelty to Brute Animals* (London, 1776) as published in Richard Ryder, ed., *The Duty of Mercy* (Fontwell, 1992).

W. H. Pyne, *Microcosm, or a picturesque delineation of the arts, agriculture, manufactures of Great Britain,* vol. II (London, 1808).

Lt Col E. H. Richardson, *British War Dogs: Their training and psychology* (London, 1920).

Benjamin Ward Richardson, *On the Healthy Manufacture of Bread* (London, 1884).

C. H. Rolph, *London Particulars* (London, 1980).

RSPCA, *Claims of Animals* (London, 1875).

—, *Domestic Animals and their Treatment* (London, 1857).

Nicolaas A. Rupke, ed., *Vivisection in Historical Perspective* (London, 1990).

Richard Ryder, ed., *The Duty of Mercy* (Fontwell, 1992).

Henry S. Salt, *Animals' Rights Considered in Relation to Social Progress* (1892, reissued Fontwell, 1980).

—, *Company I have Kept* (London, 1930).

—, *Flesh or Fruit? An Essay on Food Reform* (London, 1888).

—, *Humanitarianism: Its general principles and progress* (London, 1893).

—, *Seventy Years among Savages* (London, 1921).

Lady Burdon Sanderson and J. S. and E. S. Haldane, *Sir John Burdon Sanderson: a Memoir* (Oxford, 1911).

Siegfried Sassoon, *Memoirs of a Fox-hunting Man* (London, 1928).

Nicholas Saunders, *Alternative London,* 2nd edn (London, 1971).

Philip L. Sclater, Secretary of the Zoological Society, *A Record of the Programme of the Zoological Society of London* (London, 1901).

William Secord, *Dog Painting 1840–1940: A social history of the dog in art* (Woodbridge, 1992).

Anna Sewell, *Black Beauty* (1877, reissued London, 1994).

Sir Edward Sharpey-Schafer, *History of the Physiological Society during its first fifty years 1876–1926* (London, 1927).

George Bernard Shaw, *Prefaces* (London, 1934).

John Simon, *Experiments on Life. Address at the International Medical Conference, State Medicine Section* (London, 1882).

—, *Report on the Contagious Diseases Act* (Nottingham, 1871).

A. W. Brian Simpson, *In the Highest Degree Odious* (Oxford, 1992).

John Singleton, 'Britain's Military Use of Horses 1914–1918', *Past and Present,* 139, May 1993.

Samuel Smiles, *Duty with Illustrations of Courage, Patience, and Endurance* (London, 1880).

Carmen Smith, *The Blue Cross at War 1914–18 and 1939–45* (Oxford, 1990).

Lady Smith–Dorrien, ed., *A Book of Poems for the Blue Cross Fund* (London, 1917).

SPB (Society for the Protection of Birds), *Feathered Women,* leaflet no. 10, (London, 1893).

—, *Occasional paper for circulation among fellow workers,* no. 1, 1893.

SPCA, *Founding Statement* (London, 1824).

Colin Spencer, *The Heretic's Feast. A History of Vegetarianism* (London, 1994).

W. Gordon Stables, *Cats, Their Points and Characteristics* (London, 1876).

—, *Sable and White: the autobiography of a show dog* (London, 1893).

Jess Steele, *Turning the Tide. The History of Everyday Deptford* (London, 1993).

John Stevenson, ed., *London in the Age of Reform* (Oxford, 1977).

A. H. Stokes, *The Treatment of Pit Ponies* (London, 1910).

Florence Horatia Suckling, *The Humane Educator and Reciter* (London, 1891).

John Summerson, *Georgian London* (London, 1947).

Keith Tester, *Animals and Society: the Humanity of Animal Rights* (London, 1991).

Keith Thomas, *Man and the Natural World* (London, 1983).

Onfel Thomas, *Frances Elizabeth Hoggan 1843–1927* (Newport, 1971).

E. P. Thompson, *The Making of the English Working Class,* 2nd edn (Harmsondsworth, 1980).

F. M. L. Thompson, ed., *Horses in European Economic History. A preliminary canter* (Reading, 1983).

Lisa Tickner, *A Spectacle of Women. Imagery of the Suffrage Campaign 1907–14* (London, 1987).

Flora Tristan, *The London Journal of Flora Tristan or the aristocracy and working class of England* (1842, trans. Jean Hawkes and republished London, 1982).

Robert Trow Smith, *British Livestock. A history of British livestock husbandry 1700–1900* (London, 1959).

E. S. Turner, *All Heaven in a Rage,* 2nd edn (Fontwell, 1992).

James Turner, *Animals, Pain and Humanity in the Victorian Mind: Reckoning with the beast* (New York, 1980).

Rev. John Verschoyle, *Slaughterhouse Reform* (London, n. d.).

Brian Vesey-Fitzgerald, *Cats* (Harmondsworth, 1957).

Gwynne Vevers, ed., *London's Zoo. An anthology to celebrate 150 years of the Zoological Society of London* (London, 1976).

Dror Wahrman, *Imagining the Middle Class. The Political Representation of Class in Britain, c.1789–1840* (Cambridge, 1995).

Edward Gibbon Wakefield, *Householders in Danger From the Populace* (London, 1831).

Arthur de Noe Walker, *Address on Vivisection to the International Congress for the Prevention of Cruelty to Animals held in London 1874* (London, 1875).

Judith Walkowitz, *City of Dreadful Delight. Narratives of Sexual Danger in Late Victorian London* (London, 1992).

—, *Prostitution and Victorian Society: Women, Class, and the State* (Cambridge, 1980).

J. H. Walsh, *The Dogs of the British Isles,* 5th edn (London, 1886).

John K. Walton, 'Mad dogs and Englishmen: the conflict over rabies in late Victorian England', *Journal of Social History,* vol. XIII: 2, 1979.

James Walvin, *Slavery and British Society 1776–1836* (London, 1982).

Giles Waterfield, ed., *Art for the People: Culture in the Slums of Late Victorian Britain* (London, 1994).

Julia Wedgwood, *Why Am I an Anti-Vivisectionist?* (London, 1910).

H. G. Wells, *Ann Veronica* (1909, reissued London, 1984).

George Wenzel, *Animal Rights, Human Rights. Ecology, Economy, and Ideology in the Canadian Arctic* (London, 1991).

John Wesley, *The character of a Methodist,* 3rd edn (London, 1776).

—, *A survey of the wisdom of God in the creation or a compendium of natural philosophy,* 3 vols (London, 1770).

Gilbert White, *The Natural History of Selborne* (1788–9, reprinted London, 1987).

Ella Wheeler Wilcox, *Poems* (London n. d., 1913).

Raymond Williams, *The Country and the City* (St Albans, 1975).

David M. Wilson, *The British Museum and its Public* (London, 1982).

Stephen Winsten, *Salt and his Circle* (London, 1951).

Jay Winter, *Sites of Memory. Sites of Mourning* (Cambridge, 1995).

Anthony S. Wohl, *Endangered Lives. Public Health in Victorian Britain* (London, 1983).

Patrick Wright,*The Village that died for England* (London, 1995).

William Youatt, *The Horse* (London, 1831).

—, *The obligation and extent of humanity to brutes* (London, 1839).

William Young, *Vaccination Tracts* (London, 1879).

Zoological Society, *The Gardens and Menagerie of the Zoological Society* (London, 1831).

INDEX

Page numbers in *italics* indicate an illustration.